NEWARK SUNDAY CALL

Photo by Jake Pickendick.
BUSY SUNDAY AFTERNOON IN
MAY AT THE VELODROME

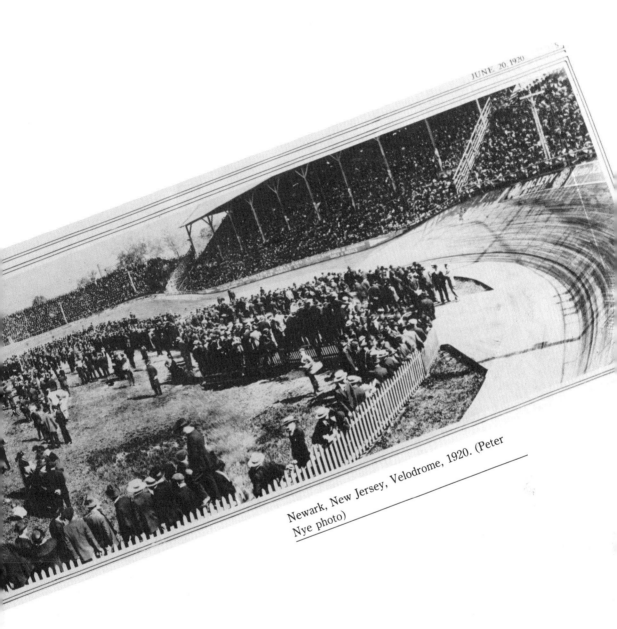

JUNE 20, 1920

Newark, New Jersey, Velodrome, 1920. (Peter Nye photo)

HEARTS OF LIONS

HEARTS OF LIONS

The History of American Bicycle Racing

PETER NYE
With a Foreword by
Eric Heiden

W·W·Norton & Company
New York   London

The text of this book is composed in the CRT version of 11.5/14 Century Old Style, with
display type set in Cochin italic. Composition and manufacturing by The Haddon Craftsmen, Inc.
Book design by Margaret M. Wagner.

First Edition

Library of Congress Cataloging-in-Publication Data

Nye, Peter, 1947–
Hearts of lions.

Bibliography: p.
Includes index.
1. Bicycle racing—United States. 2. Cycling—
United States. I. Title.
GV1049.N84 1988   796.6'2'0973   87–20331

ISBN 0-393-02543-8

W. W. Norton & Company, Inc., 500 Fifth Avenue, New York, N. Y. 10110
W. W. Norton & Company, Inc., 37 Great Russell Street, London WC1B 3NU
1 2 3 4 5 6 7 8 9 0

To Valerie and Trever,
my partners—
through thin and thin.

"Men and women enthusiasts, thrilled by the spectacle of the cyclists tearing around the pine saucer at breakneck speed, yelled themselves hoarse in a din which transformed [Madison Square] Garden into bedlam."

—*New York Times,* March 3, 1921

"It was estimated that close to 150,000 persons passed through the turnstiles, leaving their dollars and sense behind."

—*New York Times,* December 11, 1927,
reporting on the Garden's six-day race.

CONTENTS

II "Spit and Scotch Tape"

III "One Good American Rider"

FOREWORD

During the cycling season, racers are bombarded with all kinds of questions, from both the press and the public. The gamut of questions is infinite, but there are a couple that regularly pop up as people try to understand the character that makes a bicycle racer: Why did you become a cyclist rather than some other type of athlete? What's the motivating factor behind your athletic career?

The variety of responses to these types of questions is broad, but there is a common thread running through each, and a person can gain much insight into the mindset of a bicycle racer by understanding this common desire.

You see, bicycle racers—men and women—love living on the edge. They need to know the extremes of their physical limitations and often enjoy living beyond them.

How else could you explain the thrill a racer experiences flying down a narrow mountain road sandwiched within a pack of other racers? Racers constantly strive to go faster, to feel more wind on their faces. Occasionally on a descent a racer will see a friend miscalculate a corner and disappear into a cloud of dust. Never in any racer's mind are thoughts of what the consequences would be to have an accident at speeds of more than sixty miles per hour. A racer *knows* there will be no mistake, no crash.

How else can you explain the excitement sensed by a racer sprinting for the finish line elbow-to-elbow with a worthy rival? Both racers feint and dart from one side of the street to the other while in a full-out sprint. They may touch wheels, but neither will hesitate or back off. Each believes that there is no one faster.

If there weren't this need to find the limits of personal physical ability, racers would never have any desire to compete in cycling's greatest race—the Tour de France. Even though the Tour is more than three weeks long, covering some 2,500 miles for men and about one-third that distance for women, a racer cannot wait for the chance. Every racer dreams of one day racing in the Tour de France and winning, because all racers believe—they know—that they have the ability.

To reach the top a racer must push in every training workout. In a sport that is considered one of the most physically demanding, a racer knows there are no shortcuts to success. A racer must live the dedicated life of a monk, or a nun, devoting most every waking hour of every day to the sport. Rain or shine, training and racing must go on. When I have something big to do, like a demanding training program, I set aside the time I need and get into a regular rhythm, day after day. So does my sister, Beth, who has won world championships in cycling and speed skating. It is this devotion and physical suffering that binds cyclists together.

On their bicycles, racers love to push themselves to the limit. At times, they may go too far and have to pay the consequences, yet they will be greatly satisfied in having gained a greater understanding of their limitations. It is this go-for-broke attitude that many racers also live by off their bicycles.

Their escapades are often what legacies are made of. Occasionally, cyclists will live as if there is no tomorrow, and this is how many of their stories begin. The tales of many of these characters become stranger than fiction over time. As the stories are passed from one generation to the next, from father to son, to daughter, to granddaughter, their subjects become larger than life.

It has long been assumed that bicycle racing originated in Europe, but in fact it is one of America's oldest spectator sports—older, even, than basketball. Today's racers like Greg LeMond and myself owe an enormous debt to the racers who came before us, because without their courage and determination the sport would have disappeared decades ago.

Hearts of Lions describes this country's remarkably rich cycling past. There were years when bicycle racing was such a popular spectator sport that it was rivaled only by baseball. A black bicycle racer, Major Taylor, won the world professional championship in 1899 and may be considered the first black athlete to cross the color barrier in professional sports. Women cyclists have made an important contribution, especially since the 1950s when they began leading men in international competition. Without these earlier bicycle racers who kept the sport going, sometimes through very lean years of poor financial support and failing public enthusiasm, the sport would probably not exist today.

Bicycle racing is reemerging as a popular spectator sport in this country. Stars like Greg LeMond receive a good deal of media attention and are, by virtue of their celebrity status, helping to restore glory to the racers that came before them. *Hearts of Lions* tells the history of the sport through the lives of the leading racers and promoters of the past eleven decades. This book will help resurrect lost legends, rescue neglected championships, and revive the rich lore of American bicycle racing.

—Eric Heiden

ACKNOWLEDGMENTS

Working on this book took an enormous amount of research, but yielded a rich lode of Americana that kept me going. I enjoyed numerous surprises, such as discovering that some figures exceeded the legends they left behind, and that some who were legends for several decades have since been forgotten, which also fueled my interest while I traveled and interviewed and read to collect the information needed to put this story together.

Alf Goullet, Jack Simes II, Jack and Bill Brennan, and Al Toefield gave generous amounts of their time. They shared many experiences with me and never tired of answering my questions. I am indebted to them for the knowledge they imparted and the candor they shared.

I also feel privileged to have had Mary Cunnane and Katie Nelson work on this book. Mary's interest in the subject and curiosity about its history helped give this story its breadth. The manuscript further benefited from the keen copyediting of Debra Makay.

Clint Page, who has never seen a bicycle race, listened to what I told him I found, read what I wrote, and made observations and suggestions that enhanced the text. His friendship and support kept me going when I felt overwhelmed. Every writer needs a friend like Clint.

Jim Littles helped by cheerfully restoring the photo of Al Jolson firing the starting pistol of the six-day race in Madison Square Garden.

I also want to express appreciation to Lewis (Bud) Haber, who taught me to get to the source of a story, and Bill Saltzman, who always appreciates a good tale. In working on this book, I also received valued encouragement from Fred Downs, Gerry Ives, Pat Carr, Jack Simes III, Rollo Turner, Chauncey Berdan, John Wilcockson, and Owen Mulholland.

My parents, Abner and Charlotte, and in-laws, Russell and Edith Smith, always had faith in me and never insisted that I stop and do something practical like get a nine-to-five job.

Finally, I wish to express my appreciation to the Library of Congress, where I spent months scrolling through thousands of newspaper pages preserved on microfilm and leafing through bound volumes of magazines.

April 1987
Alexandria, Virginia

INTRODUCTION

On a sun-drenched August morning in 1986, I was waiting on the White House grounds for the arrival of Greg LeMond. LeMond was there for a private meeting with President Ronald Reagan, and I was there to cover it for a magazine. LeMond, from Carson City, Nevada, had just become the first non-European to win the world's most popular sporting event, the three-week Tour de France bicycle race, which dates back to 1903 and covers 2,500 miles around the inside circumference of France. His dramatic victory catapulted him to international stardom, and the American media were behaving as they always do with a new star. The *Washington Post,* which only infrequently covers cycling, suggested in an editorial on the victory that LeMond was possibly "America's finest athlete." President Reagan wanted to personally congratulate him for winning the Tour.

White House aides had been trying for a week to get LeMond to meet the president. The twenty-five-year-old cyclist's schedule was so busy that he canceled a July 30 meeting. Nobody was sure when or if he would meet the president. At 5 P.M. on July 31, a White House press aide told me that nothing was scheduled. At 9 A.M. the next day, a meeting was suddenly on for 10:45 A.M.

As I waited on the White House grounds, I thought back to an older man who had told me years earlier about two six-day bike racers, Fred Spencer and Bobby Walthour, Jr., who were so popular that President Calvin Coolidge invited them to the White House so he could meet them. The older man was James Armando of Hartford, Connecticut, a member of the 1924 U.S. Olympic cycling team. I was in my teens in the early 1960s when he came up to me one hot summer afternoon at a bike race in Connecticut.

"Don't you *ever* go swimming," he admonished me, rather harshly, as though he got to me barely in time. "That water will make your muscles soft."

I immediately saw my quadriceps turn to pulp in water. The prospect was terrifying.

Armando was in his seventies, a short, dark-complexioned man with unruly gray hair. He pedaled a vintage bicycle, its sun-faded enamel motley with chips and scratches. He had a disfigured right forearm, the result of a fall from his bicycle. A stubborn man, he set the bone himself and never sought medical treatment. He was a mason by trade and a romantic by nature, for he taught himself Esperanto, the international language that never acquired widespread acceptance. No matter how hot it was, he wore a shirt, sometimes two, buttoned to the neck, his collar turned up. He would invariably be sucking on a piece of fruit. After the pack of racers in the men's open division swarmed past, he loudly complained, "The riders today don't know what it is to really race. They're out there loafing."

As a junior rider, my event had already taken place and I watched the men's race with interest, seeing my heroes zoom by. I was offended when Armando accused them of loafing.

After a while I started to tell my coach, Joe Tosi, what I thought of Armando. Tosi had a son and daughter a few years older than I was. He worked as the Connecticut state cycling representative granting amateur licenses and giving advice on training, equipment, and diet when people asked. In the Nutmeg State, his name was synonymous with bicycle racing.

"This Armando guy—" I began, but Tosi abruptly cut me short. His deep-set, dark eyes were serious.

"It's *Mister* Armando to you, young man, and you listen to what he says. He was the best in his time. James Armando made the Olympic cycling team."

"But he says the riders today don't know what racing is," I argued. "He says they're loafing. Why, he's so crazy he told me not to go swimming because the water will make my muscles soft."

A smile crept over Tosi's face. "The business about the water and softening muscles is something they used to say when he was your age. They believed it then. But that was when riders like Bobby Walthour, Sr., Major Taylor, and Frank Kramer used to beat all the best competition in this country, when American riders were the best. Then they got on a boat and went to Europe to beat whoever was left over. They made big money in those days."

"What do you mean, 'left over'?" I asked, incredulous at the prospect. "That the best riders used to live here? I thought the best riders were in Europe—Italy, France, Belgium."

"That's right," Tosi said. "In James Armando's younger days, the best riders in the world used to knock one another over the head to get to Newark to race. They came from all around the world. Newark was known as the home of cycling. If you were any good, you went to Newark to prove it."

"Newark, New Jersey?" My teenage mind, nurtured on the irreverence of *Mad Magazine* and familiar only with the state's sooty industrial areas, read satire into the license-plate slogan "Garden State."

Tosi smiled and nodded, amused at my astonishment.

"What happened?" I demanded. "Where did it all go?"

"Ah!" Tosi gasped, gesturing with his hands raised, helplessly, a frown on his face. "What happened? A lot of things happened. But if you want to know more about riders like Bobby Walthour, Sr., Major Taylor, and Frank Kramer, you ask James Armando. He will tell you about how those guys got to be world champions. He knows all about them."

Weeks passed before I met up again with Mr. Armando. When I asked him about Walthour, Taylor, and Kramer, his dark eyes brightened. He talked nonstop of another era, of steeply banked wooden cycling tracks called velodromes, about how for more than a half-century cycling flourished in this country as a major spectator sport, rivaled only by baseball. With great animation, he told how the six-day races in Madison Square Garden in New York City were an institution and drew such high attendance that you could toss a penny from the gallery and it would never hit the floor.

When I asked him about Newark, he said the world championships were held there. Cycling was so popular year after year that when the velodrome sold out of tickets, the overflow went to watch baseball. Armando was letting me in on an open secret.

I went back to Tosi and told him what Armando had said. "Is there any truth to it?" I asked.

"Any truth?" Tosi repeated impatiently. "It's all true. When James Armando talks to you about cycling history, everything he says is true."

"What about swimming and water making my muscles soft?"

"I said history, not hygiene," Tosi retorted playfully. "When I was younger, I used to train with him. James Armando was the best in his day and I wanted to learn from him. He came into the sport a little late in life for an athlete, but he went straight to the top. He was past his prime when I trained with him in the late thirties and after the war, but even so, he could push me to new limits. In 1938 he pedaled back and forth across the country, and on the way set a national record for riding up Pikes Peak in Colorado.

"Training with James Armando made me a better rider. He taught me the most important thing a racer must have. He used to say that it's not special new equipment that just came in. And not some fancy training program that you can do in ten minutes a day." Tosi thumped his chest with a fist. "The real equipment is here. If you're going to race, you've got to have the heart of a lion. That is what makes one racer different from another, what distinguishes a winner from all the others."

"What happened to cycling in this country?" I wanted to know. "Just how big was it? And why did it die out as a spectator sport?"

"Lots of things. The depression came. Then the war. After World War II, basketball and football got strong. Baseball got even stronger. Bicycle racing in this country went by the wayside."

After the mid-1960s I left New England and never saw James Armando again. The last time I saw Joe Tosi, in 1973, he was a grandfather. He said the old Olympian had died and left his estate, including $25,000, not to his surviving brother and sister but to fund bicycle races in Connecticut. Joe Tosi was killed in August 1981, when struck by a truck while out on a training ride. I learned of his death weeks later from a friend who sent a *Hartford Courant* clipping that said 5,000 cyclists rode behind Joe Tosi's hearse. That, too, seemed like an incredible story that Armando could have told. Yet I knew Tosi, and I knew that many people would turn out on short notice to make one last ride with him.

The stories Armando told me came to mind as Greg LeMond strolled up with his wife, Kathy, who held their son, Geoffrey, age two and a half. After I filed my story, I felt compelled to find out just how popular cycling was in this country, why it faded, and how it came back.

ONE

The Golden Years

1
THE FASTEST THINGS
ON WHEELS

In today's era of high technology with satellite communications, personal home computers, and microwave ovens, it is hard to realize that less than a century ago bicycle riders were the fastest things on wheels. But they were, and Charles M. Murphy was the man who proved it.

Murphy was a prominent rider on the Grand Circuit, the national track circuit that started in northeastern cities in May and migrated west during the summer to Toledo, Fort Wayne, Council Bluffs, Peoria, Des Moines, Lincoln, St. Louis, Salt Lake City, and Denver before concluding in November with races in San Jose, San Francisco, and Los Angeles. It was a rigorous circuit. Riders competed every day but Sunday or when it rained, and track quality varied widely. Racers competed on a dirt horse track one day, a cement oval the next, followed by a banked wooden track the day after. To be a consistent winner meant that a rider had to have not just stamina to meet the demands of travel and competition but also versatility to compete on the different types of surfaces—the way tennis players do switching from clay courts to cement or asphalt courts.

Short distances were Murphy's specialty, and he won national titles in the one- to five-mile races. Period accounts describe him as having sandy-colored hair, standing 5 feet 7 inches, and weighing 145 pounds. He came from Brooklyn and was so well known that European promoters invited him for the 1896 season, all expenses paid. By 1899, he had set seven world records and seventeen national marks.

Under a clear June sky in 1899, he raced his bicycle behind a train car over a smooth, wooden track covering the railroad ties on Long Island's Hampstead Plains. He kept trying to go a mile a minute. A group of fifty timers, officials, and newspaper reporters—the penny press then constituting the media—watched from the back of the car Murphy crouched behind. After his sixth try, in 64-4/5th seconds, it was apparent that it was not the cyclist who lacked the speed but the eight-wheeled steam locomotive that set the pace.

Murphy was one of the more than 600 professional racing cyclists in the country—nearly the same number as on today's major league baseball rosters in the regular season. Racing cyclists were so popular that children collected trading cards of them the way youngsters collect baseball cards today.

He had become fixed on the idea of cracking the minute barrier while working out on a home trainer, a stationary treadmill that cyclists and triathletes still use indoors during bad weather. He consistently pedaled a mile in 37 seconds on his home trainer, equivalent to 97 miles an hour. Surely, he thought, without wind resistance he could draft behind a train car and match any locomotive's speed—even a mile a minute.

At that time, a mile a minute was the same sort of barrier that the speed of sound later was to aviators. No automobile had driven a mile a minute. Car engines were low powered, tires were unreliable, and most roads were dirt and too bumpy for such speed. Murphy at age twenty-nine was a prominent rider, but for all his stature as an athlete he had a hard time selling the project. In attempting to prove his theory of wind resistance, he unsuccessfully petitioned one railroad after another for ten years. His claim that he could break the minute barrier riding a bicycle over a smooth surface behind a train was greeted with laughter, only increasing his determination.

Finally an official for the Long Island Rail Road saw the public relations value in Murphy's attempt at a mile a minute and agreed to provide what he needed. A fleet of carpenters laid a seamless 2.3-mile pine track between the rails for Murphy to ride on, and fitted a hood over the back of the car Murphy was to ride behind to give him the best possible wind shield. Skeptics claimed that the speeding locomotive would create a suction that would pull him along. That theory was easily disproved: handkerchiefs, pieces of paper, even kites promptly fell when tossed behind speeding locomotives in test runs.

Murphy proved his point about being able to break the mile-a-minute barrier when he completed his sixth ride and the eight-wheeled steam engine was found inadequate. Another date was set in nine days for a new attempt, behind a faster engine.

On June 30, the second date for his attempt behind a train car, the same gathering of officials assembled as before. Murphy wore no helmet, and no gloves, just black woolen tights that covered his legs and a long-sleeved, light-blue jersey. His only safety measure was a protective crossbar covered in rubber that was high enough to let the front wheel of his bicycle pass under it but low enough to block the head of the bicycle frame to keep the front tire from touching the train car. Murphy's plan was to keep his front wheel close to a three-inch-wide strip of white wood at the back of the train car.

At 5 P.M. he swung a leg over the top tube of his Triumph bicycle and started his historic ride. He used a gear that moved the bicycle 104 inches every time the pedal made a full revolution, not a particularly big gear for what he was trying to do.

Unlike his previous attempt, Murphy was soon hampered by dirt and dust that swirled around him in such a cloud that he couldn't see. The head of his bike frame kept bumping against the rubber crossbar, and he felt as if the boards were flying up from underneath and rapping against his wheels.

But when he passed through the first quarter-mile in 15-⅕th seconds, the hearty cheers of officials gave him new encouragement.

The ride was jeopardized just as Murphy got his pace under control. A well-meaning official in the train car asked through a megaphone if anything was wrong. Murphy raised his head from the bent position he rode in, but before he could reply he slowed slightly and instantly fell back fifty feet.

Murphy renewed his effort and began to regain the lost ground. "It was a hot, fast, serious, life or death contract on my hands," he recounted. The half was passed in 29-⅖th seconds. The judges' earlier feelings of despair and disappointment gave way to feelings of confidence and success.

At three-quarters of a mile, Murphy was timed at 43-⅘th seconds. When he hurtled past the American flag mounted beside the track to mark the finish, officials clicked their watches off at 57-⅘th seconds.

He had beaten the odds to show he could ride a mile a minute. But before he could relish what he had done, the train engineer abruptly shut off the train's steam at the finish, sharply slowing the train. Murphy was still building speed and hit the bumper back with such force that he crashed head-on into the rear of the coach. Officials gathered there reached out nervously and pulled him aboard—bicycle and all—with just seconds to spare before the train dashed over the end of the carpet of boards he had been riding on; he would have faced sure disaster had he hit the railroad ties.

Murphy's ride generated tremendous publicity. Newspapers from coast to coast heralded his exploit. Men and women were said to have fainted at the news. The *New York Times* proclaimed that Murphy "drove a bicycle a mile faster than any human being ever drove any kind of machine and proved that human muscle can, for a short distance at least, excel the best power of steam and steel and iron."

He became a national hero. A vaudeville promoter was quick to sign Murphy up to perform on the vaudeville circuit, where he rode his bicycle in competition against other riders on home trainers mounted on stage. The following year, he retired from sports to join the New York City Police Department. He was always remembered for his famous ride, and for the rest of his life was known as Mile-a-Minute Murphy.

In Murphy's racing days, when electric lights and telephones were fast being introduced, cycling was part of the popular American culture. Cycling began as a novelty after the Civil War, progressed to a widespread hobby in the 1880s, and kept gaining popularity until the 1890s when it became a craze. On a bicycle a person could travel 10 miles an hour and faster—considerably faster than the pedestrian's 3 or 4 miles an hour. With prices ranging from $40 to $100, a bicycle was not an extravagance for the general consumer, who could never even dream of owning a horse or "horseless carriage," which cost at least five times more than a bicycle.

Men and women cyclists of all social classes took to the roads in ever-growing numbers as a bicycle touring wave swept the country in the last quarter of the nineteenth century. To meet the greater demand for sharing information on the network of roads and to promote cycling, the League of American Wheelmen was formed in 1880 in Newport, Rhode Island. Membership grew to 18,000 in 1890 before the sport took off and by 1898 LAW's membership soared to 102,600. (Considering the nation's population was less than a third of what it is today, that would represent membership of more than 300,000. Cycling's present governing body, the U.S. Cycling Federation, topped 28,000 for the first time in 1987.) Perhaps the most flamboyant LAW member was bon vivant Diamond Jim Brady, who made news when he gave the singer and actress Lillian Russell a gold-plated bicycle that had handlebars inlaid with mother-of-pearl and rubies, diamonds, and sapphires in the spokes and hubs and was presented to her in a plush-lined leather case.

One of cycling's biggest boosters was Arthur Conan Doyle, the English physician best remembered as author of the Sherlock Holmes stories. In the January 18, 1896, issue of *Scientific American Magazine* he prescribed, "When the spirits are low, when the day appears dark, when work becomes monotonous, when hope hardly seems worth having, just mount a bicycle and go out for a spin down the road, without thought on anything but the ride you are taking." His advice was heeded by vast numbers of people in this country, England, and across Europe.

Some of the best mechanical minds were drawn to making bicycles. Charles and Frank Duryea, who built the first gas-powered car in America, built bicycles first. So did Alexander Winton, builder of the first eight-cylinder engine in the country; Orville and Wilbur Wright, the fathers of aviation; and Glenn Curtiss, inventor of the seaplane. Henry Ford was interested in bicycle racing and got his hands dirty repairing racing bicycles before he built Model Ts. If these men shared any traits beyond simple mechanical talent, it might be that working with bicycles early in their careers taught them how to build light and rigid frames, and how to vary gear ratios to get maximum benefit from a particular level of power.

The Duryeas, Winton, the Wrights, Curtiss, and Ford were among the approximately 400 bicycle manufacturers who produced bicycles in America during this era. In 1897, some two million bicycles were made, compared to fewer than 4,000 cars. One of the most renowned bicycle-making centers was Chicago's Cycle Row. For nearly two miles along Jackson Boulevard, Cycle Row was lined with cycling-related stores and shops, most building bicycles with ready-made parts and fittings for shipment around the country.

It is hard to realize today, but bicycle racing is one of the country's oldest sports. The first recorded race took place in Boston's Beacon Park on May 24, 1878—two years after the National League of Professional Baseball Clubs was formed, three years after the first running of the Kentucky Derby, and thirteen years before basketball was invented. Bicycle racing grew rapidly. By the mid-1890s, there were an estimated 100 dirt, cement, and wooden tracks nationwide.

Enormous crowds turned out for the races, just as they do today for professional football and major league baseball games. It was not unusual for events, like the Diamond Jubilee in Springfield, Massachusetts, to go on for three days, with competitions from the quarter-mile to five miles, for schoolboys, novices, open amateurs (age 17 and older), and professionals. As many as 350 used to compete in a meet. Businesses sometimes closed so employees could take the afternoon and go watch. Springfield's population in the 1880s and 1890s was 35,000, but attendance at the Diamond Jubilee would top 38,000.

Most big cities had tracks. One of Indianapolis's cycling tracks that featured the latest in what we call state of the art was the Newby Oval, a quarter-mile track made from matched and dressed white pine. It boasted of a press box, telegraph office, and natural gas lights. Up to 20,000 spectators passed through the fifteen turnstile entrances that led to the grandstand amphitheaters and bleachers. As this account from the July 5, 1898, *Indianapolis News* indicates, fans followed the races enthusiastically:

Nearly every man, as well as a few of the women, who took to the oval in the afternoon took a revolver and about a hundred rounds of blank cartridges. As each heat or final was finished, the riders, as they approached the tape, were greeted with a discharge of ammunition which resembled a volley of musketry.

As indicated by Charles Murphy's performance in 1899, no small part of the success of bicycle races in the late nineteenth century was the American public's fascination with speed. After it was discovered that two wheels linked together with a board frame enabled a pedestrian to travel faster than on foot, the high-wheeled "ordinary" followed in the 1870s with pedals that fitted to cranks attached to the front wheel for better transmission. Ordinaries had an oversized front wheel and a considerably smaller rear wheel that was about the size of a dinner plate. The diameter of the ordinary's high front wheel was determined by the owner's leg inseam, and that wheel was the bicycle's only gear. Cyclists mounted from the rear and sat at shoulder height. These bicycles were made of heavy steel and were not easily maneuvered.

In 1886, George M. Hendee rode his ordinary on solid-rubber tires over a half-mile dirt track to a new world record of 2 minutes 27-$\frac{2}{5}$th seconds. It was an impressive time and showed that the bicycle represented new possibilities.

Hendee rose to prominence in 1882 at age sixteen when he won the first national championship, the mile, held that October in Boston as part of LAW's second annual convention. For the next five years, Hendee, a gentleman amateur, dominated national competition in all the popular distances up to 20 miles. Hendee captured five consecutive national championships, even defeating English champions who came over to challenge him for the title. All this helped make Hendee a hero in his hometown of Springfield, Massachusetts. When the Diamond Jubilee was held in late summer, stores, factories, and shops closed their doors. Owners were known to tack up placards on door panels and shutters bearing the announcement "Gone to see Hendee ride."

A descendant of Richard Hendee, one of the founders of Vermont, Hendee grew up in a Connecticut family whose modest fortune came from the state's silk trade. Hendee was possibly the first ever to give up college for cycling. He was bound for college until 1882 when he discovered the wheel sport and devoted himself full time to racing and traveling to meets. He became a public favorite. There were Hendee hats, Hendee suits, and Hendee cigars. Two weeks before the 1887 national championships, however, Hendee fell from his bicycle and broke his collarbone. He retired from the sport to sell bicycles.

The 1890s brought more technical improvements that opened the way for faster speeds. Pneumatic tires—invented for the bicycle by Belfast veterinarian John Dunlop, another name that links early bicycling with today's automobiles—made their way into this country in the early 1890s. About the same time, the high-wheeled bicycle was supplanted by the modern safety bicycle, with its chain transmission, diamond frame, and two wheels the same size that allowed cyclists to prevent falls by putting their feet to the ground. Wooden tracks, introduced in the 1890s, let racers reach greater speeds, and Hendee's records disappeared as riders sped faster.

In the year of Murphy's epic ride, Henry Ford was part of a small

George M. Hendee passed up the opportunity to attend college at Yale to pursue bicycle racing. He became the country's first national champion, in 1882, and kept it for another four years. (*Geneology Department, Springfield, Massachusetts, Public Library*)

group that formed the Detroit Automobile Company. Ford left the company to build racing cars. In early 1902, he got financial backing from Tom Cooper, a leading cyclist who won the national professional title in 1899. Cooper was as intrigued with speed as Ford, and in 1902 he quit cycling to form a partnership with Ford.

Cooper was part of the new wave of professional cyclists who made substantial sums from races in this country and in Europe—where he also raced—around the turn of the century. Bicycle manufacturers, as well as companies that made components, paid riders like Cooper to ride their equipment, and added lucrative bonuses for victories in key races and records set. A bicycle contract of $1,000 a year was not unusual for a top rider like Cooper, who rode for Monarch Bicycles and wore the name Monarch emblazoned across his jersey front.

In the late 1890s, Cooper emerged as a top rider renowned for his fast finishing kick against the day's leading riders, including Eddie Bald, whose sprint was so fast he was called the Cannon. Bald was the first to win three national professional championships in a row, starting with the first one in 1895. A duel between Bald and Cooper was a race promoter's delight, since crowds flocked to see who would triumph.

Photos show Cooper was a sharp-featured man of medium height and build. He was twenty-seven when the *New York Times* wrote in July 1901 that he was "arguably the richest racing cyclist in the world today. Not only has the Detroit representative some $30,000 worth of stock in the Detroit Telephone Company, but his cement business and various other enterprises, if sold, would probably net him $60,000, most of which has been won with the aid of his strong legs." That was considerable money compared with the working man's average wage of less than $500 a year. Allowing for inflation over the years, Cooper's portfolio in 1986 would be worth more than $1.1 million.

He also apparently had some mechanical aptitude, for he is credited with helping Ford design his first racing car of note. Model 999, as it was known, was cumbersome by today's standards, with a ten-foot wheelbase and weighing 3,000 pounds. Model 999 was named after a famous express train, and the car handled more like a train than a car. Few were willing to drive Ford's racing car. It didn't have a steering wheel. Instead, it was turned by handlebars like on a bicycle, and those who drove it said it took the strength of Sampson to get it through turns.

Cooper's good friend when he won the national championships was Barney Oldfield, a fellow professional bike racer who shared Cooper's interest in fast cars. Oldfield, from near Toledo, was five years Cooper's junior. He was a fearless athlete who boxed professionally long enough to get a boxer's trademark blunt nose before devoting himself full time after 1895 to bicycle racing. A few years later, he was fast enough to compete on the Grand Circuit where he became an ardent booster of Cooper. The two racers got along well and traveled together on trains around the country. It was inevitable that Cooper would introduce Oldfield to Ford, and when Cooper left cycling in 1902 to finance Ford in their partnership, Oldfield was hired as chief mechanic.

The conversion from bicycles to cars that Cooper and Oldfield made was one many others made when the public's fascination with speed shifted to cars and motorcycles. Even Eddie Bald, after he retired from bicycle racing in the early 1900s, took up car racing and afterward opened an automobile dealership. Arthur Newby, who operated the Newby Oval, abandoned cycling for a new automobile track, the Indianapolis Motor Speedway, which became the home of the famous Indianapolis 500. An amateur bicycle racer who made a bigger name for himself in the Indianapolis 500 was Fred Dusenberg, whose cars which bore his name won three Indy 500s in the 1920s. After the turn of the century, America's first national cycling champion, George M. Hendee, gave up manufacturing bicycles to found the Indian Motorcycle Company, maker of the first American-built motorcycles. For the first half-century, Indian motorcycles rivaled Harley-Davidson motorcycles in races and records.

The Cooper-Ford team's biggest rival was former Cleveland bicycle maker Alexander Winton, whose Winton Motor Carriage Company was the first to sell regularly produced cars in this country (the company subsequently became part of General Motors). Winton's racing car was so fast it was called Bullet No. 1, and lived up to its name so consistently that it was considered invincible.

Early automakers proved the quality of their cars in races. Winton's victories helped him capture the major share of the car market in America in the early 1900s. Not surprisingly, Ford was eager to have his Model 999 beat Winton's Bullet in a five-mile race October 25, 1902, at the half-mile Grosse Pointe track.

Cooper, however, was intimidated after he took Model 999 on a test drive. Model 999 had four massive cylinders, each of which was the size of a small powder keg, and their combustion together was comparable to the deafening roar of Niagara Falls. Oldfield had never driven a car before the race, but he was never one to let fear get in his way, and he knew how to compete. On race day, Oldfield pressed the accelerator to the floor from the start and never let up. He gained an entire lap on the Winton Bullet by the finish. Oldfield's new career was in high gear, and Ford was delighted to have a winning car.

Ford and Cooper soon had a falling out which resulted in Cooper selling Model 999 to Ford. In 1903 Ford formed the Ford Motor Company, which was to make cars available at prices the working man could afford ($750 each in 1904) and thus have a profound effect on the country and the world. The fledgling company got off to a fast start when Oldfield set the world speed record. On June 15, 1903, he was at the Indianapolis Fair Grounds where he revved up the engine of Model 999, hunched over the car's handlebars, and roared into automobile history when he zoomed past the mile marker in 59.6 seconds.

It was four years after Murphy's ride behind the train before a car was able to break the minute barrier. But Oldfield was just getting started in his record-breaking streak. In August, he set another speed record in Indianapolis when he went five miles in four minutes and 55 seconds.

It was a year that ushered in a new era, and cyclists led the way. While Oldfield was setting speed records and winning car races, two bicycle mechanics in Dayton were putting together the first airplane. Orville and Wilbur Wright had a successful shop where they manufactured a bicycle called the Wright Special. They were credited with inventing a rear-wheel hub and coaster brake which let the cyclist brake by pedaling backwards.

The Wright Brothers were always tinkering with ways to improve making things and became fascinated with the possibility of flying—the ultimate challenge. They made a wind tunnel and devised plans on how to use air to keep a machine aloft. Borrowing their sister's sewing machine, they stitched muslin together and stretched it over hickory sticks they glued together with Arnstein's Bicycle Cement. Their home-made contraption had two pairs of wings and was powered by a twelve-horsepower engine that turned a propeller.

In December 1903 they transported their crude machine to a place near Kitty Hawk, on the sand dunes of North Carolina's Atlantic coast. On a chilly December 17, Orville crawled between the wings, laid in the prone position, opened the throttle of the engine, and took off. For 12 seconds he was airborne and covered 120 feet. Later in the day, Wilbur went up and covered 852 feet while staying aloft for 59 seconds.

Shortly afterward, the Wright brothers set more records, including the first turn in an airplane (previous flights had been in a straight line), and the first flight over a half-hour.

Glenn Curtiss, who made bicycles in Buffalo, followed their lead. He went from making bicycles to making engines for bicycles to making engines for planes. In 1908 he won the *Scientific American* trophy for the first flight of one kilometer (six-tenths of a mile), and went on to build the first seaplane. Curtiss and the Wrights later merged businesses.

Barney Oldfield by then was on his way to becoming what the *New York Times* called "one of the greatest of the dusty daredevils of automobile racing." In March 1910 he drove a Blitzen Benz in Daytona Beach to a new world speed record of 131.724 miles an hour. Oldfield had acquired a fondness for cigars and was often depicted in newspaper and magazine photos clenching one between his teeth as he gripped the steering wheel. He made such an impression on the American public that long after he retired in 1918, his name remained synonymous with speed. "He was described as the greatest automobile driver that the world ever saw," the *Times* said, "and the side of many a youngster's scooter was inscribed with the names of his famous cars."

Advancing technology was making dramatic changes in the way people lived. More changes continued at a fast rate so that pioneers in technology were left behind. The effects of wind resistance became common knowledge after Murphy proved his theory behind a speeding train. Improved automobile engines enabled drivers to eclipse Oldfield's records soon after he retired. He went on to promote automobile safety.

Bicycle racing, meanwhile, remained relatively unchanged after the introduction of the safety bicycle. Subsequent generations of athletes who carried the sport forward may not have heard of Murphy and Oldfield, but they shared the same wind and excitement of youth, wealth of talent, and hearts of lions.

2 GENTLEMEN AMATEURS TURN PROFESSIONAL

In the late nineteenth century, the United States enjoyed an abundance of cycling talent that helped define the sport here and influence it in Europe as athletes from both continents crossed the Atlantic. What has always drawn spectators to sports events is action coupled with the drama of worthy opponents engaged in the demands of their game. Bicycle races offer high doses of both. They resemble fast-moving chess spiced with destruction—crashes or abrupt, utter exhaustion— and occasional heroics.

A plentiful stock of eager talent kept American cycling dynamic on the tracks and profitable at the box office. Out of this hotbed dashed August Zimmerman and Major Taylor, America's first international star athletes. They drew tens of thousands to track after track across the United States, Europe, and Australia. Zimmerman was the first world cycling champion and helped the sport by leading the way out of the prevailing gentleman amateur class to blaze the professional trail. Taylor modeled his career after Zimmerman and became America's next world cycling champion, in the process becoming in 1899 the first black athlete to capture a major championship in professional sports—nine years before Jack Johnson defeated Tommy Burns for the world boxing heavyweight title, fifteen years before heavyweight champion Joe Louis was born, and nearly fifty years before Jackie Robinson integrated professional baseball.

Several American cyclists—including national champions George M. Hendee and Eddie (the Cannon) Bald—had already competed in Europe, but Zimmerman was the first to win such overwhelming acclaim. Beyond chronicling his victories, the press accounts of the day routinely emphasized the graceful way he rode and the speed with which he pedaled. When Frenchman Victor Breyer, a lifelong cycling journalist and founding member of the sport's international governing body, L'Union Cycliste Internationale, reminisced about more than seventy-five years of observations, he unhesitatingly cited Zimmerman as "the greatest pedaler of all time," regardless of nationality, specialty, or time.

Breyer cited a French spectator who was moved to describe Zimmerman's style in the heat of blasting for the finish "as if the man was mounted on rails, so complete is the absence of wobbling and the semblance of effort."

Zimmerman was a lean but well-proportioned 5 feet 11 inches. Born in Camden, New Jersey, he grew up in Asbury Park and began athletics in a military school where he took to jumping and won county meets in the high jump, long jump, and hop, skip, and jump. He discovered cycling at the age of seventeen. "I liked it so well that I jumped in the game with all the spirit that was in me," he later said.

He began racing on a high-wheel bike, as ordinary bicycles were called, and soon became a top rider with a reputation for cool composure and grace in lung-bursting, muscle-burning races. Like others, Zimmerman was reluctant to part with his high-wheel when safety bicycles were taking over. But in 1891 he saw that he would have to give in to changing technology and switched. Apparently the conversion was successful because he won the half-mile League of American Wheelmen national championship and set a world record of 29.5 seconds in the last quarter-mile.

Early safety bicycles had considerably longer wheelbases than today's bicycles, and their handlebars fitted straight into the head of the frame. This put riders in a more upright and backward position that favored a rider like Zimmerman, whose acceleration and swiftness came from spinning relatively small gears with amazing leg speed. This leg speed, combined with acute timing of his sprint, earned him the nickname Jersey Skeeter and carried him to a phenomenal number of victories. He was reputed to win forty-seven races in one week (which probably included heats) from the quarter-mile to twenty-five miles, and finished some seasons with 100 or more victories—feats comparable to the 267 strikeouts in one season, or the four seasons with thirty or more victories, pitched by his contemporary Christy Matthewson.

In 1912, Zimmerman gave a *Newark Evening News* interviewer a glimpse of what the racing schedule was like in his amateur days, from 1887 to 1893. "The racing in those days extended over a greater part of the country," he said. "Nearly every state and county fair had bicycle racing as an attraction." Most often, the athletes "rode principally on dirt tracks—trotting tracks—and we made a regular circuit, going from one city or town to another and riding practically every day. It was often the case that the riders after spending several hours on a train would be obliged to go immediately to the track where they were billed to appear, and without any warming up go out and ride. This happened day after day."

Crowds of farmers and city folk packed the track bleachers and sidelines to watch thrilling finishes. The racers were amateurs who competed as hard for collar buttons and cuff links as they did for pianos, deeds to houses, and parcels of land. One of the biggest sports events of the 1890s was the Springfield Diamond Jubilee in Massachusetts every September, a three-day tournament that drew the best in the country and whatever foreign riders were competing on these shores. They raced for prestige as well as for the prize list, which included diamond tie pins. In 1892, when basketball was in its first year across town at Springfield College, Zimmerman captured the premier event, the mile. He was awarded a team of two horses, a harness, and a buckboard, valued at $1,000—more than double what the average worker earned in a year. His winnings that year, the *New York Times* subsequently reported, included "twenty-nine bicycles, several horses and carriages, half a dozen pianos, a house and a lot, household furniture of all descriptions, and enough silver plates, medals and jewelry to stock a jewelry store."

At the age of twenty-three, Zimmerman was approaching the height of his talents. His father, known as T.A., was a successful New Jersey

August Zimmerman rode on the back of this tandem with his
friend Will Laxis in 1891. Two years he later won the first
world championship. (*Lorne Shields*)

real estate broker and a member of the New York Athletic Club. Zimmerman rode for the NYAC as an amateur and wore their trademark
winged foot on the front of his jersey. Through the NYAC, Zimmerman
received an invitation from the British governing body of cycling to race
there for the 1892 season, with residence provided at the Herne Hill
track near London.

The invitation was a high honor, as England was a long-standing
major sports power. Although several distinguished American riders
had already gone to England, none had won any of the English national
championships at one, five, twenty-five, or fifty miles.

Zimmerman later complained that he did not like the gray, damp
English climate, although he said he enjoyed the company of the English

riders. He evidently adapted to their races, for he won numerous events before he rode off in July with their national championships at one, five, and twenty-five miles.

The only one left was the fifty-mile championship, and Zimmerman announced he would take it on. A sprinter, Zimmerman had no experience at racing that far, and the noted English distance star Frank Shorland was the race's heavy favorite. Nobody gave Zimmerman much of a chance. For all his victories, he set surprisingly few records. He preferred to tag along at the back of the pack and shrewdly gauge his sprint to beat the competition rather than the clock.

Zimmerman characteristically took up the challenge that the fifty-mile championship represented. He spoke often of how an athlete needed courage to match fitness as prerequisites for racing. As one of the first modern athletes, Zimmerman trained daily, often twice, avoided tobacco and alcohol, and was careful about diet, which in his case emphasized meat.

As the miles and the pace wore on during the fifty-mile championship, dozens of riders were shed from the pack. Zimmerman kept moving until, after more than two hours of racing, only he and Shorland remained in contention. Once the finish was in sight, Zimmerman unleashed his sprint and completed his sweep.

Zimmerman's triumphs also brought benefits that were both alluring and threatening to his career, as he was to discover the next year. Raleigh Bicycles gave him two bicycles, and possibly under-the-table money, as the company launched campaigns of advertising posters that showed Zimmerman riding a Raleigh. A Leicester publisher asked him to write a book, *Points for Cyclists with Training,* one of the first books on bicycle racing and training.

News of the Flying Yankee's success was dispatched to America. Soon after capturing the last English title, Zimmerman boarded a steamship and headed home. His arrival was eagerly awaited. When watchers in his hometown of Asbury Park sighted Zimmerman's ship off shore, cannons were fired from the shore, flags waved, and the entire town came out to do him honor. As soon as Zimmerman stepped on shore he was seized and a procession formed to escort him to Ocean House where he was feted as guest of honor at a dinner.

By 1893 cycling had become a craze here and abroad. National governing bodies like the LAW flourished in Europe, Australia, and Canada. That spring, leaders of the governing bodies formed a world governing body called the International Cyclists Association (predecessor to the Union Cycliste Internationale) to regulate the sport, particularly amateurs like Zimmerman who sought to expand their competitive horizons. Professionalism was seen as a threat to the purity of the sport, something cycling officials vigilantly policed by expelling any amateurs who took advantage of their sport. Any rider branded a professional was effectively banished because amateur racing was where the action was.

The association's formation coincided with the World's Columbian Exposition in Chicago. When association leaders decided to hold the first world cycling championships, Chicago was a natural choice, and August was the month.

Zimmerman launched his season that spring by once again taking a steamer to England where he expected to defend his titles and tune up for the world championships. Traveling with him was Walter Sanger, a strapping 6 foot 3 inch, 200-pounder from Chicago, who had enough brute power to occasionally beat Zimmerman in short races.

Everybody in England enthusiastically greeted Zimmerman as the returning hero—everybody, that is, except English cycling officials. They accused Zimmerman of violating amateur laws by writing his book and being featured in the Raleigh advertisements. Zimmerman was banned from racing in England. Although he was stranded briefly, and Sanger was free to compete, Zimmerman soon embarked on a successful racing campaign in Ireland and France.

The English cycling officials' accusations had no effect in America. Zimmerman was quiet and modest, preferring to let his legs do his talking, and attracted a huge following of hero worshippers. LAW officials came to his defense and inquired into why their English counterparts suspended his racing. He remained eligible to compete in the premier world championships, open only to amateur men, at distances of one and ten miles. What few professionals there were in the sport were still outside its main activities.

Meanwhile, Zimmerman was hitting his peak. Races in which he appeared drew up to 30,000 spectators. At the first world cycling championships, Zimmerman continued his winning ways. He outclassed the fields in both races, the one and ten miles, to reign as undisputed world cycling champion.

The sport of cycling was about to shift gears. A voracious demand for bicycles prompted a sharp proliferation of manufacturers who competed among themselves for a share of the burgeoning market. Their sales increased when racers won on their bikes, which led to more under-the-table payments. Most of the LAW clubs that put on races also went after the prestigious names, which also helped bid up the value of riders. In this yeasty setting, the informal arrangements with top riders like Zimmerman and Sanger rose to become open payments.

In 1894, the sport burst open with a professional class the way tennis did decades later. Utah was still two years away from becoming the forty-fifth state, yet it was already a focal point for professional racing. Dozens of bicycle makers overtly hired riders to compete exclusively on their equipment. One manufacturer was Arthur Goodwill Spaulding, cofounder of baseball's National League. Spaulding was also an entrepreneur, and he headed the pack when it came to promoting his line of bicycles. He hired Sanger and two teammates to ride Spaulding bicycles and wear jerseys with the name Spaulding across the front. He sent his pros around the country to cities on the racing circuit to appear at stores carrying his sporting goods.

Zimmerman wasted no time in turning professional. A theater agent booked the world champion for a contract in Europe that called for payment in gold for twenty-five major meets, most of which were in Paris. Raleigh had a distributorship there and put him under contract to ride their bicycles. A rough crossing of the Atlantic in March followed by foul weather in Paris put him off to an uncharacteristically slow start. In his first races, in Florence and Brussels, he lost to lesser riders.

"Then the champion suddenly found his legs," Breyer wrote in his 1947 reminiscence, "and a campaign started which may well be termed as one of fireworks."

Most of his famous races were on a Paris velodrome—the Buffalo Velodrome, a 333-meter (365-yard) track built on the site where Buffalo Bill Cody had entertained Parisians with his techniques for fighting Indians in the Plains States.

In a memorable 1,000-meter (.6-mile) race there, Scottish rider R. A. Vogt and Frenchmen André and Hermet said they were determined to beat the Flying Yankee in a match, determined by the best of three races. Zimmerman won the first decisively, prompting his opponents to loudly vow they would trounce him in the next one. Zimmerman, never prone to overstatement, reportedly told the announcer simply, "After the bell."

Zimmerman's opponents launched the next race with an aggressive pace to take the snap out of his legs. He seemed content to bring up the rear of the line they formed for two laps. When the bell rang for the last lap, Vogt sprinted with a vengeance to burn off the others. Gaps opened between riders until Zimmerman's place at the back looked hopeless in the final turn. Then he began spinning his legs faster, used the track banking to his advantage by going up it as he accelerated wide, dropped down the banking, and flew along the final straight like a homing pigeon. He sped past the other three and thus won two straight to take the match, much to the crowd's delight.

At another meet, the promoter pitted Zimmerman in a famous mile handicap against twenty-five of Europe's best. Zimmerman started on scratch, behind everybody. After the starter's pistol, he began catching competitors one by one until down the final backstretch he had half of them. Twenty thousand spectators leaped to their feet as he whipped off the final turn, his back bent low over his bicycle, and flashed past the remaining dozen riders hammering their pedals for the finish.

"The deed created a formidable impression," Breyer said. "Even today, it is cited with admiration by those who lived long enough to bear witness to that stupendous exploit."

In the summer that Zimmerman brought audiences to their feet at the Buffalo Velodrome, fifteen-year-old Major Taylor broke convention when he beat the track record for the mile that Walter Sanger set on the Capitol City Velodrome in Indianapolis. Any black rider who beat whites risked suffering backlash. LAW laws prohibited blacks from membership in every state but Massachusetts. Blacks could enter LAW races if they chose, but few did, usually preferring to compete in their own races. Track officials at the Capitol City Velodrome resented what Taylor did and admonished him never to return.

Zimmerman was on his way to San Francisco to take a ship to Australia for a season of racing when he visited Louis Munger in late 1894 in Indianapolis. Munger, a native of Detroit and a star from the

days of high-wheeled bikes, had set world records from twenty-five
miles to twenty-four hours before retiring to manufacture bicycles.

Munger's appreciation of athletic talent and social conscience must
have been offended when he heard that Taylor was banned from the
Capitol City Velodrome, for he offered Taylor, one of eight children of
a coachman, a job. Munger, a thirty-one year old bachelor, hired Taylor
to be his personal valet at home and, in those days before telephones
were common, to work as company messenger. When time permitted,
the two went riding together. Munger gave Taylor training and racing
tips. He told Taylor that if he trained hard and rigorously applied
himself, he could rise to the top and become the fastest bicycle rider
in the world. This encouragement and guidance turned into Munger's
legacy to the sport, a legacy that outlasted any of the steel machines
he made.

The announcement of Zimmerman's arrival in Indianapolis brought
a throng of admirers to the train platform where a brass band played
to welcome the star. Taylor was dispatched to meet him. It is easy to
imagine the rush of excitement that Taylor, who would turn sixteen
shortly, must have felt at the train station. Everybody else was there
just to see the champion, but Taylor was there to meet him. Taylor
made his way through the cheering throng and past the band to hand
Zimmerman a note of introduction. The two rode together in a horse-
drawn coach to Munger's home.

Articles published over the years about the popularity of cycling
around the turn of the century tend to give the impression that it was
exclusive to whites, but large numbers of black athletes were also
drawn to the sport. Bicycle racing, however, like society in general, was
segregated.

Taylor was lured into the sport by a publicity stunt two years earlier
that he unintentionally transformed into the start of his athletic career.
There were no secondary schools for blacks in Indianapolis, and after
the eighth grade Taylor went to work for the local bicycle firm of Hay
& Willits. His duties called for him to sweep and dust until 4 P.M. Then
he donned a military-style uniform with large brass buttons and went
outside to perform trick riding exhibitions in front of the store to attract
customers. His fancy mounts, dismounts, and riding stunts on an early
safety bicycle drew crowds. The uniform and snappy drills earned him
the nickname Major, which he used from then on in place of his given
name, Marshall.

For several years, Hay & Willits had held a ten-mile handicap race on Memorial Day. It was a festive affair that attracted more than 100 of the best regional riders. A band played lively music near the starting line. Red, white, and blue bunting decorated homes and storefronts, and thousands lined the dirt road to cheer. In 1892 Taylor went to watch the race; his employer, Tom Hay, told him he was entered with a fifteen-minute lead on the scratch riders, who had no handicaps and started last. Hay put the surprised youth on his bicycle and pushed him to the starting line before Taylor realized what was happening.

The frightened youth began to cry. He had never been in a race, and he could see that he was being made the butt of a joke—he was expected to line up with the experienced riders, fall behind, and then struggle in their dust for a laugh. But when Hay whispered in his ear that he could quit after he had gone down the road because nobody expected him to finish, Taylor suppressed his tears. Then, no matter what it took, Taylor was determined to go the distance to spite Hay.

What Taylor's spindly legs lacked in strength he made up for in determination. He went all out from the starter's gun and soon was riding all alone in front. He gritted his teeth and endured the pain when his leg muscles and joints ached. At the five-mile point, Hay stepped from a group of spectators into the road and dangled in front of Taylor the gold medal that would be awarded to the winner. The medal would be Taylor's, Hay said, if he could stay in the lead. Taylor renewed his effort. At last he wobbled exhausted over the finish line and collapsed in a heap.

Taylor joined the city's black cycling club, See-Saw Circle, and started to distinguish himself. Meeting Zimmerman in late 1894 and listening to Zimmerman and Munger talk about faraway cities that were wide open to a champion no doubt fueled Taylor's ambitions. Taylor was impressed with the way the two champions treated him as an equal. He became determined to become a champion himself.

After Zimmerman left for Australia, Munger apparently assessed the odds against Taylor in Indiana, because he moved his business to Worcester, Massachusetts, in early 1895, and he took Taylor with him. Worcester was also segregated, and Taylor joined a local black cycling club, the Albion Cycle Club, but northeastern riders were more liberal about blacks in competition. Taylor could compete in all the races he wanted.

———————————

Taylor developed as Munger predicted, and soon he was winning big regional races. He grew, too, to 5 feet 7 inches and 155 pounds, with even features and a square jaw. Mounted on his bicycle, he looked shorter than he actually was, because his legs were long and his torso short. He took advantage of his strong upper body and his access to Munger's machinery to design a metal extension that fitted into the head of the bicycle frame and put the handlebars several inches forward of the frame. This extension, standard today, enabled him to ride with his back stretched lower to the frame for the streamlined position long associated with racing cyclists.

As Taylor worked his way up through the amateur ranks, he set his sights on turning professional. By 1896, professional racing was only in its third season, but cycling's popularity and the cash prizes on the Grand Circuit had already attracted more than 600 professional riders. These early professionals were busy all season long keeping up with a racing schedule that had them alternating between commuting on railroad tracks and racing on bicycle tracks.

While Taylor was moving up in cycling, Zimmerman was on his way down. Zimmerman's Australian tour had its highlights, but the strain of constant racing and travel was catching up to him. He promptly followed that tour by returning to Europe, where he couldn't live up to his reputation. Breyer speculated that Zimmerman didn't even try seriously. It was Zimmerman's ninth season, and he may have been burned out.

After another mediocre season in Europe in 1896, Zimmerman was obviously no longer a contender. Yet he was already a living legend. Such were his previous achievements, on top of his low-key manner, that he captured the public imagination, particularly in Paris. The French press compared the sharpness of his sprint in his prime years to the spring of a kangaroo. Even when his legs would no longer propel him as swiftly as before, crowds flocked just to see the man who was a legend. He had charisma. His name had great marquee value. Paris promoters capitalized on this and invited *le grand Zim* back several more years to ride exhibition races. By 1905, however, Zimmerman felt it was time to watch, not ride. He quietly returned home, settled in coastal Point Pleasant, near Asbury Park, invested his savings in a hotel, and retired to operate it.

Taylor, meanwhile, turned professional to race in the December 1896 six-day race in Madison Square Garden, one of the last one-man grinds. This grueling race began at one minute past midnight on Monday morning and went straight through to 10 P.M. Saturday. It was an excruciating test of stamina made worthwhile by a purse of $10,000 in gold double-eagle coins weighing sixteen pounds. Twenty-seven riders from Canada, Denmark, Germany, Scotland, Wales, and around the United States raced for the money.

The six-day race around the steeply banked board track, ten laps to the mile, went for 142 hours of continuous competition. Each rider had a support crew to look after him and give encouragement, take care of flat tires and other equipment, cook food, and get him something to drink. But each rider was otherwise on his own to take time out to eat, sleep, and take care of other matters in the race and still ride the greatest number of laps and hence the most miles.

At eighteen, Taylor was better suited for shorter events. His impressive performance tells as much about his athletic ability as it does his character. He learned quickly and gained press attention. "The wonder of the race is 'Major' Taylor, the little colored boy who serves as a professional mascot for the South Brooklyn Wheelmen," the *New York Times* said.

Fighting hallucinations, monotony, and debilitating fatigue, Taylor churned out 1,732 miles, the distance from New York to Houston, good for eighth among the fifteen who lasted. He won $125 for his finish in the six-day and $200 for capturing the half-mile event that preceded the main event. The winner, Teddy Hale of Ireland, won so much gold he had to put it in his hat and carry it away with both hands.

The six-day proved to be a strenuous rite of passage into professional racing for Taylor, but he passed the test. He could proudly call himself a professional. Experts warned Taylor that the prolonged effort from his six-day would dull his sprint. When the 1897 season began in March, he showed he was as sharp as ever and that his stamina had improved so he could hold up better against the other pros on the Grand Circuit.

The transformation of the sport from amateur to professional appealed to entrepreneurs who moved in to take the events over from the LAW clubs that had grown up with the sport. At the vanguard of the new breed of promoters was a fast-talking theatrical impresario named Billy

Brady. Brady, who grew up over a Bowery saloon and later became one of Broadway's most successful producers, always looked for champions. He had one in boxer James (Gentleman Jim) Corbett, until in March 1897 Bob Fitzsimmons took the heavyweight title from Corbett and knocked Brady out of work at the same time. Without a boxing champ to manage, Brady looked for another prospect. He found one, not in the boxing ring, but on the bicycle track in the person of Major Taylor.

Brady became Taylor's manager and took over a one-third-mile cement oval in Brooklyn then known as the Manhattan Beach track which drew more than 30,000 spectators to each of his racing programs. Brady offered the fans top names and all-out racing: the purses were as much as 50 percent of the gate. He also branched out to promote the six-day races in Madison Square Garden.

Taylor's gunpowder sprint made him a popular attraction in meets at Manhattan Beach and around the Northeast. Like Zimmerman, he preferred to wind his sprint up from the back of the pack. After riders learned to check his sprint by boxing him in, he went to the head of the pack and rode to victories by riding off the front. The press began nicknaming Taylor the Black Whirlwind, the Ebony Streak, the Dusky Champion, and the Worcester Whirlwind; the name he said he liked best was the Black Zimmerman.

Young Taylor was earning as much as $850 a day, more than double what his coachman father, Gilbert, earned in a year. Brady also negotiated $1,000 bonuses for records that Taylor set. Brady, a gambler at heart and a battler by instinct, took advantage of Taylor's talent and the racial prejudice he faced by making side bets which paid off handsomely.

Professional cycling has always been fiercely competitive. Riders push and shove at speed, and occasionally crash. When the outcome of a race and its payoff are determined by a margin sometimes as narrow as the thickness of a tire, tempers can flare and fists fly.

As the rare black among whites, Taylor suffered more than his share of abuse. One rider he beat jumped off his bike, clamped his hands around Taylor's neck, and choked him until police broke up the attack. The race judges ruled that they should re-ride the race, which Taylor was unable to do. The incident drew outcries from several newspapers.

Some riders—like national professional champion Eddie Bald—

"drew the color line," as the expression went, and refused to race Taylor. Judges sometimes gave Taylor second place—which meant a sharp drop in prize money—when Taylor came in first by a wheel length. Most frustrating was his inability to compete in much of the 1897 national championship circuit because it extended to the South where promoters rejected his entry.

The following season got off to a tumultuous start when the riders revolted over the issue of Sunday racing. Commercial interests in favor of Sunday athletics—including baseball games—were gaining over traditionalists who wanted to preserve Sunday as the Lord's day. LAW officials adamantly opposed Sunday racing, only to find large numbers of riders and race promoters abandoning LAW for the fledgling National Cycling Association.

The issue hit Taylor personally. A devout Baptist, Taylor carried a copy of the Testament in his traveling bag and read passages of scripture in his training quarters before a race. His religious beliefs were instilled by his mother, Saphonia, who vigorously opposed her son's even riding a bicycle on Sunday. She repeatedly asked him not to ride on Sunday, and when he turned professional he promised her he would never race on Sunday—a promise that was to cause him difficulties when the NCA took over as the sport's governing body.

Despite many difficulties, Taylor kept improving. He was a big attraction on tracks from Manhattan Beach to Green Bay, from Boston to Peoria, from Asbury Park to Ottumwa, Iowa. Some attended to see him get beaten by white riders while others went to see how good he was. Writers described his style as smooth, with a compact body held in place by strong arms; his acceleration down the final stretch was so explosive he transformed races in the final yards.

Race programs typically involved men's professional and amateur events, with distances often from the quarter-mile to twenty-five miles. Promoters like Brady put on closely spaced events, with a variety of distances to keep spectator interest high, action lively. A band with as many as fifty musicians playing jaunty tunes in the infield helped generate excitement between races. Taylor and others usually rode four events in each program.

Taylor became a specialist in the matched sprints, the purest form of competition, representing a confluence of speed and cunning, where two riders compete against each other for two or three laps of the track.

Spectators like match racing for the early-race drama as riders poise on their bicycles, waiting to see who makes the first move. On steeply banked board tracks, riders play cat-and-mouse up and down the shallow banking of the straights and steeper banking of the turns. The tactics, the maneuvers, the feints, however, are just the preliminaries for the final 200 yards. Racers shoot off the final turn and blast down the final straight where the entire race comes down to who can accelerate most sharply, who can hit the fastest speed. Matched sprints have long been the high point of the program, and Taylor was winning his share of best-of-three match races, paying $500, winner take all.

It wasn't long before he saved enough money to buy a seven-bedroom Victorian home in the fashionable Columbus Park section of Worcester. Despite a heavy race schedule, Taylor was an avid letter writer and kept in touch with his family in Indianapolis. When his sister, Gertrude, fell ill with tuberculosis, he moved her to Worcester and had her taken care of in his home.

Taylor must have felt confident he was ready to fulfill Munger's prediction that he would become the fastest bicycle racer in the world, a bold prediction for the period. Blacks in American society were, as author Ralph Ellison later noted, invisible. American society, business, and sports were segregated. Even in a sport as basic as boxing, black prizefighters were confined to boxing one another repeatedly. Their best incomes came from staging a battle royal, where as many as a dozen were in the ring at one time to eliminate one another until a single winner was left. When a black West Indian heavyweight named Peter Jackson won Australia's championship and came to America as an obvious contender for the world heavyweight championship in the late 1880s, reigning champion John L. Sullivan refused to box Jackson because he was black.

In 1899 Taylor got a chance to go where no black athlete had yet gone. The world championships, after a tour of European cities following the races in Chicago in 1893, were held in Montreal in August. Four years earlier, professional events were added to the program, and by 1899 they were well established.

The world championship races opened August 9 in Queen's Park to an overflow crowd. More than 18,000 fans filled the grandstand and bleachers and thousands more were turned away. (The velodrome at the 1986 world championships in Colorado Springs accommodated

8,200 and was not always sold out.) Large white tents were pitched around the park for riders from around the United States, Canada, Australia, Belgium, England, France, and Italy. Streamers of vibrant colors hung from the grandstand spires. Vendors hawked food and beverages while bands blared merrily.

On opening day, the twenty-year-old Taylor decisively won his two heats in the half-mile to advance to the final. There he lined up against five others including Nat Butler of Cambridge, Massachusetts, and Charles McCarthy of St. Louis. From the crack of the starter's pistol it was a fast, close race around the half-mile dirt track. The crowd was on its feet and roaring with excitement. When the riders fanned across the finish line, they were so close the judges had to huddle for several minutes before reaching the decision that McCarthy had won, followed by Taylor, and then Butler. Others saw it differently—some claimed Butler had won, others Taylor—and a small riot broke out in the stands.

Differences of opinion didn't change the judges' minds, however. The next day was the premier event, the mile, and Taylor was determined not to let a world championship elude him. Twenty-one riders competed in five heats, with only winners advancing to the final. Taylor won his two heats to line up for the final against Canadian champion Angus McLeod, French champion Courbe d'Outrelon, who wrapped the French flag around his torso, and Nat Butler and his brother Tom, the reigning U.S. national champion. With the Butlers in the final, the other three worried that the brothers would work together against them; this prompted them to ride aggressively.

For the first half-mile lap, the pace was fast, then eased at the beginning of the second lap as it became a tactical race. In the backstretch, McLeod got out of his saddle and sprinted. The others chased like hounds after the hare.

"It was a beautiful sprint," the *Montreal Star* said. "McLeod was caught at the turn, and Tom Butler drove down for the finish at a great rate. Taylor caught him ten feet from the line, and just managed to hold out, while d'Outrelon made a close third."

Before the announcer delivered the judges' verdict, the *Star,* perhaps carried away with colors, noted that "the crowd, fearing that their dark-skinned, white-haired boy was going to get the worst of it, began to be a little demonstrative. The hold which Taylor has taken upon the sympathies of the people in the grandstand is something wonderful."

The announcement that Taylor was the official winner was enthusiastically received by the audience packed in the stands.

"I never felt so proud to be an American before," Taylor wrote in his autobiography, *The Fastest Bicycle Rider in the World,* of the lap of honor he rode while the national anthem played.

He also triumphed in the two-mile championship. He had risen to the top of cycling as Munger had predicted. He had beaten the best riders. He had conquered racial prejudice, though he had not set out to become a pioneer. Soon he was receiving lucrative invitations to compete in Europe.

His manager, Brady, was also managing the new heavyweight boxing champion James J. (Boilermaker) Jeffries, who won the title in June from Fitzsimmons. Brady is remembered in sports as the only boxing manager to manage two world heavyweight champions, but even more remarkable (and considerably less known) is that he also managed the world professional cycling champion at the same time.

As the century ended, cycling as a sport and industry was going through major changes. Sufficient numbers of LAW members opposed Sunday racing to vote that LAW forgo its involvement with competition altogether and concentrate on touring. Its membership was dwindling fast as automobiles and motorcycles began challenging cycling's popularity. Some of the better known tracks, such as the one in Peoria, had gone out of business. Attendance remained strong in some areas but diminished significantly in others.

In early 1900, Taylor entertained numerous offers while he continued to watch over his sick sister Gertrude. One particularly enticing offer, from a consortium of French bicycle manufacturers and track promoters, guaranteed him a $10,000 contract to race in France. But as much as he wanted to follow in Zimmerman's wheel marks, Taylor turned it down because it included Sunday competitions, to which he was opposed. Taylor didn't ride on Sundays, and he wouldn't permit his mechanic to do any repairs on the bike, either.

Iver Johnson Arms & Cycle Works of Fitchburg, Massachusetts, signed Taylor up with a $1,000 contract to ride their bikes for each of the next two seasons. They featured his photograph in their advertisements. Taylor also rode in some vaudeville home-trainer races on stationary treadmills against Mile-a-Minute Murphy before sold-out houses.

Taylor's 1900 season, however, got off to a slow start when his sister died in April, but, once started, was rewarding. He had an active season

Major Taylor in 1900 proudly wore the American flag around his waist in the fashion of the period. It designated he was the national professional champion.

on tracks from Waltham, Massachusetts, to Washington, D.C., to Ottumwa, Iowa. His riding and his personal manner earned him considerable respect. To the *New York Times* and other newspapers, he was no longer "the little colored boy," but "the colored champion."

The 1900 season culminated in Newark, New Jersey, where he reached the final of the National Cycling Association sprint championship. At stake was the national professional title and $500. His most threatening rival turned out to be Frank Kramer, a nineteen-year-old native of Evansville, Indiana, who, upon Taylor's urging the previous autumn, had made the switch from amateur to professional.

Kramer's start in cycling, like Taylor's, was accidental. When Kramer was in his early teens his parents became concerned that he might have tuberculosis, which in those days was usually fatal. They bought him a high-wheeled bicycle so he could exercise to improve his breathing and sent him east to New Jersey; they considered the air closer to the seacoast to be more beneficial than the air in southern Indiana. He grew up in the home of family friends in East Orange, near Newark. Kramer's first race, at age sixteen, was as inauspicious—he finished dead last—as Taylor's had been auspicious.

Kramer stayed with the sport, improved as he grew more robust, and became a winner. From a frail youth he grew to a little under six feet tall, with big bones, a barrel chest, and such straight bearing that he looked taller. His pronounced chin with an underbite prompted friends to call him Chisel Chin. In 1898, at seventeen, he won the LAW national amateur title, and the NCA national amateur title the next year.

In some respects, Kramer was single-minded to the point of being eccentric. He never fraternized with bike riders and had few intimate friends. Marriage was not a consideration until after he retired. Nothing interfered with his regular habits, particularly his sleep. Kramer was so punctual about going to bed every night at precisely 9 P.M. that neighbors could set their clocks when the light went out in his bedroom. His regular habits paid off, for he always had the vitality to win.

Kramer quickly established himself as a contender early in his first pro season when he beat former national champion Tom Cooper. Pierce-Arrow, a maker of bicycles and luxury cars in Buffalo, signed Kramer to ride for them. Against Taylor in the final for the national professional championship, Kramer was the one most fans put their money on. His speed made him the white hope against the black star.

But Taylor was not intimidated. He preferred going to Newark for

Frank Kramer warmed up on the Newark Velodrome before
his match race against Major Taylor for the national
championship in 1900. (*Brennan Brothers*)

the U.S. title rather than traveling to Paris to defend his world championship.

In front of a crowd of 10,000 spectators, the two Indiana cyclists competed for the match race—the best of three races over a mile on the banked wooden velodrome, six laps to the mile. The races were close throughout each lap. When Taylor and Kramer swooped down the banking of the final turn and wound up their sprints, the crowd rose in unison, shouting. Kramer led down the straight. Then Taylor whipped off his rear wheel and flashed ahead to take both the championship and the purse in the two straight. By then, word of Taylor's ability made him such a celebrity that European promoters cabled him again. This time they agreed that there would be no Sunday races, a considerable concession, for Sunday was a big day for races in Europe. Yet Taylor

was unique enough to be a Midas at the box office. As a black he was
a novelty. As an athlete he was a winner. He had a sharp sprint enhanced with tactical cunning and expert bike-handling skills.

Brady negotiated a $5,000 contract for Taylor plus all expenses and
whatever Taylor won, enough to entice him overseas to start the 1901
season. It turned into an eventful tour of sixteen cities around Belgium,
Denmark, France, Germany, Italy, and Switzerland. He won forty-two
races in a variety of distances against dozens of top riders, including
national champions Thorwald Ellegaard of Denmark, Willie Arend of
Germany, Louis Grognia of Belgium, Charles Gascoyne of England, and
Palmo Momo of Italy.

The climax of the tour came in Paris at the Parc des Princes Velodrome where Taylor was paired in a match race against the reigning
world champion, Edmund Jacquelin, a swarthy Frenchman famous for
his lightning acceleration. Some 30,000 people paid to see the two
champions compete for $7,500, a figure worth thirteen times that in
today's purchasing power. Taylor had studied the Frenchman's style,
and in their first race in the best-of-three series launched his sprint off
the final turn at the same time as Jacquelin. As the two men tore down
the long final straight, the crowd was in a frenzy. Taylor won by four
lengths.

The second race started twenty minutes later. "I worked in a bit of
psychology after both of us had mounted and were strapped in," Taylor
said. "I reached over and extended my hand to Jacquelin and he took
it with a great show of surprise. Under the circumstances, he could not
have refused to shake hands with me." Taylor wanted to show "Jacquelin that I was so positive that I could defeat him again that this was going
to be the last heat."

It was. Just past the finish, Taylor pulled a small silk American flag
from his waistband and waved it as the riders circled the track to the
audience's applause. His triumph was so upsetting to race director
Henri Desgrange, creator of the Tour de France, that Desgrange paid
Taylor in ten-centime pieces—coins like dimes—and Taylor needed a
wheelbarrow to carry his winnings away.

To American blacks, Taylor was a leading national figure. After he
returned to Worcester in 1901, he met a black socialite, Daisy Victoria
Morris, and their courtship was noted with interest in the black press.

To Europeans, Taylor was treated with the deference of a champion athlete. Paris promoters Victor Breyer and Robert Coquelle made him another offer for $5,000, expenses paid, again agreeing there would be no Sunday racing. Taylor and his fiancée married in March 1902, but the newlyweds recognized that professional bicycle racing was a business, and four days after their marriage Taylor left his bride with relatives and embarked alone on a second European racing excursion. His campaign pitted him against the best riders in Belgium, Denmark, France, and Holland. He captured another forty races before sailing home in June where the racing was lucrative enough to make him one of the best-paid athletes in the country.

But to most Americans, Taylor was just another black man in a segregated society, regardless of his athletic success. His resilient spirit kept him going in spite of petty harassment. Often he was unable to check in like the other riders to hotels near the tracks where they were to compete because blacks were not allowed, and he had to commute across town to the black section, staying in hotels for blacks or with a black family. But one rider who ruffled Taylor's pride was Floyd MacFarland of San Jose, California. MacFarland, a year older than Taylor, was a veteran of races around the United States and Australia, where bicycle racing was also popular. When Taylor returned to his homeland, he was confronted with MacFarland.

Standing a head taller than Taylor, MacFarland was 6 feet 4 inches tall, with large dark eyes and broad shoulders. He was endowed with great stamina, which helped make him a prolific winner, including two Madison Square Garden six-days. He lacked Taylor's detonation in the sprints, but he knew there were other ways to beat Taylor.

MacFarland was a shrewd judge of people. He was convivial, charming, and a natural leader. Many riders took their cues from MacFarland, and fans flocked to the track to see him compete. But MacFarland, as prejudiced as many others against blacks, harassed Taylor, who sometimes pulled a bible from his traveling bag in the changing room to wave for emphasis as he quoted scripture at MacFarland. MacFarland could use a tendency like this to work against Taylor in the eyes of other riders. In race after race, MacFarland persuaded others to ride in combinations to stymie Taylor's moves on the track. MacFarland knew just how to taunt Taylor until the black champion's usually restrained behavior suddenly boiled into anger.

When the 1902 season wound down after Labor Day, Taylor turned twenty-four and contemplated retirement. His diary showed he had won $35,000 that season, making him possibly the best-paid athlete in the nation. He had set seven world records, and had won the national and world championships. His idol, Zimmerman, had counseled retirement while "still at the top of the heap," if he could afford it, which Taylor could.

Sales of bikes, meanwhile, had fallen off precipitously. A. G. Spaulding and other retail leaders in the business got out, and Taylor's earlier mentor, Munger, was about to leave bicycle manufacturing to get into the automobile business. (Munger invented a removable automobile rim.) Billy Brady was soon to leave sports altogether, after James J. Jeffries retired from boxing in 1905, to return to the theater as William A. Brady, producer of Broadway plays. American cycling was slipping into the first of a series of falls and rises.

While Taylor contemplated retirement, he received a cable inviting him to compete for the winter season in Australia for a $5,000 contract, full expenses for him and his wife, no Sunday racing, and attractive prize lists. Australia appealed to Taylor because Zimmerman had raced there and Taylor felt that his own career would not be complete without also racing Down Under.

3
JOHN M. CHAPMAN, CZAR OF CYCLING

When Brigham Young led his small band of Mormon pioneers into a flat river valley near Utah's Great Salt Lake in July 1847, he knew he had found what he was looking for. To the east were the peaks of the Wasatch Range, reaching 8,000 feet toward the sky. To the west were more mountains—the Orquirrh Range. On the northwest side of the valley was the Great Salt Lake. "This," Young said to his people, "is the place."

The Mormons laid out a town there in the valley, built a fort and houses, explored the valley and the mountains, irrigated the land, and planted crops. More Mormons moved into the area, and in three years there were 5,000 of them. By 1868 the town was Salt Lake City, and the city became a mining center. As more settlers and more business came into the valley, so did railroads (the golden spike joining lines from the east and west was driven not far away at Promontory Point in 1869) and railroad builders. One of the builders, Captain T. O. Angell, decided that the wonders of Utah needed a showcase. The one he built in downtown Salt Lake City was a fabulous resort known as the Salt Palace, which opened in 1899.

It was indeed a palace—a glistening pleasure dome made of rock salt

from the shores of the lake. Slabs and blocks of salt provided the
building materials for the structure. Salt-encrusted wood was used for
exterior wall panels and molding. Salt was mixed with plaster for the
wainscoting. The exterior lights were set in sparkling crystal-covered
bells that covered the towers of the palace. An electric star sat atop the
dome. At night, the Salt Palace was an enormous jewel that twinkled
in the dark.

The interior of the dome was not salted, but it was as spectacular as
the rest of the Palace. Each of its sixteen panels was painted in irides-
cent colors to display the name of a western state. One, of course, was
Utah, which had been a state for only three years when the Salt Palace
opened.

Besides its exhibits of Utah's copper, gold, zinc, and other mineral
resources and its displays of agricultural industry, the Salt Palace of-

The Salt Palace was an architectural marvel and had a
velodrome on its grounds which drew crowds of 5,000 when
the city's population was 90,000. (*Utah Historical Society
Library*)

fered on its grounds an outdoor wooden velodrome one-eighth of a mile around, where races were held twice a week. Sellout crowds of 5,000 were common; bicycle racing was a major spectator sport at the turn of the century, and the 90,000 people of Salt Lake City included a high proportion of fans.

Fifty years after Young and his followers arrived in the valley, Salt Lake City had become, among many others, one of the stops on the bicycle racing circuit. For the riders, Salt Lake City meant speed: the thin air at 4,400 feet let them ride faster, and speed records became commonplace. For the sport in general, Salt Lake City meant something more. For if it was *the* place for Young and his Mormon followers to found a city, it turned out to be the place as well for one itinerant bicycle racer to learn the business of promoting races—a business that launched the sport into its golden era.

Dozens of world records were set on the Salt Palace Velodrome by riders who took advantage of the city's 4,400-foot altitude. (*Utah Historical Society Library*)

That racer was John M. Chapman, who became what the *New York Times* described as the "undisputed czar" of the sport. "More than any other man," the *Times* said, "he was responsible for the growth of the sport as a popular attraction in this country."

Chapman is one of the most overlooked figures in American sports. In many ways, he was the quintessential Horatio Alger character who came from a humble background and went on to great fortune. He was even born in a log cabin in College Park, near Atlanta. His father was celebrated throughout Georgia for the excellent brandy he distilled from peaches grown on his farm. In 1894, at the age of sixteen, young John bought a bicycle, which began his involvement in the sport that was to be his life.

Two years later, he started racing in Atlanta. He showed promise in his first year, and the next year found him also competing in Nashville and Chattanooga. By the end of the season, he was a regional star, with an income of $800—impressive at the time.

Chapman was one of the best, but he was not quite in the same class as another Georgian—Bobby Walthour, Sr. They were the same age and competed against each other often. Walthour, a few inches taller than Chapman, was Arthur Zimmerman's size, and won so many races that newspaper accounts indicate he was as well known in the state as Robert E. Lee.

Walthour and Chapman competed on the track, and, as it turned out, in romance. Chapman fell in love with a petite redhead named Blanche Bailey a year or two after he started racing. She was with him at races and somewhere along the way she and Walthour met. By 1898 Walthour's competition with Chapman gained another dimension, though this one would end with a clear winner. On a soft summer night when the moon was full Bobby and Blanche eloped on a tandem bicycle.

The next day an Atlanta newspaper carried a picture of the couple riding their tandem, with cupid perched on the handlebars. Accompanying the artwork was a verse that went:

> He was a champion scorcher
> She was a lady true;
> They sped away at the close of the day
> On a bicycle built for two.

Walthour's descendants, and a number of contemporary newspaper accounts, say that the elopement inspired the popular song "Daisy, Daisy," sometimes better known as "Bicycle Built for Two." It's a pleasant romantic notion, but records at the Library of Congress show the song was copyrighted in 1892, when Bobby was thirteen and Blanche ten.

The elopement caused a falling out between Walthour and Chapman. Chapman left the South to become an itinerant bicycle rider. He competed on tracks from New York to Michigan to British Columbia, and then to San Francisco. Finally, in 1899, he arrived in Salt Lake City, where he lived for most of the next eight years.

At the Salt Palace Velodrome, Chapman had his best racing years. The local press dubbed him the Georgia Cyclone. Thistle Bicycles hired him to ride for their team and promote their product. At the end of the 1899 season and again the following year, Chapman and Iver Lawson, one of Chapman's fiercest competitors, traveled to Australia to race. In 1901 in Salt Lake City, Chapman teamed with Lawson to set a world tandem record of 9 minutes 44 seconds for the five-mile race; it stood as a U.S. record for more than fifty years. All the racing, however, may have been too much for Chapman's constitution for he was having such a difficult time in the 1902 season that he retired.

By then Chapman had enough of a following that he was offered the job as manager of the Salt Palace Velodrome. His inaugural term as track manager was highly successful. He learned to set up a racing program involving professional and amateur races, arrange for purses to draw the better pros and merchandise for the amateurs, and attract publicity to draw spectators to the track. Chapman became so confident about his abilities that at the end of the 1903 season he left the Salt Palace and invested his savings in another track in the Salt Air Amusement Park on the shore of the Great Salt Lake. His business acumen was not up to his confidence, apparently, for the enterprise flopped in 1904 and Chapman went broke.

Out of money as well as a job, and out of contention as a racer, Chapman was ready to seize any opportunity when he heard of a gold rush in Goldfields, Nevada. There he met another prospector, a former cowpuncher and marshal from the Lone Star State named George Rickard, better known as Tex. Rickard had already struck it rich once in the Klondike gold rush in northwest Canada's Yukon Territory. With that money, he set up a saloon and gambling hall that made him even more money, but he lost everything on a bad bet. He worked as a lumberjack long enough to earn some more money and opened another saloon in Alaska that was more profitable than the first—and lost that as well in worthless gold claims. Rickard had won and lost enough money to make Chapman's losses seem like small change.

The two became friends, but eventually decided they weren't going to strike it rich in the gold rush. Rickard invested what money he had left to establish another gambling house, the Northern Bar Saloon, in Goldfields, and Chapman returned to Salt Lake City where he landed a position as manager of Hogel's Saloon. Another twelve years were to pass before the two prospectors met again at the other end of the country, to strike it rich at the top of American sports.

While Chapman was falling out of racing, his rival Walthour was charging to the top of the sport. In 1899 when Chapman arrived in Salt Lake City, Walthour and Blanche settled in Newark, which was becoming a center for the sport in the Northeast. Walthour competed in many races that Billy Brady put on at Manhattan Beach and in the December six-day that Brady helped promote in Madison Square Garden. The Georgian continued to win. He became a darling of the penny press, which called him the Dixie Flyer. The *New York Times* later said, "Bobby Walthour was to bike racing what Babe Ruth was to baseball."

The Garden's six-day races, which had been held yearly since 1891, were on their way to becoming part of American popular culture. The Garden itself was synonymous with sports and entertainment in New York City—from Annie Oakley shooting glass balls out of the air in Buffalo Bill's Wild West Show to circuses to beauty contests—and the six-day bike racers were part of it.

Critics felt the six-days were punishment to the body, and in 1898 the New York State legislature passed a law forbidding any competitor to ride more than twelve hours a day. Fans and promoters feared that the event was dead, but they need not have worried. With a showman like Billy Brady involved, the event became more lively. Two-man teams were introduced, with each rider competing only twelve hours a day, and, like tag-team wrestlers, the teams could use their discretion on when each rider would race. This made the sixes more exciting than

Bobby Walthour, Sr., kept his head down when it came time
to race and won two gold medals and a silver in world
championships for the glamorous but dangerous motorpace
event. (*Brennan Brothers*)

ever and drew even bigger crowds. Two-rider team races have been
known worldwide ever since as Madisons.

In the 1901 six-day in the Garden, Walthour teamed with Archie
McEachern of Toronto against fifteen other teams. After 142 hours of
nonstop racing, Walthour and McEachern were tied with four other
teams for the lead. They had covered 2,555 miles—the distance from
Atlanta to San Francisco. When the bell rang for the final lap, a tenth
of a mile, Walthour took off so fast that only one other racer could stay
with him. They shot into the final turn, where Walthour blasted ahead

to win and clinch the race for himself and McEachern, earning $4,000 in prize money and product endorsements.

Walthour was the one who consistently got singled out in newspaper reports. When he raced, everyone was assured of action. When motorcycles were introduced after the turn of the century and cyclists raced behind motorcycles for motorpace racing, Walthour became the top motorpace racer. In 1902 he won nearly every competitive motorpace event, including the U.S. title, which he captured again the next year. He found that by reversing the frame's front fork and using a smaller diameter wheel he could lower his center of gravity to gain a better wind shield, riding 50 miles an hour and faster. In a motorpace event on the one-third-mile Charles River cement oval in Cambridge, Massachusetts, Walthour set twenty-six world records in a thirty-mile race.

Motorpace racing was glamorous but dangerous. Falls were common, largely because bicycle tires tended to burst at speed. The riders wore neither helmets nor gloves. They depended on fast reflexes, the rude health of youth, and luck. Despite having all three, Walthour collected an impressive (or dismaying) inventory of injuries over his career: twenty-eight fractures of the right collarbone, eighteen of the left, thirty-two broken ribs, and sixty stitches to his face and head. Once, according to family history, he was given up for dead in Paris and taken to a morgue, where he regained consciousness on the slab.

The injuries are only one measure of how much Walthour put into his races. The wins are another, and Walthour continued to win. In 1903 he and his teammate Bennie Munroe of Memphis won the six-day at Madison Square Garden. By then Paris race promoters Victor Breyer and Robert Coquelle were wooing the Dixie Flyer with attractive offers. In 1904, he went under contract to Paris, where he blossomed to international superstar status. He won sixteen out of seventeen motorpace events, making him such a hit that he was put under another contract to race through the end of the season.

That led to his entering the 1904 world cycling championships, held late in the summer on the grounds of London's Crystal Palace, a Victorian architectural marvel made of glass and steel. He won against a field of riders from seventeen countries in the 100-kilometer (62.5-mile) motorpace event.

The 1904 world cycling championships in London remain a high-water mark for American cycling. In addition to Walthour's triumph, Chapman's former tandem and traveling partner, Iver Lawson, made off with the world professional sprint championship. New Yorker Marcus Hurley rounded out the medals when he won the world amateur sprint championship. Both Lawson and Hurley remain the last American men to win those titles abroad.

What is remarkable about Lawson's victory is that he nearly lost the chance to compete. In February he was matched against Major Taylor in a two-mile race in Melbourne, Australia. In front of a crowd of 20,000 people, Taylor crashed heavily on the cement track, suffering multiple cuts and abrasions that put him in the hospital for two weeks. Lawson was charged with knocking Taylor down. The League of Victorian Wheelmen conducted an inquiry and found Lawson guilty of unfair riding. They imposed a twelve-month, worldwide suspension.

Lawson immediately appealed. He pleaded that the suspension would deprive him of his livelihood and cost him his contract with Cleveland Bicycles. After another inquiry involving about twenty witnesses, the board told Lawson they considered him guilty of careless riding, but they reduced his disqualification to three months, making it possible for him to compete in the world championships seven months later. He promptly returned to America, along with Floyd MacFarland, who had also raced in Australia until he and Taylor clashed once too often on the track and Australian officials banned him.

Taylor had deeply mixed feelings about the 1904 Australian tour. His wife gave birth to their only child in Sydney, a city the couple loved so much they named their daughter after it. Their first trip there the previous year had been a great success. Taylor's diary showed he won more than $23,000 in four months. His victories and the records he set led to a third European excursion that also included a few weeks of racing in England.

But Taylor's second trip to Australia was spoiled when his nemesis MacFarland showed up. Taylor felt MacFarland enlisted others to ride against him in teams.

Meanwhile, the stress of prolonged international travel and the pressure of high-level competition were getting to him. Before leaving Australia in June, he accepted another contract to compete in Europe where he was planning to race in the world championships in London. But he was becoming increasingly distraught. His return to America was marred when he and his family were refused service in a San Francisco restaurant. The contrast between Taylor's experiences abroad, where he was accorded celebrity status, and the treatment at home, where he was constantly relegated to being second class, made for a disquieting life.

Taylor returned home to Worcester for a brief vacation, but instead of enjoying a rest, he collapsed and suffered a nervous breakdown, forcing him to cancel his fourth annual European tour. His French promoters, Victor Breyer and Robert Coquelle, sued him for $10,000 for breach of contract. The National Cycling Association agreed with the French promoters and suspended Taylor for not fulfilling his contract.

By the time the world cycling championships took place, Taylor had quit riding altogether. He had brought back from Australia a baby kangaroo, a joey, and was more interested in raising it as a pet for his daughter than in racing.

Chapman got another chance at race promotions at the Salt Palace Velodrome when the track went through a lean period and management asked him to return in 1907. His first act was to import talent, a tactic he used for the rest of his career. From his racing days Down Under, he knew Jackie Clark, the Australian national champion famous for his explosive sprint. Chapman sent Clark an invitation and money for passage to Salt Lake City.

Clark was a colorful man, about 5 feet 6 inches, who dressed to the nines, drove the biggest automobiles available, and loved women. He came from North Shepparton, Victoria, where nobody attracted attention when they walked with rifles on the dirt streets. At twenty-one, Clark was a handsome, photogenic man with a sunny disposition, and his world records and his after-hours life made good newspaper copy.

The first to recognize his marquee value was Floyd MacFarland, who tried his hand in 1906 as a manager of talent. MacFarland got Clark an invitation to race in America for the season and managed Frank Kramer as well. MacFarland tried to link his two charges with a mutual name based on a period expression, "I've got you, Steve." He dubbed Kramer as Big Steve, and Clark as Little Steve. The nicknames didn't quite work because the American press was so impressed with Clark's explosive sprint that they named him the Australian Rocket. But the name Big Steve stuck with Kramer. After the season, Clark returned to Australia and MacFarland went back to racing.

In Salt Lake City, Clark attracted the kind of attention that Chapman needed to fill the velodrome seats again. While Clark was the big attraction, he had stiff challenges from Iver Lawson, who set several world records there; a San Jose native named Hardy Downing, who had competed around the country and in Australia; and several other experienced pros. But after a year in the same city, Clark was growing restless. He wanted to take on Frank Kramer, who was burning up races in the Northeast.

Kramer's speed was known in Europe, and in 1905 Paris promoters Breyer and Coquelle offered him an attractive contract. The climax of the tour was the Grand Prix de Paris, an event equal in grandeur to the world championships. In Paris, Kramer faced his toughest challenge in a three-rider match race against Frenchman Gabriel Poulain, who won the world championship later in the summer in Antwerp, Belgium, and the emerging Emile Friol, who was to win the world title two years later and again in 1910. Kramer prevailed to nip the Frenchmen at the line.

Races between national champion Frank Kramer and Australia's champion Jackie Clark were always exciting and helped pack the stands. (*Frank Mihlon, Jr.*)

The French were enthusiastic about his victory. They invited him back the next year where he won a second Grand Prix de Paris. Both his European trips were great successes. His first trip abroad resulted in fourteen wins in twenty-three starts; his second trip ended with seventeen wins in twenty races. He won decisively, but his personal life was so regimented and disciplined that the worldlier French found him bland and lost interest in him.

After that, Kramer remained in the United States. Although he lost the national championship to Taylor in 1900, Kramer clinched it in 1901 and appeared to have a headlock on it. But it was open to foreign challenges, and that appealed to Jackie Clark.

In August 1908, Chapman left the Salt Palace Velodrome and took his charge Clark east for match races against Kramer. Clark occasionally beat Kramer and promised to be Kramer's biggest threat in years for the national championship. Their races filled the grandstand and bleachers. On September 12, the national cycling championship was held in Madison Square Garden. A full program of amateur and professional races was held, but two events—the half-mile and mile—between Kramer and Clark were the central events. In the first race, the half-mile, Clark jumped away from Kramer and appeared to have it. Then Kramer made a great spurt, overtook the Australian, and finally won by a length. In the contest for the mile, Kramer trailed until the last lap when he again outsprinted Clark.

Chapman's success with the Salt Palace Velodrome and promoting such cyclists as Clark earned him a considerable reputation as a man of power and cunning. When he met Frank J. Mihlon, owner of the Long Bar Saloon in downtown Newark, a few miles from the velodrome, he impressed the saloon owner enough to persuade Mihlon to buy the Newark cycling franchise the next year and put him in charge. Chapman showed Mihlon how the network of railroads linking the cities of the Northeast made it possible for them to set up a franchise circuit based in Newark that extended to New Haven, Providence, Boston, and Philadelphia. This would give riders daily competition and net Mihlon a percentage of each race's gate. Mihlon thought the idea was a good one and backed him in the entire project.

As manager of the Newark Velodrome and director of the franchised circuit, Chapman earned a salary of $50 a week—a princely salary in those days. His races paid $50 to the winner, down to $5 for fifth place, and each meet had two to four races for the riders to compete in daily.

The better riders earned far more money than typical workers; automobile assembly line workers earned less than $2.50 for an eight-hour day. That was enough to live on at the time, however, as haircuts and movie admissions were twenty-five cents, thick corned-beef sandwiches cost a dime, and a saloon patron got free lunch for a nickel beer.

Among professional athletes, bicycle racers were the best paid. Baseball players were routinely underpaid, and frequently not paid, factors that contributed to the Chicago Black Sox scandal in the 1919 World Series. Professional football was still a raffish, underworld sport; basketball was decades away from having a league; and hockey was chiefly a Canadian phenomenon.

Over the next couple of years after 1908, Chapman was establishing himself as a promoter. In the winter months, he traveled to Europe where he attended indoor six-day races and developed contacts with foreign promoters and riders, many of whom began coming to America to race in his circuit. They included German champion Walter Rutt and Denmark's Thorwald Ellegaard, who won six world professional championships.

It was not all smooth going, however. He kept his distance from his former fellow riders, who complained privately that they felt he tried to make them feel subservient. Photos of Chapman show a stiff-looking man in a starched white shirt and collar, his tie always in place, wearing a business suit, button shoes, and rimless eyeglasses, looking sternly at the photographer. He was notoriously tightfisted with money and except for rare instances—such as with Kramer and Clark—refused to pay appearance fees.

His race circuit increased in importance as other tracks disappeared. The Grand Circuit that flourished around the country in the 1890s vanished as cars and motorcycles overtook the popularity of bicycles after the turn of the century.

Chapman had a penchant for importing talent. As he had with Clark, he also arranged passage to this country for Alf Goullet, another emerging Australian racer. There is no denying that Chapman could spot talent. Goullet was nineteen when he came to the United States in 1910, and he went on to win more than 400 professional races on three continents and set numerous world records, including one that stands today, the distance covered in a six-day race.

This foursome filled the seats when they were involved with races. Left to right are Frank Mihlon, who funded tracks; Frank Kramer, who raced on them; and two of Mihlon's track managers, John M. Chapman and Nat Butler. (*Frank Mihlon*)

Chapman persuaded Mihlon to build a new velodrome in the Vailsburg section of Newark. This board track measured six laps to the mile and accommodated 12,500 spectators. Its construction in the spring of 1911 marked the dawning of the sport's golden days, and Newark was well on its way to becoming known around the world as the home of cycling.

Major Taylor in 1910 was winding down his career in Salt Lake City when fire destroyed the great Salt Palace on August 29—eleven years to the day after it opened.

Taylor had settled out of court three years earlier with the two Paris promoters after they agreed to drop the suit in exchange for his return to Europe—including Sunday events. Taylor protested against the Sunday competitions, but Robert Coquelle, who made the trip to Worcester from Paris exclusively to get Taylor to sign a new contract, had the upper hand. Taylor wanted to get back to competition to support his wife and daughter, and the price he had to pay was to give in to Sunday races.

Taylor had gained forty pounds during his layoff and the extra weight showed. But he trained hard, trimmed down, and made a successful comeback in Europe. Once he got back into condition, he beat all the crack riders of Europe, except for French champion Jacquelin, who beat him when Taylor first arrived there. But later when Taylor regained his lightning form, he refused to take a return race with Jacquelin who had lost his form and was getting beaten by second- and third-rate riders.

At the close of the 1907 European tour, Taylor announced his retirement. It could be that Taylor fully intended to retire, for he always wanted to go out as a champion the way Zimmerman had advised. However, two main factors may have influenced the proud Taylor to change his mind and accept the many offers to race that he continued to receive. One was his anger at the widely held perception of black inferiority, a perception Taylor worked hard at dispelling. The other was the responsibility he felt toward his wife and daughter. Offers from Breyer and Coquelle kept him returning to race in Europe. But his last trip, in 1909, was so disappointing to the thirty-year-old Taylor, who was consistently beaten by inferior riders, that he regretted ever going.

He might have retired then, too, except that in America's highly charged racial climate, he didn't want to appear to back down. Black boxer Jack Johnson defeated Canadian Tommy Burns in 1908 for the world heavyweight championship, which prompted the white public to cry out for a "white hope" to regain the title. Tex Rickard, choosing another way to prospect for gold, promoted a fight between Johnson and James J. Jeffries, who came out of retirement to be that hope. Rickard built a special arena in Reno, and refereed the fight on July 4, 1910. Johnson knocked Jeffries out. The outcome bitterly disappointed whites around the country while blacks were euphoric. Major race riots broke out in Los Angeles, Kansas City, Washington, D.C., Norfolk, and Jacksonville.

When Taylor returned from Europe, he decided to race one more season, confining his races to America "with those dirty sandbaggers," as he wrote in a letter to his wife, describing those who let MacFarland influence them at his expense. In August 1910, Taylor competed at the

Salt Palace Velodrome against other pros like Iver Lawson, Hardy Downing, Jackie Clark (who returned to Salt Lake City to be near his fiancée), and his nemesis, Floyd MacFarland.

It was the beginning of the end for Taylor. His first appearance was on August 5, when he rode a quarter-mile exhibition behind a motorcycle. According to the *Salt Lake Tribune,* "The Negro rider was not the hero of any wonderful performance, but he gave a good exhibition behind the motor."

Not two weeks later, a match race between Taylor and Lawson, two former world champions, packed the stands outside the fabulous resort with 5,000 spectators. The two men competed in Taylor's specialty— the best of three one-mile match races on the eighth-mile velodrome for an $800 purse: $500 to the winner and $300 to the loser. Taylor, the master bike handler, maneuvered behind Lawson at the start of the first match. Lawson countered by taking Taylor up and down the steep banking to tire Taylor's legs and possibly get around behind him, to take advantage of drafting and to monitor his every move. But Taylor followed Lawson closely as they snaked up and down the banking for six and a half laps. They were high up the banking when Taylor abruptly cut down the inside of the track and burst for the finish. It was a standard tactic, and it gave Taylor a lead of several bike lengths and built speed before Lawson could react. Such a move executed between two riders of nearly the same ability normally would have won the race, yet Lawson shot down the banking, quickly caught Taylor, and beat him comfortably.

The second race was a similar defeat for Taylor. He was shut out of his specialty by a man two years older and only slightly taller. Three days later in a match race against Clark, he was again defeated. Taylor's career was clearly on the decline.

On August 28, Taylor and other racers competed in a benefit program to start a fund for riders injured on the Salt Palace Velodrome. The races drew another full house. Four world records were set in the course of the evening's program. One rider, S. H. Wilcox, clipped a second from Taylor's world quarter-mile motorpace record while Taylor watched from the sidelines. Taylor managed a second-place finish in a half-mile race against three others, and later competed against two others and finished last.

At three o'clock the next morning, fire broke out in a concession stand of the Salt Palace and reached the roof. A heavy wind fanned the flames to overwhelm the Palace and spread the short distance to the velodrome. Remarkably, as soon as the velodrome fire was doused, the manager had a fleet of carpenters repair the damage, and racing resumed three days later under the Utah sky.

On Labor Day, the final race of the season, Taylor won his heat in the quarter-mile race but got a bad start in the final and quit. Next came the mile handicap for professionals. Taylor started, but pulled out. The race just wasn't going well for him, and he didn't want to lose badly. He went home to Worcester and finally retired from athletics.

His eventful sixteen-year career ended profitably. He owned his home and his records show savings of $75,000—a considerable sum. After cycling, what interested him most was a mechanical trade. Taylor applied for admission to Worcester Technical School but was turned down because he lacked a high school diploma. The extension he designed for his handlebars had become a standard feature of bicycles, and he was fascinated with developing shock absorbers for trucks. He decided to use his capital and go into business with the Taylor Manufacturing Company to manufacture them.

Chapman's franchise circuit based in the Vailsburg section of Newark was a big commercial success for him and Frank Mihlon, except for the New Haven track, which was closed after the 1911 season. Australians traveled twenty-two days by ship and three days by train across the continent to come and race in Newark. Europeans traveled a week across the Atlantic to dock in New York and then take a short train ride to Newark to race. Newark was settled by immigrants from Germany, Italy, Poland, and Ireland, who went to watch racers from their homeland.

At the close of the 1911 season Chapman faced a crisis. Floyd MacFarland retired from racing and arrived in Newark to launch a new career as a promoter. Big Mac, as he was known, had distinguished himself in many events, especially six-day races against top international competition in Berlin, Paris, Brussels, and Vienna. MacFarland was also well known in this country, especially in Madison Square Garden, where he won six-days in 1900 and 1908.

Most of the top riders who traveled widely and raced hard liked

MacFarland. He was a gregarious man, and when the opportunity arose, he drank and told stories into the night. He was considered well educated for the period, with a high school diploma, and he could talk to anybody about anything. Yet he was not without his faults, and, not surprisingly, often clashed with Major Taylor. In the rough-and-tumble life of the professional athlete, Big Mac could also hold his own against anybody. While at a champagne reception in Camperdown, in Victoria, Australia, MacFarland was reputed to have deliberately insulted Bull Williams, a professional boxer. The two men squared off and MacFarland knocked his opponent flat.

In early 1912, with the racing season still some weeks away, thirty-six-year-old MacFarland began his career as a promoter by taking over the management of the Salt Palace Velodrome, where attendance had failed to return to the level enjoyed before the fire. He had a vision of where he wanted to take the sport, which included expanding franchises in the West and Canada the way Chapman did out of Newark. But first, he prevailed on old friendships. In the spirit of camaraderie, he easily persuaded many of Chapman's best pros to leave Newark for Salt Lake City. MacFarland recruited about twenty professionals, a good number for the Salt Palace Velodrome.

Chapman, meanwhile, did not sit idly behind his rolltop desk in his office upstairs in Mihlon's saloon. He used his contacts within the Union Cycliste Internationale and was granted the world cycling championships. The championships gave him considerable clout in signing contracts with top talent from abroad. Heading the list was two-time world champion Emile Friol of France, current French champion Andre Perchicot, and Australian champion Alfred Grenda of Tasmania. This gave Chapman a top lineup and assured him of a great season in Newark, culminating in the world championships.

Back in Salt Lake City, MacFarland's career as a promoter was off to a flying start. A local newspaper account proclaimed the 1912 season "the best season of racing which Salt Lake City has ever seen." Alf Goullet led with the first of about a dozen new world records set there. He won $150 in silver coins his first day. (Racers were never paid with paper money in Salt Lake City.)

World records put the Salt Palace Velodrome back in the news again.

According to Goullet, Mac was the only man who had the ability "to do a race right." If a race began at 3 P.M. on a Saturday, then the stands were packed at 2 P.M.

Floyd MacFarland holds up Jackie Clark, one of the riders MacFarland managed. (*Frank Mihlon*)

The main distinction between MacFarland and Chapman was personality. MacFarland's friendliness came across to the riders and spectators, whereas Chapman tended to remain aloof. And MacFarland was also extremely adept at coming up with new events, whereas Chapman preferred to stay with races that had worked in the past. Chapman lacked MacFarland's inherent feeling for the abilities of the riders so that the competitors could be closely matched. Then, as now, spectators lose interest in a race where the outcome is obvious long before the finish. Races are more than just athletes blasting away from the starting line. MacFarland was in his element when devising a racing schedule for spectators and riders alike.

Word of MacFarland's successes traveled to Newark, where riders were getting frustrated with the way Chapman treated them. So many riders were dissatisfied with Chapman that they sent MacFarland a cable that was published in a Newark newspaper:

Great majority of riders favor your immediate presence here. We are prepared to race at motordome across the street under your management. Motordome people will reconstruct track and also install lights upon advice from you. Proposition looks good. Chapman must be canned.

The motordome was a quarter-mile track that had opened on July 4, 1912. Motorcycles were the new rage, and motordomes hosting motorcycle races were opening in many cities around the country. The owner of Newark's motordome was Ingles Moore Uppercu, a pioneer automobile distributor, whose decision to convert the motordome into a velodrome was made in the aftermath of a tragic motorcycle accident that killed two racers and six spectators. MacFarland, however, was not prepared to discuss details until the close of the season.

By today's standards, the 1912 world championships late in the summer were simple. No road races were held. Nor were there races for women, who were still eight years away from the right to vote. Radio was a novelty and television was not to arrive until the next decade, so coverage was restricted to the penny press. Competitors were amateur and professional men who raced on the outdoor track in the summer sun for the right to be known as the best.

Kramer had been the reigning national champion every year since 1901 and was the highest-paid athlete in the country. In 1911, Ty Cobb of the Detroit Tigers held out all winter to increase his salary from $4,500 to $10,000; Kramer was already making more than $20,000. As reigning champion for twelve years, Kramer was under considerable pressure to win the world professional sprint title in the mile event, six laps of the velodrome. When he was among friends, the man they called Big Steve admitted concern about getting too nervous and not racing up to his ability. In his trial heat against three opponents, he apparently felt right, for he had no trouble winning to advance to the next round three days later. Before he left the velodrome on the first day, however, his chances for a world championship literally crumbled beneath him.

Emile Friol talked him into being his partner in the tandem races on opening day. A wiry and cheerful athlete, Friol had won the French national championship four times and the Grand Prix de Paris three times. He was the rider Kramer later named as his favorite. The American argued that if he were to ride a tandem in the world championships, which he didn't plan to do, he should choose a compatriot. Friol talked him out of it, explaining they were forming an all-star team.

When the tandem championship got under way, it looked as if the all-star team had it won on the last lap. Two of the best sprinters in the world were winding up their sprint off the far turn, where the banking went from 25 degrees on the straight to 52 degrees on the turn. Suddenly, their rear wheel collapsed and they slammed against the boards at speed. Friol was knocked unconscious. His face was scraped and his right eye was swollen nearly shut. Kramer's right arm and elbow suffered abrasions. They were forced to quit the race.

Three days later, Friol lined up for the next heat against former Australian champion Ernie Pye and two others. Friol's face was still swollen, and his right eye still nearly closed. Yet he was a feisty competitor and won, advancing to the semifinals three days later.

Kramer's heat pit him against Fred (Jumbo) Wells of New Zealand and two others. He won and thus qualified for the semifinals as well.

In the semifinals, Friol was eclipsed by compatriot Andre Perchicot who advanced to the final. Kramer defeated compatriot Walter DeMara to line up in the final against Perchicot and Alfred Grenda of Tasmania, a muscular yet lean six-footer.

The stands and the infield were filled with spectators as trainers held

START of the FINAL.

John M. Chapman held the world championships in Newark in
1912. Shown is the start of the final in the professional sprint
championship. From the left are Tasmanian champion Alfred
Grenda, American champion Frank Kramer, and French
champion Andre Perchicot. (*Brennan Brothers*)

the three finalists up on their bikes for the start of the six-lap race. After
three laps, Grenda zipped past Kramer for the lead. Perchicot tried to
catch Grenda's rear wheel, but Kramer's reactions were quicker and he
got there first. For the next two laps, Grenda put his head down, locked
his arms into a streamlined position, and steadily quickened the tempo
to keep the lead.

As the bell rang to signal the last lap, spectators yelled for Kramer.
He stayed behind Grenada, and with fewer than 300 yards remaining,
the screaming spectators feared Kramer would let them down. The
Newark Evening News reported:

"Make your jump now, Frank!" and "Go on, Kramer!" were shouts that were heard from all quarters as the men swung to the first turn on the last lap, and everybody who hadn't already stood up jumped to their feet. Everybody knew that within a few more seconds a world's championship would be won and lost, and pretty near every mother's son and daughter of them wanted Kramer to win it. They thought he could win it, too, but the tardiness made them fearful. Should he falter after the twelve years of campaigning when the crown was in sight should be disheartening.

Midway through the first turn, Kramer moved up on Grenda, who pedaled faster to hold him off while Perchicot drafted comfortably at the rear. They were barreling at more than 30 miles an hour down the back straight when Kramer pulled even with the tall Tasmanian. But Grenda still held Kramer off. When they leaned into the 52-degree banking of the final turn, Grenda forced Kramer to take the turn wide and gained a length on the American when they hit the final straight. It was do or die when Kramer unloaded his sprint. The *Evening News* continued:

First, his advance was slow, and then he came faster, but come he surely did, and as each yard passed under him he was nearer Grenda's front wheel and after the halfway mark in the stretch was reached it was seen that he could win. There were already exultant shouts from the spectators, and, as Kramer came on, they increased, so that when he finished a yard from the tape they broke into bedlam. The race was over. It was a great race and fairly won and fairly lost.

Grenda lost by inches, with Perchicot finishing higher on the track, only a wheel's diameter behind. Kramer became the last American to win the world professional sprint championship.

Chapman's world championships reaped a good profit for him and franchise owner Mihlon. But a few days after the worlds, the accident at Uppercu's motordome occurred and everything changed. Uppercu announced that he was prepared to convert the track for bicycle racing. He was ready to hire the riders necessary to have the new track compete against the Newark Velodrome, and he had considerable capital to back up his goal. As Mihlon and Chapman tallied their receipts for the year, a battle was shaping up between Uppercu and Mihlon to determine who would survive the next season.

MacFarland left the situation in Newark alone. He and all his riders boycotted Chapman's world championships. At the conclusion of his successful season in Salt Lake City, MacFarland took a coterie of his riders, including Goullet, off to Europe and set up indoor events for them in Berlin, Prague, Brussels, Copenhagen, and Paris. He had developed many contacts during his racing career and used them wisely on this 1913 tour.

Floyd MacFarland's riders passed up the world championships and afterward went to Europe for the winter season where they took on the best riders. One of MacFarland's charges, Alf Goullet, on the far left, lines up in the Velodrome d'Hiver in Paris for a match race against 1909 world champion Victor Dupre of France and the redoubtable Thorwald Ellegaard of Denmark, who won six world professional sprint championships between 1901 and 1911. (*Alf Goullet*)

Within two weeks of arriving in Paris, MacFarland had lined up a six-day event. It ran from January 13 to 19, and drew a top international field at the famed Velodrome d'Hiver. MacFarland signed up sixteen teams, most of which were made up of household names of the period, including Tour de France winners Octave Lapaize and Lucien Petit-Breton of France, Maurice Brocco of Italy, Cesare Debaets of Belgium, and Bobby Walthour. Goullet, teamed with Joe Fogler of Brooklyn, won the race after riding 2,600 miles.

For races in Berlin, MacFarland wanted to sign up former German champion Walter Rutt, a friend of MacFarland's who had won two six-days in Madison Square Garden. But twenty-nine-year-old Rutt had dodged the draft for compulsory military training and could not return to his homeland. Yet MacFarland's good relationship with Emperor Kaiser Wilhelm II, a great fan of bicycle racing, who in 1909 had given MacFarland and partner Jimmy Moran each a pair of gold cuff links for winning the Berlin six-day, quickly solved this problem. Rutt was allowed to race.

At the conclusion of the winter season, MacFarland returned in early April with his riders to Newark. He visited friends and was quickly informed about the latest friction between Mihlon and Uppercu.

Mihlon by then was a saloon owner who had moved up socially through his cycling connections. The velodrome circuit that Chapman managed for him generated considerably more income than the Long Bar Saloon, with its brass foot rail running the long length of its bar, and walls that were festooned with hunting trophies such as ten-point bucks. Mihlon was an affable man who hobnobbed in high social circles. He was a bachelor of thirty-five and soon to marry the lovely Minnie Yetter, a Gibson girl and movie actress at Fox Studio in nearby Fort Lee. Mihlon's cycling connections extended to Madison Square Garden, where he reaped a percentage of the highly profitable six-day events, and extended even further to investment opportunities in Europe where he soon would become part owner of velodromes in London and Rome.

Above all, Mihlon was a businessman. The Long Bar Saloon had been in the family for decades, and he understood what he risked by going against Uppercu, who had considerable economic resources at his disposal. When MacFarland approached him with a suggestion for preventing a confrontation, Mihlon was receptive.

MacFarland brought the two track owners together. He recommended that Mihlon let Uppercu buy a half interest in the Newark Velodrome in exchange for Uppercu's closing the velodrome. This left Mihlon with the rest of his enterprises untouched. He would rather have Uppercu on his side than against him, and he graciously agreed to MacFarland's recommendation.

MacFarland's strategy was opportunistic. He had proven what he could do while managing the Salt Palace Velodrome and the races he put on in Europe, and he was intent on taking over the Newark Velodrome. As the diplomat who prevented a potential commercial war, the new co-owners hired him to manage the velodrome, which aced Chapman out altogether. The prestigious franchise Chapman was in large part responsible for establishing was taken out of his hands. There was not much for him to do but return with his wife, Martha, to the family farm in Georgia.

4 A BIZARRE TWIST

MacFarland became the premier cycling promoter of competitive cycling in America. He paid out more appearance money than ever. Alf Goullet was paid $3,000 in appearance fees in 1914, won another $5,000 in prizes, and won $3,500 more in the six-day race in Madison Square Garden that November for a total annual sum of $11,500. That was a prestigious income at the time when Henry Ford's workers took home the unprecedented figure of $5 for an eight-hour workday, or $1,300 a year.

Goullet's voice is still strong and resonant, his face is remarkably unlined, and his blue eyes are so good that he does not need glasses for driving during the day. Born in 1891, he grew up in Emu, 150 miles north of Melbourne, where he made his own dirt track. He hitched a horse to a heavy log, dragging it to clear away grass on ground that had natural bankings. In 1908 he competed in his first race—a quarter-miler—which he entered as a professional. It was a near disaster. The trainer became so nervous holding him up that the firing of the starter's gun startled him and he pushed Goullet to the ground. Goullet, however, scrambled back on his bike, finished third in the heat, and went on to win the final, establishing a reputation that earned him an invitation to Newark in 1910.

The transition from Australian racing to competition in America was enormous. Goullet had to become faster and smarter in order to compete. At the 1914 six-day in Madison Square Garden, he was teamed with Alfred Grenda. The Tasmanian six-footer, who stood a head taller than Goullet, was an extremely strong man who had spent his off-seasons in northern Australia chopping down trees for furnaces that generated steam in the mines. In late 1911 when Goullet returned to Australia to win the Melbourne and Sydney six-days, Chapman cabled him to sign up two riders. He signed up Grenda, figuring "that was all that was needed." Their dispositions made them natural foils: Goullet was high-strung and inclined to fret; Grenda didn't worry as long as he got six or seven meals a day and could take an occasional nap.

The six day in the Garden was the major event of the year for racers and a big social opportunity for the city. Anytime of the day or night there was at least one band playing lively music on the infield. Crowds attended around the clock to watch the riders. Every day New York's thirteen daily newspapers would compare the present teams' mileages to those of past racers. The crowds drew song pluggers who hired pianists and sang through a megaphone on the bandstand in the track infield. Sometimes the song pluggers had help from cabarets. When the Harlem cabarets closed for the night, the jazz bands and combos would head for the action of the Garden's six-day. While the racers were pedaling their way toward world records, the song pluggers were peddling songs like "For Me and My Gal," "Peg o' My Heart," and "Road to Mandalay."

The nightclub atmosphere, combined with the fierce competition—which invariably opened with riders covering fifty or so miles in the first two hours—generated so much excitement that riders rarely slept in the first twenty-four hours. On the second day, they became saddle sore, while their wrists, arms, legs, and necks began to ache. The aches and soreness usually continued until the final day. Then the racers approached the finish in a rush of adrenaline. The final hours of the race turned into one hard chase after another. Audiences relished these and called them "jams."

At the 1914 six-day, which ran from November 16 to 21, MacFarland was the general manager. Wearing a dark three-piece suit and bowler hat, he seemed to be everywhere—up in the stands and down at trackside—always monitoring the race. He kept the race pumped up with more than $2,000 for designated sprints; for teams that "lapped the field," that is, broke away from the front and continued all the way around to catch the others from behind, thus stealing a lap; and for teams leading in distance. He also adapted a new ending. Instead of the last-mile sprint, he introduced racing over the final hour. Teams a lap or more behind the leaders would be withdrawn to leave the leaders alone to sprint every fifteen laps (1.5 miles) for points, with six points awarded to the winner, five to second, down to one for sixth.

Most of MacFarland's premiums for designated sprints were $10, although some from audience donations rose as high as $250. The premiums—called premes—kept the riders sprinting, and soon after the race began the leaders were ahead of the record of 2,751 miles that Goullet had set the previous year with his Paris six-day partner Joe Fogler.

By the fourth day, the aggressive pace had taken a toll on the eighteen starting teams. Several riders were forced to withdraw. Those whose partners dropped out formed new teams after losing a penalty lap. But on the fifth day, many of the riders banded together and threatened to quit if MacFarland did not stop offering premes. They complained that they could not get any sleep because of all the premes, and that the competition was becoming distorted. Teams that were behind in the race could hit up a terrific pace during the sprints to win money and then rest by dropping back a few laps, while teams in the lead had to fight to keep up the pace or be dropped.

MacFarland reminded them that they had known about the sprints for the premes when they entered the race and that no change would now be made. He also warned them that, if they quit, they would be ruled off all tracks for violating their contracts. The dissatisfied riders grumbled, but all continued.

Between accidents on the velodrome and the duration of the event, a majority of the riders incurred minor injuries. Through it all, the team of Goullet-Grenda managed to stay in control of the race. By 5 P.M. Saturday, with the finish still five hours away, the Garden's stands and infield were filled to standing room only. The *New York Times* commented:

The arena was one vast mass of humanity, packed in as close as sardines, as every available seat was taken, and the crowd was literally hanging on the rafters. Early in the evening the place was kept in an uproar by the desperate efforts of Clark and his partner, Root, to make up the lap which they lost Friday night, and which divided them from the six leading teams.

Nobody in the top six teams wanted to contend with riders like Clark and Eddie Root in the final hour, and they fought to stave off the aggressive attacks that Clark and Root launched. Clark's partner, a thirty-four-year-old Bostonian, was an established star on both sides of the Atlantic; Clark himself had won Garden sixes in 1909 and 1911. Root was famous for having won a six-day in Brussels in 1909, resting one day, and then competing in the Paris six-day, which he also won. He had a taste for the ironic, and for years he raced with Number 13 over his back. From 1904 to 1906 he had ridden on consecutive winning teams in the Garden sixes.

The attacks and counterattacks in the 1914 six-day continued hour after hour. The hot pace and taut drama kept spectators yelling and on their feet. But not even stalwarts like Clark and Root were able to make up their lost lap. During the final hour, the top six teams were left to fight among themselves to determine who would win the $1,600 for placing first, $1,000 for second, down to $350 for sixth.

In that final hour, the audience was electric with excitement. Grenda was struck with an attack of appendicitis, forcing Goullet to do most of the racing for their team. Goullet won eight of the sprints to lead his team to victory with 2,759 miles and one lap—the distance from San Francisco to Buffalo. They set the world record that still stands today.

MacFarland's success in the Northeast had a consequence in Salt Lake City. The Salt Palace Velodrome closed. Local pros had either gone east or quit. Hardy Downing, age thirty-six in 1914, was one pro who retired. He opened a local boxing gym that promoted amateur and professional cards on Monday nights. In 1915, a reedy-voiced Mormon youth who called himself Kid Blackie and used to run errands for Downing years earlier asked for the chance to break into professional boxing. Kid Blackie won his first bouts in Downing's gym, changed his name to Jack Dempsey, and soon was slugging his way into American sports history.

MacFarland, meanwhile, seemed to have a golden touch, for success after success came of his ventures. Everyone seemed to win, for the sport's popularity enhanced the lesser promoters and a majority of the riders.

For the 1915 season, MacFarland had several plans in store. Although the war in Europe forced suspension of the world championships after 1913, MacFarland planned to hold a spectacular world championships in Newark, Philadelphia, and Boston in 1915, or whenever the war ended and the worlds were resumed. He also established a track in Chicago with a local promoter named Paddy Harmon that was scheduled to open with the 1915 season, and he planned another track in Toronto. Big Mac, who had gained a few pounds and started to fill out, enlisted Chapman for the Toronto management. MacFarland knew Chapman had the expertise to develop a racing circuit based in Toronto and modeled after the one he had put together in Newark.

Chapman arrived in Newark in the middle of April to discuss details with MacFarland and Mihlon, who was funding the Toronto venture. Neither one could have anticipated that Chapman, who had been completely removed from the sport for two years, would be returning to take over big-time cycling for good.

On Saturday, April 17, 1915, the weather was chilly as athletes geared up for a new season. Newspaper sports pages that day said that Ty Cobb was on his way to his ninth straight American League Batting Championship, and that a field of seventy-five runners were signed up to run in the nineteenth annual Boston Marathon which would be held in two days. In Newark, about 150 fans, chiefly men and boys, put up with the chill to watch riders in wool clothes practice on the velodrome that afternoon in preparation for the early-season races, set to begin the next day.

Those at the track saw MacFarland get into a heated argument with David Lantenberg of Brooklyn, who ran a concession selling refreshments at the track. Lantenberg, a twenty-seven-year-old with dark hair, had been mounting posters on a velodrome wall when the advertising manager—Wally Howes—told him the signs were not allowed. The screws that Lantenberg used to mount the posters loosened and fell to the track where they caused tire punctures. Lantenberg protested that he was authorized to post the signs to promote his business. The two argued until Howes left to take the matter up with MacFarland, who angrily rushed over to Lantenberg.

MacFarland was reputed to have a bad temper. He and Lantenberg got into a shouting match. Lantenberg, who came only to MacFarland's chest and weighed 120 pounds, insisted he was going to put up his signs no matter what MacFarland said. He turned and used the screwdriver he was holding to drive a screw into the wall. MacFarland grabbed his arm, and both men lost their tempers. Witnesses told police that Lantenberg lashed out with the screwdriver and MacFarland, who quickly turned his head, could not avoid the blow. The point of the screwdriver struck the back of MacFarland's head behind his left ear, pierced his skull, and penetrated his brain. He dropped senseless to the ground.

Lantenberg's anger vanished when MacFarland collapsed. Alfred Grenda rushed to the quarrel in time to pick up MacFarland, with Lantenberg's help. They carried him to Lantenberg's nearby car and rushed him to Newark City Hospital.

The screwdriver had penetrated five inches into the back of MacFarland's skull. He never regained consciousness. At his bedside were his wife, Frank Mihlon, Frank Kramer, and Alf Goullet.

MacFarland died at 9 P.M. He was thirty-nine.

"I felt empty," Goullet says. "It was a real loss."

Lantenberg was arrested at the hospital and taken to Seventh Police Station. He was initially charged with assault, then with homicide, and finally with manslaughter; he was acquitted on June 23.

News of MacFarland's death was carried on page one the next day in newspapers from Newark to New York City. A crowd of 1,500 attended the funeral at the home of Frank Kramer, who escorted MacFarland's widow during the service. A thousand gathered at the cemetery where the casket was kept temporarily until it was sent for burial in Buffalo, his wife's hometown. Eighty-five floral offerings were received, requiring three horse-drawn wagons to carry them to the cemetery. Foreign cyclists sent a horseshoe-shaped floral arrangement bearing the colors of the countries they represented.

A week after MacFarland died, the *New York Times* ran a feature on his career, complete with a portrait two columns wide, a practice reserved for important figures. The *Times* acknowledged that MacFarland was a master at arranging a race program and could suggest more new turns to a race than anyone else connected with the sport.

———————————————

Races at the velodrome were suspended for a week. Co-owners Frank Mihlon and Ingles Uppercu discussed the situation with Chapman, who had signed a contract to manage the Toronto Velodrome. On April 22 Mihlon and Uppercu announced that Chapman would succeed MacFarland as manager of the Newark Velodrome, and a resident manager would be appointed in Toronto under Chapman's supervision.

The *Newark Evening News,* carrying the announcement as the lead sports story that day, acknowledged the "dissension in the ranks of the cyclists" in 1912, when a majority of the riders wanted Chapman canned, but it endorsed Chapman by saying, "With a vast amount of money and great fortune at stake, it is no time to experiment with an inexperienced man." Comparing the two promoters, the *Evening News* observed, "Chapman lacks the magnetism of MacFarland. He is more of the cool, calculating business man."

The newspaper said others had been briefly considered for the post but praised Chapman as "the best man for the position," adding, "Chapman knows the game thoroughly. The present success of cycling in America is largely due to his ideas, and it was the foundation laid by him in 1911 and the two years following that put the sport on a firm basis here in Newark."

Through a bizarre twist and by being in the right place at the right time, Chapman was back in charge.

He returned to his old office over Frank Mihlon's saloon on Market Street and from there oversaw the operations his late rival had set up. The managers of the other velodromes tended to be retired professional riders, like Walter Bardgett, who took over the Chicago track, and Nat Butler, who oversaw the Boston track. In their youth Bardgett and Butler had competed around the United States and in cities across Europe with Bobby Walthour, Major Taylor, and Floyd MacFarland.

Over the next few years, Chapman supervised an active schedule of races that strengthened his hold on the sport. As he gained more control of the cycling business, his old crony Tex Rickard showed up in New York City after a detour that had taken him to Paraguay where he had raised cattle for six years. Rickard was on his way to becoming the biggest boxing promoter ever. He and Chapman palled around together. Rickard gave Chapman a small trophy of a boxer for his rolltop desk. Chapman introduced him to bicycle races, and Rickard became an instant fan, especially of the six-day events that Chapman organized in Madison Square Garden.

During this time, Bobby Walthour was still racing in Europe. Despite the war, bicycle racing continued and Walthour was in high demand in Paris, Leipzig, Berlin, Milan, and other cities. For a decade he had won every European motorpace classic. He won a third world championship medal when he placed second for a silver in the 1910 motorpace event in Brussels. (The U.S. Cycling Federation incorrectly lists it as a bronze medal.) By 1917 he had also won fourteen six-day races, the greatest number in the world at the time.

But late in the summer of 1917, in a motorpace event in Paris, he suffered his most severe crash. His front tire blew out, throwing him to the track where other riders and motorcycles ran into his prostrate body. By the time rescuers reached him, his head was split open, his left shoulder was broken, and his arms and legs were severely cut.

French physicians gave up hope and didn't bother replying to his wife's cables from Newark asking about his condition. The U.S. embassy in Paris had been instructed to take care of his remains if he died and to see to the flowers.

Three weeks passed before he was able to open his eyes. Another four weeks went by before he could leave his cot and board a ship for home.

Aside from Kramer, Walthour was the last of America's world champions still competing. Iver Lawson, forty, was working for Chapman as a clerk. Lawson had saved nothing during his career and had a drinking problem that was attributed to grief over the death of his brother, Gus, in a motorpace crash in Cologne, Germany. Zimmerman still had his hotel in Point Pleasant. Riders like Goullet occasionally went there to drink a pint. Major Taylor continued to live in Worcester, and word in the cycling community that summer had it that Taylor was going broke with investments turning sour. Property he bought as a revenue source wasn't panning out because his tenants wouldn't pay their rent. A home-heating company that he formed was draining him. The Taylor Manufacturing Company was losing money as well.

It was also that summer that the inevitable happened—Frank Kramer was finally beaten in the national professional championship after winning it for sixteen consecutive years. The title was won by a newcomer, a robust twenty-year-old from Toronto named Arthur Spencer.

Kramer's defeat, news of Taylor's misfortunes, and Walthour's near-fatal crash may have produced a sentimental moment for the normally unsentimental Chapman. Or perhaps he saw an opportunity. For whatever reason, he organized an old-timers' race at the Newark Velodrome for Sunday, September 16.

Goullet, recalling the event in 1986, said it was the only old-timers' race he ever heard of at the Newark Velodrome. "There should have been more races like that to help generate public interest in the sport," Goullet contends. "Bicycle racing was a badly managed sport after MacFarland died."

Chapman invited Taylor, which prompted local sports writers to question whether Taylor would accept because he had never raced on Sunday in America. Besides, Chapman, always tightfisted, was not paying travel expenses. But Taylor cabled back that he had returned from a hunting trip and would be in Newark for the race "with both feet."

Zimmerman, forty-eight, declined because he was ill with rheumatism. Mile-a-Minute Murphy, forty-six, was unable to race because of a pulverized kneecap suffered while on duty as a New York City motorcycle policeman. But he came to watch and was appointed official starter.

Taylor's mentor Louis Munger made the trip down from Middletown, Connecticut. On the way, Munger was involved in a car wreck, borrowed another car, and drove night and day—typical for the road conditions of the period—to arrive in time to hold Taylor up for the start.

Taylor looked older than his thirty-eight years. In street clothes he appeared trim, but once he was in racing uniform the extra weight he had gained over the years showed. He rode a bicycle that Goullet lent him, a Redbird, made by hand at the Columbia Bicycle Company. All the components came, however, from Europe—a reflection of how the bicycle-making industry in America had fallen off.

The stands were filled to capacity with 12,500 spectators on the day of the old-timers' one-mile race—six laps around the velodrome. Goullet recalled that Taylor was relaxed as he rode his warm-up laps and waved to the audience who cheered for him and the others.

Eleven riders entered the event, which the *Newark Evening News* in a preview story called the "Rheumatic Stakes Feature." Chapman entered, along with Taylor's rival from the 1899 worlds, Nat Butler.

The *Newark Evening News* declared, "Major Taylor is the best of ancient pedal-pushers," and added: "The dusky demon won and won as he pleased with yards to spare, making a show of his Caucasian brethren."

In the regular program, Goullet won both the half-mile and the five-mile handicap races for professionals. Frank Kramer, who had lightheartedly lined up for the start of the old-timers' race until photos were taken, triumphed in the professional mile match race against two opponents.

By December, Walthour was sufficiently recovered from his injuries to sign a contract to race in the Garden's six-day. Even when he was getting back to fitness he was a better rider than most others on their best days, and was always a great crowd attraction. Not long after the event got rolling, however, his partner took ill and both riders were forced to withdraw. A week later, Walthour slipped on ice while walking near his home. His left leg broke in two places between the knee and ankle.

The Garden's six-day was continuing to gain a bigger following. This time the song pluggers were introducing patriotic tunes like "Over There" and "It's a Long Way to Berlin, But We'll Get There from Here."

In 1917, Chapman lengthened the race from 142 hours to 144 so that it ended at midnight Saturday. He also introduced the Berlin Points System to heighten the action. A series of ten two-mile sprints were introduced for the matinee, evening, and late-night shows. For these races, six points were awarded for a win, four for second place, two for third, and one for fourth. In the final hour, from 11 P.M. to midnight, the racing got hotter. There was a sprint every mile, with seventy-two points awarded to each winner; points then decreased precipitously— from five points for second to one for fourth. A race's outcome could change drastically in the last hour.

That year, boxing lost at political roulette in New York and was declared illegal. Chapman's pal boxing promoter Tex Rickard was shaping the career of boxing's new sensation, Jack Dempsey, who could knock an opponent out with either fist. Rickard traveled to Toledo, where he set up a championship bout for July 4, 1919, pitting Dempsey against 260-pound Jess Willard. The Ohio Ministerial Association denounced the fight. The Ohio legislature passed a resolution requesting that the governor ban the fight. But all the opposition accomplished was to promote Rickard's fight, which Dempsey won with a third-round knockout.

In 1920, New York State senator James J. Walker, who would be the mayor of New York City a few years later, helped arrange passage of what was known as the Walker Law which permitted boxing again. Rickard moved fast, and before the law was signed, he had leased Madison Square Garden from the New York Life Insurance Company for ten years at $200,000 a year. He then took over the management. With Dempsey as the new heavyweight boxing champion, and his old prospector friend Chapman in charge of bicycle racing, Rickard was ready to usher the Roaring Twenties into Madison Square Garden.

Not one to let opportunities pass by, Rickard had Chapman start up the six-days with a spring event that March to augment the long-standing winter six-day in the Garden. On August 1, 1920, Rickard signed a five-year contract with Chapman to jointly hold two six-days a year in the Garden with $50,000 purses each, and Rickard announced their plans to import more foreign talent than had ever been seen in the history of the sport.

Cycling's golden days were rolling.

5
WONDERFUL NONSENSE IN THE GOLDEN DAYS

In 1920, eleven football teams that would eventually form the National Football League went on sale for $100 each. One could have bought the entire NFL for $1,100. The better bicycle racers made almost that much—$700 to $1,000—in a good week. Chapman's race programs paid $200 to the winner of the open race, $100 for second, on down to $10 for sixth place, and $100 to the winner of the handicap race, down to $10 for sixth place. Professional riders usually raced in at least two events in each program, and some riders like Goullet and Kramer made up to $350 more for winning match races. The prize money had gone up after Chapman raised the velodrome general admission fee in 1919 to fifty cents, matching the cost of movie tickets.

Fortune smiled upon Chapman after he took over from MacFarland. He bought a hilltop mansion in nearby Summit and improved his family's College Park farm in Georgia where he and his wife spent winters. The log cabin he was born in was torn down and replaced by a modern house. Then he apparently had second thoughts and built another log cabin to show how far he had come.

Construction started in 1920 on the New York Velodrome, which opened in 1921 and was considered the best in the country. Located at

225th and Broadway, the track was at the end of a rail line that cost only five cents to ride. People who drove to the velodrome could park for free. Chapman managed the velodrome for co-owners Ingles Uppercu, the Cadillac distributor, and John Ringling, the circus entrepreneur.

The circuit Chapman managed was rigorous, with eight outdoor programs a week for seven months of the year. Racing began Sunday afternoon on the Newark Velodrome, then moved Sunday night to the New York Velodrome. On Monday night events were in Providence or the Revere Beach Velodrome in Boston, followed by Tuesday again in New York, Wednesday in Newark, Thursday in Philadelphia, Friday night in New York, and Saturday night in Newark. Cycling was so popular that Massachusetts had tracks in Worcester and New Bedford that were independent of Chapman.

The races were fiercely competitive. In the open events, fields of fifty to sixty went hard and fast around the velodromes, which were only twenty-two feet wide. The riders zipped around these narrow tracks at speeds approaching forty miles an hour, and there was a lot of body contact through the turns. Bike races on the boards were like hockey on wheels. Riders slammed each other into the boards of the outside railing or crunched together in mass pileups that twisted wooden wheel rims and steel frames like pretzels. Falls could be serious. Dan Pischione of Providence was killed by a splinter that drove into his abdomen when he fell. Reggie McNamara of Australia, called Old Ironman for the punishment he endured, left a tooth imbedded in the track boards after one crash.

The action, and the attendance, appealed to Tex Rickard. Wearing his trademark Stetson and carrying his cane, he was seen often at the races. Leading sports and entertainment celebrities were traditionally official starters for the six-days in the Garden. For the March 1921 event, Rickard took the liberty of firing the starting pistol. The following March, Jack Dempsey did the honors. Other official starters included Oklahoma humorist Will Rogers, who toted his own six-gun to start a six-day; Al Jolson, whose movie *The Jazz Singer* introduced sound to film; and entertainers Eddie Cantor, Jimmy Durante, and George Jessel.

Chapman's outdoor velodromes were the same size, six laps to the mile, but the New York Velodrome had the largest seating—20,000 filled the stands three times a week. Publicity generated by the outdoor circuit helped bolster enthusiasm for the winter indoor six-days. The

Al Jolson was a six-day fan and fired the starting pistol for this six-day in Madison Square Garden. (*Brennan Brothers*)

six-days in Madison Square Garden took over as the primary events of their kind at the beginning and end of each season.

By the late teens, six-day fever had spread around the country. Chapman created an international circuit of six-days that included Buffalo, Philadelphia, Pittsburgh, Cleveland, Toronto, Montreal, Detroit, Indianapolis, St. Louis, Kansas City, and Chicago. Riders would rest up two or three days before boarding a train to travel to the next event. Promoters in western cities also held six-days that Chapman sanctioned through the governing body, the National Cycling Association, which he ran out of his office. North America had as many six-days as Europe.

All this gave Chapman tremendous international power in cycling. His races were among the best paying in the world, and the circuit he controlled offered the best opportunities anywhere. The $50,000 purse for each of the two annual Garden six-days gave Chapman the pick of the best racers from three continents.

Chapman took a tip from Rickard, who was quick to put up money. Beginning in 1920, Chapman paid Alf Goullet $1,000 a day as appearance money to ride in six-days in New York and Chicago. Goullet was fast; he was known as the Australian Bullet. His personal traits appealed to Chapman; he was flamboyant on the track, which attracted crowds and the press, yet he was reserved and gentlemanly off his bike. Besides the six-day distance record Goullet set with Grenda in 1914, Goullet had five other world records, all unpaced, from two-thirds of a mile to fifty miles. His fifty-mile record, in 1 hour 49 minutes 8 seconds set on the Newark Velodrome, which stood for fifty years, is still one that few can touch today on better equipment.

Goullet generated the kind of news coverage Chapman liked. "That dark and sinister villain, Alfred Goullet, again held the center of the stage last night in the six-day cycling drama at Madison Square Garden," the *New York Times* reported on March 13, 1920, in telling how Goullet helped his American partner Jake Magin win the inaugural spring event. "While the fans booed and groaned with their usual gusto, he circled the track in front four out of six sprints, and maintained the team lead despite repeated onslaughts by the other ten combinations."

Goullet's trademark was a scarlet silk jersey with black trim on the sleeves. He rode with his back low to the frame, yet without his knees hitting his chest. When he sprinted, he stayed on the saddle while the middle of his back arched up like an attacking cat.

A match race between Alf Goullet, left, and Frank Kramer
always kept the audience on its feet. (*Alf Goullet*)

Goullet and other riders sweated hard for their pay, but at its best,
the life of a bicycle racer who could make the grade gave back what few
other endeavors could match. Peppering the action on the track were
three sprint programs with ten two-mile sprints in each, beginning at
the 3 P.M. matinee, 9:30 P.M. evening show, and 2:30 A.M. session for the
theater crowd. The sprints whipped audiences into a frenzy that in-
duced heavy spending for premes.

The 1920s were wonderful nonsense, and the Garden's six-days
were part of it. Actress Peggy Joyce—whose wealth and style
prompted Cole Porter to pen, "My string of Rolls Royces is longer than
Peggy Joyce's"—liked to serve up $200 premes several times a night

to keep up the tempo. Once, while the band played "Pretty Peggy with Eyes of Blue," she had a grand time watching the riders tear around the track for her $1,000 preme.

Mike Delores, known as the Mad Hatter from Danbury, got into the Garden at the end of one evening sprint session, but he was allowed to extend the sprints as long as he posted two and three century notes at a time until he turned his pockets inside out. He then came back for the morning session with an even bigger roll than before. The Mad Hatter from Danbury put up his entire roll for a two-mile sprint preme. It came to $2,400.

The Garden's six-days grew so popular that it was not unusual for two bands to perform along the back stretch and another two on the home stretch, each band playing a different song as the riders charged round and round on what sportswriters of the period called the human squirrel cage.

Entertainers who regularly attended were Enrico Caruso, Mary Pickford, Douglas Fairbanks, John Barrymore, Bob Hope, and Jimmy Durante. Theatrical impresario Florenz Ziegfeld rented a box by the week and brought along beautiful showgirls to fill it. Crooner Bing Crosby went regularly and was known to pick up hospital costs of injured riders. Others who stopped by to watch—and not necessarily cover the event—were celebrated newspaper writers Damon Runyon, Heywood Broun, Westbrook Pegler, Herbert Swope, and James M. Cain. Before Cain became famous for his novels, and successful movie adaptations— *The Postman Always Rings Twice, Mildred Pierce,* and *Double Indemnity*—he wrote editorials on the six-day races for the *New York World.* Crowds streamed through the Garden's doors until the fire marshal ordered them closed.

Into this colorful, endless whirl rode Bobby Walthour, Junior. In 1921, Walthour's son won the national amateur track championship at the age of nineteen, and soon afterward turned professional to follow in his father's tire marks.

"He was really proud of his dad," says Bobby Walthour III. "My dad used to brag about him. My dad took a big chance trying to fill his dad's shoes, but he gave it a good try."

The son had his father's easygoing disposition and straw-blond hair.

He grew up around velodromes on both sides of the Atlantic and lived in Germany long enough to become fluent in German. The Walthour family originally came from Germany. The first Walthours settled in Georgia, and a Walthour built the first railroad line connecting Atlanta to Savannah. The family became wealthy landowners near Savannah, where Walthourville is.

By the time his son turned professional, Walthour Senior was no longer involved in American cycling. After he recovered from his broken leg, he was given a commission in 1918 to head the YMCA Division formed for service with the French Army in France. He returned to Newark in 1920 after more than a year of duty in France to find his wife involved with another man. Too many long absences from the hearth brought an end to the marriage of the couple who had pedaled to a parson on a bicycle built for two. Just after Valentine's Day in 1920, Walthour traveled to Atlanta and filed for divorce in Fulton County Superior Court. He charged that his wife had become infatuated with another man and alleged that she tried to kill him with a butcher knife.

Walthour's career was for the most part over by then, although he had earned such a name for himself that he still could get contracts in Germany, where he went to live.

When Bobby Junior won the national amateur track championship at the end of the summer of 1921, he posed for photos on the Newark Velodrome, clutching a bouquet of flowers and with the American flag wrapped around his shoulders. Next to him also wrapped in the flag and holding flowers was the professional champion—Frank Kramer.

Kramer was still on top at the age of forty-one. His defeat for the title in 1917 interrupted his reign but did not end it. When he lost the national title at the age of thirty-seven, Kramer realized his legs had slowed slightly so he converted to a bigger gear, from one that propelled him 91 inches with each pedal revolution to one that moved him 104 inches. The bigger gear took getting used to, but after he mastered it, Kramer found the bigger gear packed more wallop. He came back to win the title in 1918 and again in 1921.

In 1922, when Walthour Junior was working his way up the professional ranks, Kramer still ruled as monarch of bikes. He was on his way to capturing yet another national title. In performance and longevity he was in the same class as baseball's Christy Matthewson, Cy Young, and Ty Cobb. But that summer he began having difficulty falling asleep. His physician told him his insomnia was mental, but he felt it came from all the years of training and racing.

In the third week of July, Kramer performed well in the preliminary heats of a championship race that earned points counting toward the national title, but he faltered in the semifinals and was eliminated. Those sleepless nights were affecting his performances. Some spectators razzed the champion. They called him an old man. They told him he had lost it. In his dressing room, the door of which had borne the words "Number One" for twenty-one years, he was unable to hold back tears. He protested to close friends that he didn't deserve harassment.

Kramer pondered the situation and emerged from his dressing room to announce he was going to make one last ride, appropriately, against the clock. He was going to shoot for a world record on which to end his career. Kramer chose to go after the world record of one-sixth of

The finish of a match race between Frank Kramer (left) and Iver Lawson of Salt Lake City. Lawson won the world professional sprint championship in 1904 in London, eight years before Kramer won the title in Newark. They remain the last Americans to win the title. (Frank Mihlon, Jr.)

a mile—a popular distance and one lap of the Newark Velodrome, his home track.

Kramer's retirement, at age forty-two, was a national event. The *New York Times* ran stories for three days leading up to his last ride as the sultan of speed, on July 26. The *Newark Evening News* assigned four reporters, two photographers, and a cartoonist.

Jack Brennan of Irvington, New Jersey, recalls Kramer's final ride with excitement in his voice. Brennan's father, Pop Brennan, was a master bicycle mechanic known throughout international cycling and was virtually an institution at six-days around the country. He took his son to witness Kramer's last ride on the velodrome on South Orange Avenue in Newark.

"I was just a kid," Jack Brennan says enthusiastically. "But I remember the excitement at the track. It was like the second coming of Jesus Christ."

When the grandstand, bleachers, and infield were crammed, Kramer was feted with one photo after another and one more award after another presented to him. Fellow professional Goullet had taken up a collection among the other professionals based in Newark. "We collected about $200," Goullet says. "Kramer liked to smoke occasionally in the off-season, and we knew a jeweler in town who could give us a good deal, so we bought Kramer a gold cigarette case. When I presented Kramer with the case, I teased him, 'Don't smoke too much.'"

Even Kramer's former trainer, Jack Neville, who hadn't spoken to him for years, came forward to shake his hand. After winning the world championship, Kramer returned to race in Europe in 1913 and 1914. On the last trip, he thought his carefree, partygoing trainer needed discipline and relegated him to steerage class while he himself traveled first class. When they finally shook hands, a band at the center of the velodrome played "Hail, Hail, the Gang's All Here."

At last Kramer swung a leg over his nickel-plated bicycle and warmed up for several laps around the velodrome. In the days before chrome was available, he preferred nickel-plated frames to enameled frames. He warmed up with Alfred Grenda, who paced him for a flying start. When the champion was ready, Grenda pulled him to within a few feet of the start line and then dropped back. Kramer had a flying start and was on his way with a crack of the starter's pistol.

Wearing his trademark white silk jersey over black wool shorts,

Kramer hurtled through the first turn. His legs rolled sharply as they had through so many titles and so many races. At forty-two, he was considered the oldest professional athlete in the country and the highest paid, with an income of at least $20,000 a year for twenty-two years.

As he streaked down the back straight, the crowd boisterously cheered him on. He was going after the world record of 15-⅖th seconds set by a former rival, Albert Krebs of Salt Lake City. As he barreled through the final turn, the crowd of 20,000 was on its feet, cheering madly. This was it. Kramer was sprinting for the last time down the final straight.

When he burst across the finish, the cheering stopped. Everyone sat hushed. They waited until announcer Willie Sullivan picked up the megaphone and said that Kramer had equaled the world record. A brief silence followed. Then pandemonium broke out. It was an emotional moment that brought tears to many eyes. The band played "Auld Lang Syne," then "The Star Spangled Banner." Kramer wrapped Old Glory over his shoulders and clutched it tight to his chest with one hand and rode his last lap of honor to a tumultuous audience.

It was a high note on which to end his long competitive career. He was retiring as the incumbent national champion, and he ended by tying a world record while lowering his own mark for the distance by two-fifths of a second.

When Kramer finished cooling down and got off his bike for the last time, his remarks were characteristically brief. Ever the methodical man and not comfortable speaking before the public, Kramer had prepared a written statement.

"I want to thank you for your interest shown in me and your appreciation of my efforts in the last twenty-seven years," he said. "I'm only sorry that I am not fifteen years younger, so that I might continue to entertain you. However, I have no alternative, and must bow to Father Time."

Another thunderous ovation followed. Hats and programs were thrown in the air, and everyone rose again in honor of Kramer as the band struck up the national anthem for the second time. It was a fitting tribute to a national champion—an athlete who embodied the American ideals of integrity, perseverance, and courage. The following day reporter George Bancroft Doren published this poem in the *Newark Evening News:*

When dusk creeps in and silence treads the bowl
And shadows crouch in every vacant seat,
He will come back in fantasy to ride
Each winning and defeat.

His last race run, the crown upon his head,
And yet I know, though others look in vain,
A silent form bent low across the bars
Shall ride that track again.

He will still come, a watcher in the crowd.
And yet in mind, in heart, in soul, I know
He will be there beside the panting men
Who ride in the bowl below.

With six-day events to help pay the rent in the Garden, Rickard reached across the Atlantic to France and signed up the dashing European heavyweight champion Georges Carpentier. On July 2, 1921, in Jersey City, Rickard put Carpentier against heavyweight champion Jack Dempsey. Rickard billed it as "The Battle of the Century" and nearly quadrupled the previous gate record, to $1.8 million. Not only was this the first million-dollar gate but it also was the first time commentary was broadcast over the radio.

Dempsey knocked Carpentier out in four rounds. But Rickard knew a gold vein when he saw it and looked abroad again to arrange another bout for Dempsey—against Luis Firpo of Argentina. Firpo was called the Wild Bull of the Pampas, and on September 14, 1923, at the Polo Grounds in New York City he gave Dempsey a wild fight before Dempsey knocked him down for the ninth and final time in two rounds. That bout produced Rickard's second million-dollar gate.

After the Firpo fight, Goullet had lunch with Dempsey. "Jack Dempsey wanted to race bikes more than anything," Goullet says of their discussion. "On Decoration Day [Memorial Day], he was about fifteen or sixteen and he wanted to ride a race. He told the barber that he wouldn't be at work the next day. Then the barber said, 'No, you can't because tomorrow I will start you off with your own chair.' He wouldn't give Dempsey the day off. So Dempsey had to quit his job to race. It was twenty-five miles each way, out and back. Dempsey got to the turnaround when his chain broke and he had to walk all the way back. After that, he got involved in boxing."

Bicycle racing continued to be one of America's biggest-paying sports for those at the top. Sam Gastman of Irvington was paid $150 a day, plus whatever he won, for the twenty-two six-days he rode for Chapman in the 1920s. Gastman points out, however, that it was hard-earned money, and Chapman always got his way. Once, to help promote the November 1923 Chicago six-day, Chapman had Gastman and nine others pedal their track bikes—which lack brakes and have a fixed gear that doesn't permit coasting—from Newark to Chicago, about 850 miles.

"The roads were horrible," Gastman recalls. "There were a lot of cobble roads. Most of the roads that were paved had broken pavement. Sometimes we rode through backyards because the roads were so bad. After we got to Chicago, we rested three days. Then we had to race the six-day. There was a lot of competition to get into Chapman's races. There was a limit to the number of teams in the six-days, with fifteen to eighteen teams, and half the riders came from this country, the other half from Europe and Australia. When you rode for a living, you had to do what Chapman said."

In 1925, the New York Giants football franchise was sold for $500. The February 13 *New York Times* trumpeted that Chapman signed burly Pete Moeskops of Holland to race in the spring Garden six-day for twenty times that amount. Once Moeskops arrived, Chapman signed the four-time world champion to race the season on his circuit.

About the time Moeskops arrived, New York Life Insurance Company officials told Rickard they planned to demolish the Garden and replace it with a forty-story building that would become the company's main office. Never one to shut off a money machine, Rickard came up with nearly $6 million from Wall Street backers to construct a new "palace of play" twenty-five blocks uptown. It would accommodate his passion for boxing, as well as for other indoor sports, like hockey, which he recently discovered and promoted. (He named the New York Rangers hockey team after the Texas Rangers. For a while they were known as Tex's Rangers.) To keep tradition, he decided to call the new building Madison Square Garden.

The famous Garden closed its doors forever on May 5, 1925. Its successor opened in November with a six-day bicycle race that set a new attendance record—15,475 attended the final night's action to watch Belgians Gerard Debaets and Alphonse Goosens win.

It was Goullet's last race. At thirty-four, Goullet found the demands of racing daily all summer, with two to four six-day races in the winter, too strenuous. To sweeten the departure, Chapman paid the newly married man $10,000. He retired after eight six-day victories in the Garden, and a career total of fifteen, the most in the world at the time.

First Kramer, then Goullet. Chapman's stalwarts were retiring, and he was becoming increasingly dependent on foreign talent. America was headlong into its love affair with automobiles. A hundred manufacturers with names like Marmon, Dusenberg, Oakland, Flint, Star, Hupmobile, Reo, Maxwell, Nash, and Moon were producing more new cars every year. An Automotive Industries census in 1928 put the number of cars in this country at 17.7 million, with 3.6 million estimated for the rest of the world.

Fewer Americans were becoming involved in cycling. Cars like Fords or Chevrolets, which cost around $600, were not a great deal more than racing bikes, which cost at least $100 and required a lot of time for training. Americans sought luxury, not fitness. Weighing increasingly against the sport in America was that Chapman was not building a farm system, such as those run by baseball teams to cultivate new talent. Rather than spend money to develop new young riders, he spent large sums to import experienced talent, a propensity that was contributing to the sport's downfall in America.

It was generally acknowledged that Chapman was grooming Walthour Junior to succeed Kramer as the big name in the sport. When Walthour's parents separated and he was still living at home, Chapman quietly provided for the family. Race results showed, however, that the youth lacked his father's snap in the sprints, although he had quick recovery, which made him a champion six-day racer.

When eighteen-year-old Fred Spencer of Plainfield won twenty-eight consecutive two-mile races as an amateur on the Newark Velodrome in the 1923 season, Chapman paid attention. Only a close second-place finish broke Spencer's streak. But the robust, raven-haired Spencer came back to win the next fourteen two-milers before the season ended.

"In 1924, Chapman turned me professional," Spencer told me. "Didn't even ask me about it. I was nineteen going on twenty. I had to lie about my age to ride in my first six-day because you had to be twenty-one to ride in them."

He quickly went straight to the top, and he was just what Chapman needed. Spencer, like Kramer, whom Spencer admired, even preferred nickel-plated frames, and when chrome became available after the mid-1920s, he had some of the first chrome-plated frames in the country.

"I don't know why Kramer preferred the nickel-plated frames," Spencer says, "but I rode them because he looked so good on them and I found I could look at the down tube of the frame and see the reflections of the riders behind me like looking in a mirror. That helped me keep track of what was going on behind me."

At the March 1925 six-day, Pete Moeskops's $10,000 appearance fee made him the top moneymaker in the Garden, but Spencer teamed with Walthour Junior to beat the sterling international field and take top honors. Moeskops was huge—6 feet 3 inches and a solid 230 pounds. A former wrestler, he liked to playfully push riders around, except for Alfred Grenda, who was developed enough to hold his own. Moeskops had tremendous power and he had come to America as the world professional sprint champion for the last four consecutive years. He stayed the season with the intention of taking home the U.S. title.

Moeskops was in for a surprise when he met Spencer for a one-mile match race in April. Spencer's preferred style was to take the lead, which suited the Dutchman. Spencer kept Moeskops even with his hip as they covered the inconsequential early portion of their first heat, and when the world champion made his move the American matched him pedal stroke for pedal stroke down the banking and all the way to the line. Spencer repeated in similar style to win the match. The first off his bike to congratulate him was Moeskops.

Chapman initially signed Spencer up for forty match races at $200 each. He went undefeated, taking the U.S. title along the way, and Chapman upped the ante to $350 a match for the next six years, with a guarantee of at least thirty matches a season.

Moeskops returned to Holland at the end of the season without the American national championship, but he won a fifth world title in 1926 in Milan.

In October 1925 Spencer teamed up again with Walthour as "The Little Old New Jersey Team" and captured the Chicago six-day. Both riders had gained a national following. More than 100,000 fans watched them ride to victory in the March six-day in New York. Nearly as many people saw them win seven months later in Chicago. Walthour became well known in Chicago for the five consecutive six-days he won there.

Pete Moeskops of Holland won five world professional sprint championships, but the American title eluded him in 1925, the year he was paid $10,000 to ride in the Madison Square Garden six-day. (*Brennan Brothers*)

Spencer got a lot of attention when he became the first racer to win a six-day and the national championship in the same year.

They were such celebrities they were invited to the White House. In 1986, Spencer recalled what it was like meeting President Calvin Coolidge. Spencer has lost some of the bulk he had in his prime, and his hair has turned mostly white. But the Rahway, New Jersey, resident was light on his feet and moved with ease at age eighty-one.

"The way President Coolidge shook my hand, I thought he had a broken finger because he had a funny grip. President Coolidge was not a cycling fan. But being that Walthour and I were so popular, the president wanted to meet us."

Fred Spencer of Plainfield, New Jersey, sits on his bike at the Newark Velodrome after he finished the 1925 season as national champion. Here he shakes the hand of Bobby Walthour, Jr., his six-day partner, shortly before they left for the White House to meet President Calvin Coolidge. Between them is Spencer's trainer Dick O'Connor. Canadian champion Willie Spencer, no relation, is on Walthour's left, with Australian champion Cecil Walker on his right. (*Fred Spencer*)

After meeting Coolidge, Spencer and Walthour traveled by car to Atlanta where Walthour left Spencer to meet his fiancée, Margaret Murray. When Spencer and Walthour met again at Chapman's farm in College Park, Walthour arrived and announced he and Margaret had eloped in Georgia to keep up family tradition.

A crack showed up in the sport's structure when velodromes in Worcester and New Bedford were dismantled in 1926 after going out of business. The two tracks were not part of Chapman's circuit, and observers said the tracks failed because Chapman's circuit had the best competition. Bay Staters stopped going to the Worcester and New Bedford tracks when they saw inferior riders, or races that were increasingly fixed.

At the top of the sport, meanwhile, six-day purses at Rickard's "castle of competition" jumped 50 percent to $75,000, and attendance records were climbing. There never was a shortage of the Hollywood celebrities that attracted spectators as much as the racing action did. The March 11 *New York Times* chronicled that, after midnight, Douglas Fairbanks and Mary Pickford went to the Garden, followed by Theodore Roosevelt, Jr. Fairbanks paid out premes of $200 each for two one-mile sprints. Mary Pickford posed for a photo taken with Fred Spencer.

On July 12, 1926, fire swept the grandstand of the Newark Velodrome and part of the track. Firefighters responded quickly. They worked under constant danger that trolley wires would drop on them. Tongues of flame licked up and the heat was so intense that steel frames of bicycles stored in a shed nearby were buckled and bent. Damage to the track was estimated at $25,000; insurance was limited to $10,000.

Ingles Uppercu paid for the repairs. Since becoming involved in the sport, he had made more than a million dollars from the Newark and New York velodromes. Five months older and slightly shorter than Chapman, Uppercu had fine facial features and blond hair that he combed straight back. He was born in Evanston, Illinois, where his father was a lawyer, and after graduating from the Brooklyn Polytechnic Institute he attended Columbia University Law School until he gave up law to become an automobile mechanic. It wasn't long before he branched out into other wide-ranging and successful projects. He owned extensive gold, silver, and manganese mining interests in Mexico, Montana, and North Dakota. During World War I, he was president of a company that made seaplanes for the federal government. The government paid him a salary of a dollar a year and issued him a paper barring his arrest or delay under any circumstances. From 1914 to 1917 he operated a passenger airline between Miami, Nassau, Cuba, and Key West. A yachting enthusiast, he reconditioned a full-rigged clipper ship, the *Seven Seas,* and sailed in West Indian and other waters.

He influenced John Ringling's involvement in the New York Velodrome in 1920. Ringling was a man renowned for his common sense. Ringling trusted Uppercu's judgment and spent $50,000 to buy into the venture, an investment that paid each back more than tenfold.

In 1925, Uppercu became president of the National Cycling Association. Promoting sports was still a relatively new enterprise when he became involved. But as Rickard showed in boxing and Chapman in cycling, the attendance and money were there for the taking.

With the Newark Velodrome repaired and back in operation, Chapman continued to bring the best riders to Newark. It is hard to reconcile today's Newark—for the most part blighted, burned out, boarded up—with the Newark that was called the home of cycling. But the list of those who competed on the track in the Vailsburg section comprises a Who's Who of the sport. Since the days of Major Taylor, every world professional champion and most national amateur and professional champions from Europe raced there. Attendance was so good that when the bleachers and grandstand were full, those who could not get in would go watch the Newark Bears play baseball at Ruppert Stadium.

Races like those in Newark and elsewhere in Chapman's outdoor circuit were an enormous attraction, but the Garden's six-days had a passionate following. *New York Times* sportswriter John Kieran examined the phenomenon in his March 10, 1927, column "Sports of the Times":

There are several problems that still baffle the scientists, and one of them is the dreadful six-day bike bacillus which twice a year ravages the peaceful population of this more or less fair city. Once bitten by the "bike bug," the victim bids his family farewell, takes up a leaning position on a rail at Madison Square Garden and for an entire week alternates between periods of coma and hysteria.

At times the patient gives no sign of life at all. That is during those hours when the weary pedal-pushers circle the track at a funeral pace. But as the riders come to life the patient goes into fits of delirium. While a "jam" is on he shouts, weeps, gnashes his teeth, stamps on his coat, tosses his hat in the air and subsides exhausted only when the clanging of the bell tells him that some luckless rider has crashed to the track and the pace is slowed down to pick up the wreckage.

If the spill occurs at the end of the track the patient is in his glory. He will buttonhole everybody coming into the Garden and tell about it, with gestures.

"Mac tried to cut inside—clipped Dinale's hind wheel—down they went— Goosens rode into the pile—turned a somersault—landed on his nose—murder! Sure, I was standing right there—MacNamara had Dinale's front wheel around his neck when they picked up—here's a couple of spokes for souvenirs."

And thus the dread disease runs its course.

What kept the riders in the race? Kieran suggested there was no logical answer but added there was at least a plausible explanation:

Money makes the wheels go round. Except for a trifling matter of breakage in bones, bike riding is a profitable profession.

"We must have bloody noses and cracked crowns," said Percy Hotspur in *King Henry the Fourth,* and bike riders turn these necessities into profit. An ordinary six-day pedal-pusher might average $5,000 or better during any given year. Reggie MacNamara sometimes makes as much as $25,000 or $30,000 a year, but Mac plays more circuits than most riders. And he's the flower of the six-day flock.

New York is not the only city which suffers from the six-day fever. It's an international disease. There are six-day grinds in Chicago, Berlin, Antwerp, Brussels, Paris and Milan. This clearly indicates that no nation has a monopoly on insanity.

Spencer corroborated Kieran's explanation. "What kept me going so well," Spencer told me, "was the money that I earned. It was very exciting. I liked the fans. They treated me real nice."

In December 1927, Spencer was teamed with New Yorker Charley Winter and was hard at it in the Garden's forty-third international six-day. Winter had taken up cycling on a dare. His brother-in-law told him it was a rich man's sport that took all day to train for. Winter got a racing bike, won two national amateur championships, and set a national record for one-third of a mile that still stands. He was a rookie pro when he raced with Spencer in the six-day.

They were five laps down on the leaders, a team from France, when Spencer was awakened from a nap as Winter raced around the track. Spencer woke up surprised to discover it was Major Taylor.

"He said I was aces," Spencer recalls.

Taylor was apparently enjoying himself at the race, although he was having a tough time personally. With his fortune dwindling since his retirement, he and his wife by 1925 had sold off most of her jewelry and disposed of their seven-bedroom house to move into a smaller home in Worcester. These developments were leading the couple to irreconcilable differences. Their daughter had graduated from the Sergent School of Physical Culture in Cambridge (now the Sergent School of Allied Health at Boston University) and had left home to embark on a teaching career. Taylor attempted to recapture some of his better years and turn them into cash by writing his autobiography, which he dictated to a student from the local business school. About that time, Taylor's wife left him to live in New York City.

Alone and broke, but with his spirit intact, Taylor may have already completed his autobiography by the time he visited Spencer. Taylor was unable to interest a publisher, so he published the book in 1928 at his own expense through the Commonwealth Press of Worcester, and had them list the publisher as the Wormley Publishing Company. *The Fastest Bicycle Rider in the World: The Story of a Colored Boy's Indomitable Courage and Success Against Great Odds,* in 430 pages, replete with numerous photos from his career, describes his travels and races. It is dedicated to Louis Munger.

Taylor's faith in Spencer was justified. The Spencer-Winter team rallied to overcome their deficit and turn the race around. Then Spencer won the final sprint by six lengths to capture another Garden six-day. Twenty-one thousand fans, a new record attendance, went wild in appreciation to show that they, too, thought he was "aces."

A short time later, Rickard invited fifty millionaires to a banquet he put on to celebrate what he called the "Kings of Sport." It was at the Waldorf-Astoria Hotel, and it remains memorable for being perhaps the greatest single gathering of America's top athletes of the 1920s.

Babe Ruth, who in 1927 had belted sixty home runs, was there. So was Gene Tunney, who reigned as world boxing heavyweight champion after defeating Dempsey twice in two bouts that produced more than $3 million for Rickard. Bill Tilden, the first American to win at Wimbledon, had already won six U.S. singles tennis championships. Atlanta golfer Bobby Jones was well on his way to winning thirteen U.S. and British championships and achieving golf's grand slam—winning four major tournaments in one year. Bill Cook was the hockey star on the New York Rangers' first line credited with scoring the team's first goal in Garden history. Johnny Weismuller, the Olympic swimming champion, was soon to become best known for his Tarzan movie roles.

Joining these Kings of Sport were Spencer and Winter. When the eight monarchs assembled for the photographer, Spencer sat next to Jones, a golfing buddy. Jones gave him a pair of steel clubs that the cyclist had Pop Brennan, one of the country's premier bike mechanics, use as seat stays for a new bicycle frame Brennan made for him.

Only a brilliant promoter like Tex Rickard could gather the most popular athletes of the mid-1920s and convince them to give up their regular uniforms for tuxedos. Standing, left to right, are Babe Ruth, Gene Tunney, Johnny Weismuller and Bill Cook; seated left to right are Bill Tilden, Bobby Jones, Fred Spencer, and Charley Winter. (*Helen Winter*)

With such enthusiasm and money backing the sport, the year 1928 began like a six-day jam. In January, Rickard formally announced that Chapman was appointed vice-president and assistant general manager of the Madison Square Garden Corporation. Two weeks later, on February 5, Rickard announced that Chapman was representing him on a London trip to "look over the situation" there for a possible title bout in London's Wembley Stadium. Rickard wanted Chapman to give him a report while Rickard went on vacation to Miami where he owned property and spent winters.

The second announcement came in tandem with news that the forty-seventh congress of the Union Cycliste Internationale had awarded the 1929 world cycling championships to the United States. Frank Kramer, chairman of the Board of Control of the National Cycling Association, attended the UCI meeting in Paris. On Valentine's Day, in New York City, he told reporters that the events would be held eighteen months later at the New York and Newark velodromes. He said the UCI member countries gave assurances that they would be sending their outstanding riders to compete in the worlds.

The news was warmly received in Newark. On February 16 Howard Freeman, a sportswriter and cartoonist for the *Evening News,* wrote, "The two-wheeled racket does not need any stimulation, for it runs along on an even keel from season to season, paying great dividends to the moguls. But Chapman believes in serving the customers with a delectable dessert once every decade just to break the monotony of a menu that's pretty much the same year in and year out."

Freeman predicted that additional stands would have to be erected to accommodate greater audience attendance. He published a cartoon of Chapman, in spats, greeting Kramer who held a bundle labeled "World Cycling Championships" in his hand.

But the biggest fumble in American cycling was about to take place, and soon afterward the sport would get knocked galley-west.

6
SPUTTERING TO AN END

American culture was going through changes. Millions of listeners could hear in the comfort of their homes radio broadcasts of six-day races from Madison Square Garden's station, WMSG. By 1928, radio had become such an accepted way of life that E. M. Statler invested a million dollars to equip 7,700 rooms in six Statler hotels with loudspeakers and headsets so that guests could "feel at home." Some visionaries were predicting that before many years passed they would be able to watch the six-day races without leaving home, thanks to a new device called television. Prototype television sets used a screen four inches high and eight inches long to receive a picture that made a squealing sound when transmitted.

The relationship between Rickard and Chapman, too, was undergoing transformation. Rickard, seven years older than Chapman, was known for the thousands in cash he carried around in his pocket. He never hesitated to give money to an athlete who needed it, or to lay a wager when the mood struck. In a relaxed moment with Fred Spencer, he pulled the embroidered metal handle out of his cane to reveal it was actually the grip of a pistol fitted into the cane, which he carried as much for style as for protection from robbers.

Chapman never carried more than pocket change. He paid a few select riders well and let everybody else fend for themselves. Even though attendance was greater at the new Garden's six-days, Chapman paid his star Spencer only up to $800 a day and not the $1,000 he paid Goullet. Most riders were grateful just to get the chance to compete in his races. Chapman was not above taking advantage of that. Riders ruefully nicknamed him Stingy Johnny.

He was notorious for appropriating the national team sweaters that riders from France, Italy, Belgium, and other countries brought with them to ward off the chill of the drafty, cavernous arenas where the six-days were held. Stingy Johnny took the sweaters without asking, as though extracting a tithe, and collected them by the trunkload. Each winter he took them down to his Georgia farm to give to his farmhands.

Chapman's publicist, the former *Newark Morning Star* reporter Harry Mendel, published a story in the *Newark Evening News* about the first night he spent at Chapman's Georgia farm. He looked out a window the next morning and saw so many workers scurrying around doing chores in foreign team sweaters that he thought a bike race was about to start.

To his credit, Chapman's reputation with finances was pristine. According to Spencer, Chapman required that money for the premes the riders valued so highly be paid up front before any announcement was made. "Mr. Chapman never accepted an IOU," Spencer says. "When you won a preme, you got an envelope with the money right away." Spencer and Goullet said Chapman always paid promptly. From time to time other promoters tried to break into cycling. Some quickly disappeared after they slipped quietly away with the receipts, and none of the few honest ones could pay anywhere near what Chapman's races did.

As Chapman's tenure directly under Rickard developed, differences between the two became issues. One involved how to spend money to promote the Garden's six-days. Rickard insisted on handing choice tickets to his legion of friends around town. Chapman insisted that cycling was doing fine without giving away free tickets. Following the December 1928 six-day, Chapman resigned after nearly a year as Rickard's vice-president and as assistant general manager of the Garden's corporation.

Ostensibly, Chapman resigned on the grounds that he felt the public would be deprived of the chance to purchase choice seats to the six-days if tickets were given away. But within the corporation, Chapman was seen as an outsider who was awarded his position as patronage for the high profits of the Garden's bicycle races. On a personal level, however, Chapman was not an endearing man, and he did not get along with corporation members personally or politically. Garden officials publicly praised his work as they reached an amicable compromise in which Chapman agreed to resign to devote more time exclusively to his cycling interests.

On New Year's Day 1929, Rickard was operated on in Miami Beach for acute appendicitis. His appendix had been aggravating him for seven years, but he dreaded surgery so much that he ignored all suggestions —and constant pain—to go under the scalpel. Following the operation, infection from his gangrenous appendix spread through his abdomen. Rickard was fifty-seven when he died on January 6 in Miami Beach.

Rickard lived and died with superlatives. His body returned to New York aboard the train the Havana Special in a bronze casket that weighed 2,200 pounds. Eighteen policemen and firemen were needed to carry it. His body lay in state in the Garden's arena in keeping with the character of the myriad events he staged there. Jack Dempsey covered the arena with a blanket of orchids six feet deep and the message "My pal."

Rickard had raised boxing from a fugitive sport to one where thousands from the Social Register filled the audience right along with the common people. Five of his prize fights generated million-dollar gates, something that would not happen again for nearly fifty years. His slogan, he once said, was "Give the public what they want, the way they want it, and not the way you think." It served him well. The former cowpuncher died leaving an estate valued at $2.5 million, including a million dollars in cash.

Among Rickard's pallbearers were Dempsey, John Ringling, and John M. Chapman. Although it was widely speculated that Chapman would succeed Rickard as president of Madison Square Garden, that post was subsequently filled by Colonel John Reed Kilpatrick, a former all-American end on the Yale football team, a decorated army officer, and a member of the Garden's board of directors.

For the rest of the country, 1929 opened auspiciously. The stock market's first day of the year started with a new record of 5,413,610 shares sold. The rush of orders established big gains. General Electric was the best seller, up twenty-three points. In Detroit, the Ford Motor Company plant in early January picked 600 out of an army of 25,000 jobless, shivering men outside the plant who were applying for work. The company announced 30,000 were to be added to the payrolls as the plant was planning to go to a six-day workweek with production expected to rise 20 percent.

The 1929 cycling season opened unevenly. The New York Velodrome remained a big draw, while attendance declined so much at the Newark Velodrome that Chapman abandoned Saturday events and cut the velodrome to two days of racing a week. Rain forced cancellation of many races on the rest of his circuit.

Chapman's high card was the 1929 world championships, but even they were in trouble. The Union Cycliste Internationale requested that American organizers put on its full program—which had expanded to include separate road races for amateurs and professionals. In Chapman's 1912 world championships, events had been confined to the track.

Road racing didn't interest Chapman. Nor did amateur racing. All his attention was directed at professional cycling on the velodromes. His National Cycling Association held amateur events in every race program and staged an amateur national championship each year, but to Chapman amateur races were something to warm up the audience for the pros.

As a result, U.S. cyclists did not perform as well in Olympic cycling events as the level of professional riding would indicate. In 1920 the Amateur Bicycle League of America was founded in response to the poor state of amateur racing. After jurisdictional jockeying, Chapman begrudgingly tolerated the ABL as long as its races stayed off the velodromes, and as long as ABL officials didn't hold professional events.

Chapman turned fifty shortly after the UCI awarded the world championships to the United States, and he had long been a man fixed in the way he did things. He was a quiet, soft-spoken man, but he was czar of the sport in America, accustomed to running the show, and wanted to organize the world cycling championships in 1929 the way he did seventeen years earlier. The only possible compromise would be to hold just the velodrome events and make a substantial cash contribution to the UCI, something that Chapman's nature rebelled against.

Newspapers that had trumpeted the news of the 1929 worlds being awarded to the United States, such as the *New York Times* and the *Newark Evening News,* were mute on what followed. But retired pro rider Walter Bardgett, then associate editor of *American Bicyclist and Motorcyclist,* suggested in his magazine that "the running of the road championship was probably the straw that busted the camel's suspenders."

The 1929 world cycling championships were held in Zurich, Switzerland. Nearly a half-century was to pass before UCI awarded the worlds again to the United States.

With attendance declining at the Newark Velodrome, Chapman was reluctant to keep it in good condition. A standard temporary repair was to cover a bad spot with a car license plate. Nineteen-year-old Sergio Matteini of New York's Greenwich Village was a rising star that year. He won both 1929 amateur titles—the NCA and ABL championships. He told me that the Newark Velodrome had several such patches where the pine was worn. Matteini and Spencer recall that the practice was more common in 1929 than in the past.

"The splinters were terrible at the Newark Velodrome," Matteini says. "After crashes there, I was always pulling out splinters. It was an old track and needed a lot of repair. But they used to get some good crowds watching."

About the time that the world championships would have been held there, the Newark City Commission discussed the advisability of removing the track for more new streets to relieve traffic congestion in the neighborhood. The issue was raised because the lease that Frank Mihlon and Ingles Uppercu had to the land the track was on was set to expire on January 1, 1931.

Then came Black Tuesday: the stock market crashed. On October 29, 1929, Wall Street was swamped with 12,894,650 shares of stock up for sale; the ticker lagged for hours. Two days later, $15 billion in stock market "value" had been wiped out.

At the Newark Velodrome, attendance continued to decline throughout 1930. Chapman cut back the prize money to $75 for first place, and upped the general admission fee to a dollar. Sports promotion, which suffered when Tex Rickard died, took another blow when Chicago sports promoter Paddy Harmon was killed in a car accident that July. Then on a sweltering August night while the eastern half of the country was suffering under one of the worst heat waves on record, the New York Velodrome went up in flames.

The three-alarm blaze, reported at 3:30 A.M. on August 4, lit up the sky for miles. The fire spread so fast that firefighters abandoned their efforts to save the velodrome and worked to keep the blaze from spreading. Showers of sparks rained on hundreds of residences in the vicinity, and their occupants were awakened by the brilliant light. Scores of homes were without electricity as fire destroyed many electric lines.

The cause of the fire was reportedly a lighted cigarette left over from the race the night before. Goullet shakes his head emphatically when discussing the cause. "It was a deliberate fire," he contends. "There was no question about that."

The fire followed the opening two weeks earlier of the Coney Island Velodrome. On July 19 the new velodrome began operation with a full card of twenty-three cycling events. Like the Newark and New York velodromes, it was six laps to the mile, and had seating for 10,000. Chapman had granted sanction approval to the new velodrome's management, but stopped short of authorizing the top riders to compete there, which could have been the factor that sparked the New York Velodrome's demise.

The owners of the New York Velodrome did not replace it. In 1928, Ingles Uppercu had invested in the Uppercu Cadillac Building in Manhattan, a modern twelve-story structure to store the Cadillac and La Salle cars his company—the Uppercu Cadillac Corporation—sold and serviced. For many years he had been storing his inventory in six locations around metropolitan New York. The building was a considerable financial commitment that put him in a bind when the depression hit and the sales of his cars dropped sharply. And, according to the *New York Times,* velodrome co-owner John Ringling, at age sixty-four, was then mainly interested in acquiring "the biggest and best art collection."

The Newark Velodrome appeared destined for oblivion as well, since its property lease expired at the end of the year. It was generally expected that Frank Mihlon would build a new velodrome on the six-acre plot he owned directly behind its present location because he had made a fortune from the velodromes Chapman managed for him. When

Ingles Moore Uppercu helped pilot cycling in its golden years. Here Uppercu is about to take Jackie Clark aloft for a ride in his sea plane. (*Frank Mihlon*)

Prohibition took effect and the sale of alcoholic beverages became illegal, Mihlon sold the Long Bar Saloon. He bought land around Newark to provide for family members, and there was every reason to believe that he would also provide for the cycling community.

On December 4, 1930, the track on which so many stirring battles had been fought and world records set was torn down so the site could be returned to its owners in the same condition as when leased. The location that had been so vital for thirty-three years, where every world professional sprint champion in that time had raced, was knocked apart by the wrecker's ball.

All winter, rumors circulated about the fate of cycling in Newark. On February 13, 1931, *Evening News* columnist Willie Ratner wrote that there was a move under way to fund a new velodrome in the aptly named Dreamland Park section of Newark, with Alf Goullet as manager. Riders themselves raised $38,000 to fund the venture. But the sum fell short. Chapman was not willing to invest. Uppercu could not. Mihlon was equivocal.

The source of Mihlon's indecision that winter may have been across the Atlantic, in Berlin, and not locally in Newark. Frank Mihlon, Jr., recalls that his father had lost a considerable sum in Berlin where a velodrome he had invested in burned down in 1930 not long after it opened. It was the Rutt Arena, named after Walter Rutt, the German champion who won the 1913 world professional sprint championship. Mihlon and Rutt got to know each other well over the years that the German raced in Newark and New York before and after World War I. When Rutt retired in the 1920s, he prevailed upon Mihlon for capital.

"I recall that Mother and Dad got into an argument over the amount of money that Dad took in a suitcase over to Berlin to finance construction of the track," Frank Mihlon, Jr., says. Postwar Germany was hobbled by hyperinflation of at least 200 percent a week and construction costs would have been expensive. "Dad dropped a lot of money there, and he didn't get any of it back."

Not until early March 1931 did Mihlon make up his mind. Bill Wathey, sports columnist for the *Newark Star-Eagle,* wrote on March 9 that Chapman told him that Uppercu and Mihlon could not afford to rebuild tracks in Newark that year.

Soon after, Chapman and his wife left and traveled around the South. He was considering building a velodrome in New Orleans when he suffered a mild coronary there. The couple returned to Newark where he recovered, and the plan for the Crescent City Velodrome was scuttled.

The 1920s roared for bicycle racing, but the 1930s whimpered, and American cycling was on a definite downward spiral. Attendance at the tracks remaining in Chapman's circuit steadily declined as the depression tightened its grip: one-third of the nation's work force could not find jobs; business failure rates tripled from 48 per 10,000 listed enterprises in 1920 to 154 in 1932; suicides hit a rate of 15.6 per 10,000 population in 1930, the highest ever in American history.

The Revere Beach track in Boston closed in 1931 and was torn down, along with the rest of the circuit's tracks in Providence and Philadelphia. All that remained was the Coney Island Velodrome and attendance was declining. The Grand Circuit of the 1890s was history, as was the circuit that Chapman had watched over for many years. All that remained for Chapman to oversee were the six-day events in the Garden and other cities.

Some of our better riders went abroad. Sergio Matteini got an invitation from Georges Kaiser of Paris to race for him in 1931. Kaiser, who

Sergio Matteini won both the amateur road and track championships in the same year, 1929, and raced successfully as a pro in Europe for several seasons. (*Sergio Matteini*)

billed himself as "Agent of the Stars," had a stable of the most outstanding sprinters of the decade. They included English champion Sydney Cozens, French champions Lucien Faucheux and Louis Gerardin, Italian champion Mario Bergamini, and Belgian champion Jef Scherens.

Matteini's style of pedaling was smooth, with no torso movement, so that he looked like he was floating when he rode. He was small but had a high strength-to-weight ratio. With his movie-idol features, he became known on both sides of the Atlantic as Adonis of Bikedom. He settled just outside Paris for most of the next four years.

His 1931 season was remarkable for winning a three-man match race on the Buffalo Velodrome in Paris like Major Taylor and Arthur Zimmerman had before him. Matteini beat Scherens and former world amateur champion Willie Falck-Hensen of Denmark to raise expectations for another American medal at the worlds. Two weeks before the worlds, however, he wound up in a Paris hospital with typhoid fever. Falck-Hensen won the 1931 worlds, with Scherens third.

Matteini became good friends with Scherens, who went on to win the 1932 world pro title and six more. Matteini accompanied Scherens in 1933 for the hero's welcome Scherens received in Brussels, complete with horse-drawn carriages and ticker-tape parade. Scherens dominated sprinting well into the next decade, even after the hiatus brought on by World War II.

Like Scherens, Matteini was a pure sprinter who specialized in match races. Kaiser lined his racers up with matches that paid them $200 to $350 a race, even during the depths of the depression, and had them racing often. (Allowing for inflation, $200 in 1932 was worth $1,150 in 1987.)

Matteini competed all over France, Italy, Denmark, and crossed the Mediterranean to race in Casablanca. He was even made an honorary citizen of the French city of Niort, near Bordeaux, where he won the Grand Prix de Niort.

Major Taylor was selling copies of his autobiography door to door to support himself. Those close to him in his prime could no longer help him. Louis Munger died suddenly at age sixty-six of a heart attack in 1929 in New York City. Taylor's former agent, William A. Brady, lost everything in the stock market crash. Brady was sixty-five and was wiped out of everything he had set aside for retirement.

Word of Taylor's predicament reached Chicago and a former competitor named James B. Bowler. Bowler got in touch with Taylor in 1930. Bowler was alderman for Chicago's twenty-fifth ward, and told Taylor he would get him a job if the old champion would come out. Taylor sold what little he had left, including his house and collection of bicycles, piled a cart high with copies of his autobiography, and left Worcester.

Chicago held promise for Taylor. He had a brother living there, and he was still remembered from his racing days. Taylor took up residence in a YMCA and took a job. Photos taken in his Chicago days show him dapperly dressed in a suit and tie, but with sad eyes, often downcast. His resilient spirit had gone with his youth, and by age fifty he started to suffer health problems.

In the spring of 1932 he was admitted to Chicago's Provident Hospital. He was a patient there for a month and then was moved to a charity ward in Cook County Hospital. On June 21, 1932, Taylor died of an apparent heart attack. He was fifty-three.

His death went largely unnoticed, except for the *Chicago Defender,* a weekly newspaper for blacks, which ran a story on July 2 entitled: "Major Taylor Dies Here in Charity Ward." According to an article by Robert Lucas in the May 1948 *Negro Digest,* "barely enough mourners to fill a single automobile" accompanied his body to Chicago's Mount Glenwood Cemetery—a sad end to the young man who won two world championships that were so well attended that thousands were turned away at the gate. The athlete who drew as many as 30,000 paying fans to a meet was buried in an unmarked grave.

After the mid-1940s, an organization called the Bicycle Racing Stars of the Nineteenth Century Association based in Chicago got together with distinguished black athletes to do something about giving Major Taylor a better resting place. On May 23, 1948, a memorial service was held in the Mount Glenwood Cemetery, with members of the association, black athletes, and members of the Olde Tymers Athletic Club of the Wabash Avenue YMCA attending. They had Taylor's body moved to the cemetery's Memorial Garden of the Good Shepherd.

Delivering the main address at the memorial service was Ralph Metcalfe, the black track star who won a gold medal at the 1936 Olympics and was to become a congressman. Other black athletes who attended were National Football Hall of Fame players Claude (Buddy) Young and Frederich F. (Duke) Slater and 1936 track Olympian John

Brooks. Walter Bardgett covered the memorial service for *American Bicyclist and Motorcyclist.*

Frank Schwinn, president of the Schwinn Bicycle Manufacturing Company, provided a tombstone for Taylor. The cycling association donated a bronze tablet sculpted with Taylor's image. It was placed on his grave with the inscription: "World's champion bicycle racer—who came up the hard way—without hatred in his heart—an honest, courageous and God-fearing, clean living gentlemanly athlete, a credit to his race who always gave out his best—gone but not forgotten."

American cycling appeared to revive when a new velodrome opened on June 4, 1933, in Nutley, a quiet residential community northeast of Newark. Frank Kramer was consulted on the design and recommended that it be seven laps to the mile so the turns would be sharper and tighter to provide more speed and excitement for the spectators.

For a while a true renaissance seemed about to occur. Even though admission was only forty cents, attendance was high enough that the track paid for itself by the second season, rather than in five as planned. Velodrome owner Joe Miele, a local businessman, said he did not expect to get rich from it but just wanted to give bike fans a break and help promote the sport. Managing the velodrome was Chapman's aide, Harry Mendel, who also managed a car track, promoted prizefights, and continued to help Chapman promote six-day races.

A new crop of professionals was dazzling audiences. William (Torchy) Peden of Vancouver, Cecil Yates of Australia, Norman Hill of San Jose, and local rider Tino Ribaldi were proven world-class competitors and were local heroes in Nutley.

But those auspicious seasons were only an Indian summer before the cold winds of January 1935. Mendel had a falling out with Miele and left to manage the Coney Island Velodrome, a split that harmed both tracks. Mendel and Miele discouraged professional riders from signing contracts with the other track, a departure from the past track circuits. The Nutley and Coney Island velodromes scraped along fitfully for a few more years, carried more by memories of cycling's heyday than by receipts.

At the end of the 1934 season, Sergio Matteini decided it was time to return to the United States. "Something was in the wind," he explains.

"Crowds at the races were falling off. People were preoccupied—they had no money and they were tightening their belts. You could see the war was coming."

The last American competing in Europe was Bill Honeman, national professional champion from 1934 to 1936. For five winter seasons through 1935, Honeman returned to Europe to compete on the indoor velodromes, chiefly in France and Belgium, but also in Denmark.

French promoters felt that Honeman should wear a national champion's jersey in their races. The national jersey was designed in 1934 by a Parisian sporting goods store called Unis, Honeman recalls. The jersey featured a blue field with white stars on the upper part and vertical stripes below. The design quickly became popular and soon was adopted as the official jersey of U.S. champions.

In 1936, the entire country was struggling in the grip of the depression. Even baseball, the nation's pastime, was having a difficult time. The total major league baseball payroll had been scaled back 25 percent in five years, from $4 million in 1931 to $3 million in 1936. The average annual salary for players dropped from $9,800 to $7,500.

The champions of early years continued to die. America's first international cycling star, August Zimmerman, died in Atlanta on October 20 at sixty-seven of a heart attack. Shortly after Christmas, Frank Mihlon succumbed to a heart attack in his home in Belmar, New Jersey, at fifty-nine.

Far from being out of cycling, Chapman was still busy promoting six-days. With the economy staggering and times hard, the two annual sixes were a welcome source of revenue to Madison Square Garden's shareholders. Twice a year the galleries were packed with crowds that came to watch dazzling performances of the best European and U.S. riders. Chapman signed up luminaries like Alfredo Binda, Italy's three-time world champion who was so overwhelming that race organizers of the Tour of Italy once paid him the equivalent of the winner's prize not to race; the famed German duo Heinz Vopel and Gustav Killian, the most consistent team winners in six-day history; and Frenchman Alfred (the French Comet) Letourner, who was to ride into the history books when on May 17, 1941, he pedaled his bicycle behind a race car in Bakersfield, California, for a new cycling speed record of 108.92 miles an hour.

In December 1936, another Walthour rode into the Garden's winning circle, making the Walthours the premier family of American cycling.

LEFT. John M. Chapman could smile while his six-days were helping Madison Square Garden pay the bills during the depression. (*Sergio Matteini*)

BELOW. Jimmy Walthour, Jr., won the national road and track championships in 1927, then enjoyed a successful pro career like his cousin and uncle before him. (Jack Simes II photo)

Jimmy Walthour, Jr., was the son of the first Bobby Walthour's twin brother, Jim. Between the three of them, they had garnered seven national championships and each rode to victory in a Garden six-day.

Chapman also promoted other six-days that kept him busy around the country. They were held in places like the Butler Field House at Butler College in Indianapolis, municipal auditoriums in St. Louis and Kansas City, and the Washington, D.C., armory.

On December 7, 1937, Chapman announced in Madison Square Garden that he was quitting. Garden president Colonel John Reed Kilpatrick tried to persuade him to remain, but Chapman was firm. Harry Mendel succeeded Chapman as promoter of the Garden's six-days.

Chapman's retirement influenced Frank Kramer, who had been working as chief referee at indoor and outdoor races since his last ride. Kramer said he wanted to leave the sport with Chapman, so two men whose names were synonymous with the sport called it quits.

The next year, Mendel put on only one six-day in the Garden—the first time in nineteen years that two weren't held. In December 1939, the sixty-sixth and final international six-day took place. Because of previous Garden bookings, the race was shortened to five days. Only half the seats were sold, a marked contrast to long-standing tradition. With Britain and France declaring war on Germany that year the supply of foreign talent was cut off, which effectively dealt a *coup de main* to the sport that was already waning on these shores.

A boisterous, robust era in sport had come to an end. Kramer and Chapman had enough money to live comfortably the rest of their lives. In 1924, when he was forty-four, Kramer had married Helen Hay of East Orange. He was a natty dresser and smoked cigarettes with a gold holder. After he left cycling with Chapman, Kramer became police commissioner for East Orange and afterward managed a nonprofit ambulance service in Orange. He was active in the Boy Scouts movement and became a member of its National Court of Honor. Kramer, who had a fondness for cars, became a special inspector in the New Jersey Department of Motor Vehicles.

Neither the Kramers nor the Chapmans had children. The Chapmans went to the West Coast in 1940 and subsequently bought a house in the Los Angeles suburb of Santa Monica. It was said that Chapman preferred the sea view there, but it is more likely that he wanted to be near Bobby Walthour, Jr., who had already settled in Santa Monica with his wife and children. Walthour worked in the MGM film library in Culver City.

Chapman was said to have mellowed. His voice became gravely from years of smoking. He joined the Santa Monica Pinochle Club and started playing at 9 A.M. Everybody called him Colonel. He enjoyed trading old bike stories with the racers who migrated to the mild weather of the West Coast, but he never went to sporting events of any kind again. When summer came, he and his wife traveled east to visit friends, until his last years when he was too weak to travel. He became so frail that he could hardly raise his hands to play pinochle. Chapman died at sixty-nine, in Santa Monica, on March 20, 1947.

By 1947 the focus of cycling had shifted to Europe. The cadre of professional cyclists in this country was forced to abandon the sport and find other work.

When Bobby Walthour III came of age after World War II, all the wooden velodromes in this country were gone. The competitions held by the Amateur Bicycle League of America on roads in remote locations on early weekend mornings to avoid car traffic was all that remained of competitive cycling.

About the time Walthour III was setting swim records for Santa Monica High School and St. Mary's College, a *Newark Evening News* reporter interviewed Kramer, who still had a full head of hair, albeit completely white, and a spritely walk. When asked what he thought it would take to revive bicycle racing as a spectator sport in this country,

After World War II, cycling in the United States fell on lean times: races were held in remote areas and rarely drew spectators. This is the finish of a 1946 race on Staten Island, New York. Ted Smith, far right, is narrowly beating Jack Heid. (*Ted Smith*)

Kramer considered the question and replied, "Only one good American rider."

During the years that followed, the story of U.S. cycling was to be one of individuals working against sometimes overwhelming odds to become that rider.

T W O

"Spit and Scotch Tape"

7
THE JACK ARMSTRONG OF AMERICAN CYCLING

One summer night in 1948, five-year-old Jack Simes III was tuning a shortwave radio for the BBC broadcast of the Summer Olympics from London. In the living room of the family's vacation cottage at Beaver Lake, New Jersey, young Jack heard the news that a rider his father coached, Jack Heid, had won a 1,000-meter (1,100-yard) cycling match race to advance to the next heat in his quest for an Olympic medal.

The five-year-old listened attentively as the BBC announcer told how Heid won his qualifying match by twenty yards to advance against Clodomiro Cortini of Argentina—South America's best sprinter. Heid was racing on the 503-yard Herne Hill track, an outdoor cement track in a quiet, tree-shaded residential borough of metropolitan London. Cortini took the lead with 400 yards remaining. Heid drafted snugly behind Cortini's rear wheel and started to pass him in the final 200 yards. At the finish, the two racers were so close, their heads down, their backs arched, that judges had to consult a photo of the finish before they ruled for Heid, who progressed to the quarterfinal.

That same summer, fifteen-year-old Art Longsjo of Fitchburg, Massachusetts, was planning to quit high school and train full time to make the Olympic speed skating team. Seventeen-year-old Nancy Neiman

Baranet of Detroit was taking courses in shorthand and typing to prepare for a secretarial career. Herb Francis, eight years old, was getting ready to move north from Miami with his parents. Perry Metzler, seven years old, was living in Yazoo City, Mississippi. In Los Angeles, another seven-year-old, Mike Hiltner, was learning to play the flute. Audrey Phleger McElmury was five and turning cartwheels in La Jolla, California. All of them, including Simes III, would follow Heid into cycling, taking the sport where no American cyclist had ever gone. They helped keep the sport alive through cycling's lean years in this country.

Amateur cycling had not been vigorous here since the League of American Wheelman had withdrawn from racing at the turn of the century. Under LAW's successor, the National Cycling Association, professional racing had thrived, but the influx of foreign talent actually masked the neglected state of domestic amateur ranks. The sorry state of amateur cycling led to the formation in 1920 of the Amateur Bicycle League of America (referred to as the ABL), which bumped along with the aid of volunteers. When the velodromes disappeared and John M. Chapman retired, the NCA vanished, too. The ABL, the organization that Chapman reluctantly tolerated, was all that was left to sustain the sport. After World War II, American cycling was held together, in the words of one cycling official, "with spit and Scotch Tape."

For decades, the NCA had held races all week long on velodromes and charged admission. The ABL events were relegated to remote areas to avoid car traffic, and they were free to anyone willing to get up for the 6 A.M. starts on weekends. Sometimes the finish line for ABL events was even changed during the race—police chased officials away from residential areas for waking up neighbors.

Raising funds to send athletes to the Olympics was mostly up to each sport's governing body within the U.S. Olympic Committee. Not even when the NCA flourished did Chapman provide money for Olympic cyclists. The ABL relied on donations. It lacked the resources to provide masseurs or mechanics for Olympic riders, although providing support personnel was standard in Europe at the time and is in this country today. Moreover, riders like Heid and the others were on their own for equipment because sponsorships did not exist. All of these hindrances made Heid's progress in the Olympics noteworthy.

Heid next drew Axel Schandorff, the Danish champion who towered over him by six inches and had finished second in the 1946 world championships. The Dane eliminated Heid in the Olympics and went on to win the bronze medal. Heid had to serve a rigorous apprenticeship before he could turn the tables and eliminate Schandorff in international competition. In the meantime, Heid next tightened his toe straps for the kilometer time trial. A tire punctured soon after the start, however, and he had to wait hours for a second ride, at dusk in a drizzle. He rode to seventh of twenty-one riders, slower than his Olympic trials qualifying time, but the best finish by far of the other U.S. Olympic cyclists.

Heid was determined to succeed in the sport, and the London Olympics were a stepping stone to Europe, where he had the courage to go and race against the giants of cycling. Heid would become the Jack Armstrong of modern American cycling. "I had to go there and do what everybody else did to get better. I used to say that I would eat shit if it would make me ride faster." But to get to Europe on his own, Heid first had to overcome prevailing ABL complacency.

"Frank Small, the ABL president and manager of the Olympic cycling team, told me I couldn't stay in London after the Olympic Games," Heid recalled. "He told me I owed it to the cycling community to go back to the States and race in the nationals. But I asked him who would pay for my way back here. We argued back and forth until I told him I was prepared to give up my U.S. citizenship to stay. He saw I was determined and gave in. I got $210 return fare for the U.S.S. *America,* the ship we went over on, and with the $600 I had saved, I went out to conquer Europe."

Born on Manhattan's Lower East Side in 1924, Heid saw six-day racers train in Central Park. The way the men in brightly colored jerseys handled their bikes, pedaling fluidly, maneuvering easily around traffic, rolling up hills and zipping down them as though the bicycles were extensions of their bodies, fascinated him.

When his family moved to northern New Jersey, he got a track bike so he could emulate six-day riders. In 1941 he won his first race, a half-mile handicap on the Coney Island Velodrome. Young Heid grew to 5 feet 8 inches, had a boxer's sloping shoulders and dark curly hair and a broad smile. His leg muscles gained mass and definition as his career began to take shape in 1942, when he entered his first year of open competition at the age of eighteen.

His early mentor was Jack Simes II, the 1936 national ABL champion. Simes II raced professionally for a year after his championship until he was seriously injured in a crash in the December 1937 six-day in San Francisco. Simes retired to open a bicycle shop in Westwood, the northern New Jersey town where Heid grew up. Retirement did not stop Simes from going to races. His shock of curly red hair was a familiar sight on the starting line. Simes loved stories about racers and their personalities. Heid used to visit the Westwood bicycle shop to ask questions and soak up the atmosphere.

Heid was on his way up in 1942 when he beat Furman Kugler of Somerville, the 1940 national ABL champion and three-time state champion, for the state ABL title. But the Japanese had bombed Pearl Harbor in December 1941, and after Heid won the state championship he enlisted in the navy as an aviation mechanic.

"Most guys in the service dreamed of their girlfriends back home, but I dreamed of my bicycle and what I would do when I resumed my racing career," Heid said.

While Heid was stationed at Treasure Island in San Francisco, a fellow New Jersey rider, Ray Blum of Nutley, also received orders for the base. Blum, dark-complexioned and a few inches taller than Heid, had begun racing on the Nutley Velodrome. He also took up speed skating, which uses similar leg muscles and tactics, and established a national reputation in both sports. Until Blum was transferred to the Great Lakes Naval Base in Illinois, the two shared the sole rental bike at a local cycling shop. When the war ended and they were released from the navy, they resumed their friendly rivalry.

After the war, American riders still used track bikes with fixed gears on the roads, even though the stiff frames of track bikes are jarring when riding on anything other than a smooth surface. Decades earlier, Europeans had switched to road bikes with longer wheelbases that made them more comfortable than track bikes, and in the 1930s began equipping bikes with derailleurs—multiple-speed rear-wheel sprockets that enabled them to vary gears up and down hills.

Derailleurs date back to shortly after the turn of the century, when Frenchman Paul de Vivie came up with two concentric chain-rings that required manually lifting the chain from one front ring to the other. Not long after came other manufacturers introducing their own models. Early versions with two or three speeds tended to be troublesome; they jammed easily. Only tourists who had time to fuss over them used derailleurs.

Racers preferred riding in hilly races with rear wheels that had a sprocket on both sides of the hub. One sprocket had the standard fixed gear on track bikes, which did not permit the rider to coast; the other sprocket permitted the rider to coast. Standard practice in road races was for everyone to stop on an arduous climb, remove the rear wheel by unfastening wing nuts that held the wheels to the frame, turn the wheel around for the free wheel which had a smaller gear for pedaling up grades, then coast down the descent. Later they would stop again and revert to their fixed gear.

A breakthrough came in 1928 when Frenchman Lucien Juy invented a double-pivot derailleur. It had two spring-loaded pivots that kept the chain taut underneath the rear hub where the chain could be shifted up and down as many as five sprockets to give the rider a selection of five gears. Juy founded Simplex derailleurs, which became a household name in cycling. By the mid-1930s, European road racers were riding bicycles with derailleurs.

American racers resisted derailleurs partly because they were difficult to come by, but mostly because the prevailing wisdom dictated that fixed gears made riders better pedalers. Better pedaling had its price: it was not uncommon to see a veteran fixed-gear rider with a joint or two missing from the finger of the right hand from getting the finger caught between the chain and front sprocket while tightening a toe strap.

The first racer to use a derailleur in this country may have been James Armando in 1929 during a sixty-two-mile race in New York. Jack Simes II was among the spectators lining the road when they discovered that Armando was riding a bicycle with three speeds. Simes recalled the moment for me with enthusiasm:

"Armando rode a Cyclo derailleur, made in England. It was a crude contraption that literally had a complete figure eight in the back to keep the chain tension, and it sounded like a coffee grinder. But the crowd just loved it. They kept yelling at him, 'Throw it in high gear! Let's see what you've got! Throw it in high!' "

America led the world to changes in industrial technology but fell behind Europe in cycling. The first significant change in America's bicycle racing in the 1940s was for aluminum rims to replace wooden rims. America's biggest change was the ABL helmet law of 1946. Armando may have been an early proponent of derailleurs, but spoke for many in resisting helmets. Helmets made cycling look dangerous, he said.

The chief influence on cycling—and all amateur sports in America—after the war was Avery Brundage of Chicago, known as the "Mother Superior" of amateur athletics. Brundage became what the *New York Times* described as "the most powerful figure in the history of international sports." He was heavily influential in the International Olympic Committee—as vice-president from 1945 to 1952, then as IOC president through the 1972 Munich Summer Olympics.

Brundage was so devoted to amateurism that he was called "Slavery Brundage," "the nation's No. 1 common scold," and "a male Carry Nation, hacking away with a hatchet of righteousness at those who are trying to undermine the amateur idea." He tended to be undiplomatic and tactless, prompting one critic to describe him as looking like Oliver Cromwell's idea of God—righteous and inflexible.

When Heid and Blum and others raced after the war, Brundage's controversial fight to keep amateur sports pure was felt by all amateur athletes in this country. Racers often packed four into a car to drive ten hours one way to race for a trophy or maybe a pair of bicycle tires.

"But we all went because we loved the sport and money never entered our minds as it just wasn't there," Heid said.

In contrast to today's national-class amateur riders who benefit from corporate sponsorship, Heid and other amateurs of his day were on

Jack Simes II, second from right, retired from racing in 1937 after he won the national championship, but he remained active in the sport. On the left is Ray Blum and Jack Heid, and on the right is Don Sheldon. (*Julia Heid*)

their own. When Heid accepted invitations in 1947 and 1948 to compete in the Caribbean Olympics in British Guiana (now Guyana), the British Guiana Amateur Cycle and Athletic Association covered all expenses—flight, accommodations, meals—with no expectation that the ABL would return the favor.

Athletes like Heid and Blum trained and raced with an eye toward making the Olympic team. On early Sunday mornings when there were no races, a group of Olympic hopefuls used to meet to ride 50 to 100 miles around New Jersey and southern New York. Most in the group, which also included Don Sheldon and Don McDermott, trained diligently. When one of the group couldn't make the Sunday morning ride—usually because he had been out too late on Saturday night—somebody would joke that the absent rider was "out painting a barn."

Blum was the first to make the Olympic team, in 1948, as a speed skater bound for the Winter Olympics in St. Moritz, Switzerland. His versatility and virtuosity on a bicycle attracted Robert LeRoy Ripley's attention. The result was a "Believe It or Not!" cartoon in which Ripley heralded Blum as "The World's Most Decorated Athlete."

Another member of the New Jersey group was fifty-year-old Gerard Debaets, the Belgian who had won the December 1925 six-day in Tex Rickard's new Madison Square Garden. Debaets was a Chapman import who settled in northern New Jersey and opened a bike shop when he retired. Debaets had thick dark hair combed straight back and a prominent nose. He was a man of indomitable spirit. In the early 1930s, he felt ill after winning the Chicago international six-day and checked into a hospital for tests that revealed he had a congenitally bad heart—his aorta valve leaked with each beat. Yet he was a prolific winner—including the Tour of Flanders, a Belgian classic he won twice, and he won eighteen six-days, as many as current Belgian national hero Eddy (the Cannibal) Merckx.

"I went to Debaets for help because I wanted to stay in Europe to race after the Olympics," Heid remembered.

Debaets cheerfully helped. He advised Heid in tactics and training, and introduced him to massages that sped the recovery of tired muscles. A bike rider's legs are the pistons of his engine; they have to be treated carefully. Cyclists shave their legs to help keep them clean and aid massages. Debaets's advice took some getting used to in the 1940s; no American man would shave his legs, let alone have them rubbed in a massage. But the Belgian pointed out that Heid was going to have to look at cycling differently if he wanted to get to the top. Debaets had something perhaps more important than advice as well—contacts with race promoters in Europe, and a sister in Antwerp, Belgium, who would give Heid a place to live while he made his start on the Continent.

Any doubts Heid had about whether he should go to Europe to compete were dismissed during the 1948 Olympics. Teammate Ted Smith of Buffalo was the best prospect for a medal in the road race until he incurred the wrath of ABL officials. Smith had won two national championships and decisively captured the 138-mile Olympic trials qualifying race in Milwaukee to claim first spot on the road team. When athletes arrived at the Olympic facilities, Smith entered several English races which also drew some of the other foreign Olympic cyclists. But the ABL Olympic coach ordered U.S. cyclists not to race them, because any rider who fell risked not being able to race in the Olympics.

Twenty-year-old Smith did well in some of the races, which he entered to test himself against the competition he would face in the race for the Olympic medals as well as to adjust to racing with a derailleur, a new development for him. The reaction of the ABL officials was typical of the state of American cycling. They gave his berth to another rider in the road race.

"I trained eight years to make the Olympic team," Smith remembers, his disgust still strong after all these years. "The Olympics were my dream. I won the Olympic trials qualifying race by a minute and got replaced in the Olympics by some ham-and-egger."

None of the four U.S. riders in the road race even finished. Smith was put on the four-man, 4,000-meter (2.5-mile) team pursuit, which was doomed when one rider broke a wrist in a fall and pulled out.

Another of Heid's Olympic teammates liked the idea of remaining in Europe to get better. Al Stiller of Chicago, who rode in the tandem event but was eliminated early, said he would join Heid. A graduate of the University of Utah who also liked to ski, Stiller was powerfully built but nowhere as aggressive as Heid.

"I used to say that Al was too nice a guy to be a bicycle racer," Heid remembered. "I was an animal."

Olympic cycling team manager Frank Small, after arguing with Heid, quickly granted Stiller permission to remain behind with Heid.

Following the Olympics, Heid and Stiller traveled to Antwerp and met Debaets's sister, Ernestine, who helped them set up a base residence. The two Americans signed up for a team race in Antwerp, where they won in their first foray.

The next stop was Amsterdam for the 1948 world cycling championships. There Heid got the full effect of what he was up against. He saw that cycling at the top level was unforgiving. Riders on national teams had full-time coaches and trainers, masseurs, and mechanics. He and Stiller, strictly on their own, had each other.

Heid also discovered that he had to discard some misconceptions and reexamine basics. He was eliminated early in the match-race heats and was left, with Stiller, in a 10-kilometer (6.2-mile) consolation race for losers under the track lights after midnight.

Sixty riders made an aggressive race around the 500-meter (550-yard) cement oval. In the final two laps, the pace was sizzling. Heid positioned himself behind the rear wheel of Australia's champion sprinter Sid Patterson, who, like Heid, was trying to win so he could stay on the Continent.

When they sped around the final turn, Patterson jumped to the front of the surging pack. He put his head down, pulled on the handlebars, and went all out for the line as racers spread all over the track like sparks. Patterson held off a challenge by another rider to win, with Heid a close third. That got the American an expenses-paid trip to race in Copenhagen on the Ordrupp Velodrome, an outdoor cement track. Stiller went with him.

In Copenhagen, Heid won a race, which helped generate more invitations. After a couple of weeks, Heid and Stiller returned to Antwerp to break into the Belgian circuit. They won some team omniums—four events—but found the going more intense than they had ever experienced before. On occasion, Heid could hardly walk after a race.

Unlike in the United States, amateurs racing in Europe were paid modest amounts of cash. European riders who had survived the ravages of World War II had far more use for money than silver trophies. Riders on the velodromes had a contract for every race they rode. A standard contract at the Antwerp and Ghent velodromes was about $30 a program for amateurs racing four events.

Heid and Stiller found that Belgians still fondly remembered Gerard Debaets. "All I had to do was mention his name and doors opened," Heid recalled. Belgian champions Jeff Scherens—Sergio Matteini's old

LEFT. Al Stiller of Chicago, left, and Jack Heid enjoy a victory lap following their win in an international omnium (four events) at the Antwerp Sports Palace in Antwerp, Belgium, in October 1948. (*Julia Heid*)

OPPOSITE. While Jack Heid raced in Europe, Ted Smith stayed active. Here Smith is racing in eastern Canada, riding second behind Art Lauf of Hydes, Maryland, and ahead of three-time Olympian Dick Cortright of Buffalo in third place. (*Julia Heid*)

friend—and Stan Ockers sought them out for training rides. Shortly before Christmas, Heid won a miss-and-out (where the last rider at the end of each lap drops out until one is left) on the Antwerp track. He won about $25 and a bouquet of flowers. Stiller, who came in tenth, did not seem as determined to make it in Europe and left to return to Chicago for Christmas.

While Heid was getting ready for his next season in Europe, Art Longsjo, back in Fitchburg, Massachusetts, burned with the same competitive fire for speed skating. In the pantheon of American athletes, Longsjo—who made his mark in not one but two sports—remains one of the most overlooked.

As an eleventh-grader in 1948 at Fitchburg High School, Longsjo decided to quit school because he wanted to train full time and be an Olympic skater. He was inspired to get into speed skating in the early 1940s when Carmelita Landry of Fitchburg won the national championships. She was so popular that local kids went out and bought speed skates with the long blades, not hockey or figure skates.

At sixteen, Longsjo was a wiry 6 feet 1 inch, broad shouldered and deep chested. He had a light olive complexion and chestnut hair. His facial features were well defined but not delicate, with a chiseled nose and cheeks. His family spoke Finnish and always said that if one word characterized Longsjo it was *sisu*—Finnish for guts. Fitchburg itself, an industrial town in north-central Massachusetts, is named after John Fitch, an eighteenth-century explorer whose name represented heroism.

Longsjo was a quiet, high-spirited youngster. When he was eleven he joined the Mirror Lake Skating Club of Fitchburg, which got him into skating events on frozen ponds and indoor rinks around New England. He competed in age-group events from 220 to 880 yards.

Dick Ring, an athlete who grew up with Longsjo, remembers going with him to the Boston Silver Skates Derby in Boston Garden, the speed-skating equivalent of boxing's Golden Gloves: "We clipped out an entry from the *Boston Record-American* and sent in twenty-five cents. We got back a postcard and a number. We were just in awe at the Garden. There were fifteen-thousand-plus people packed into the stands. As youngsters we got buried by the veteran salts. But we came back the next year and did better. Eventually we became some of the heavy hitters, too."

By 1947 Longsjo was under the tutelage of Alex Goguen, a national-class skater who had won several national five-mile championship races in the 1930s. Goguen, who was twelve years older than Longsjo, was regarded as a fox when it came to racing. He lived near Longsjo and gave the youngster rides to races for the company and helped work on Longsjo's form.

"He could hardly stand on his skates as a youngster," Goguen recalls. "But he was happy going to meets. He had a ball. He always thought he would do well because he was a Finn."

For such a small country, Finland has turned out a high proportion of world-class athletes, and that sports streak was continued by the Finns who settled in Fitchburg, which also supports a Finnish newspaper. In 1925 when the great Finnish runner Paavo Nurmi toured the United States, he stopped in Fitchburg to compete in a track meet. The elder Longsjo won a sprint event. Nurmi won the handicapped mile, where he ran a mile and a half against competitors who went just the mile. The elder Longsjo was a member of the local Reipas Athletic Club, a Finnish club where members discussed stories of track, skating, and skiing the way baseball and football stories are bandied about in American Legion halls.

Goguen got Longsjo skating more smoothly. "I saw the kid was slowing down on the turns because he was digging the front of his skate blade into the ice on each stroke as though he were running," Goguen says. He told the youngster to lift the blade front up first as he pushed the skate blade level on a stroke that was at right angles from the body.

Speed skates are set lower to the ice than hockey or figure skates, which makes them harder to balance on. "Sometimes I couldn't tell if he was listening to me," Goguen recounts. "He had his own ideas about things. But then I would watch him and I could see he was trying it."

Goguen broadened Longsjo's competitive radius to major events in upstate New York and around New England. Often Goguen and Longsjo won races in their divisions. Longsjo felt that he had what it took to make the Olympic team. His parents were highly concerned about his dropping out of school at age sixteen, but they finally gave in.

This big change in young Longsjo's life coincided with Goguen's move to Pittsfield, nestled in the Berkshires 100 miles west of Fitchburg. Goguen, twenty-eight, went to work for the Pittsfield Parks Department in a job that included coaching a speed-skating team. After a talk with Goguen, Longsjo's parents let their son go to Pittsfield with him. In Pittsfield, Longsjo could get the coaching he needed, and Goguen could get him a seasonal job with the Parks Department. Later in life, Longsjo told reporters that he thought that was "heaven on ice."

Heid adapted to the austere life-style of postwar Europe and learned to speak French and Flemish. He lived in the home of Ernestine Debaets, on a street near a dock where heavy loads were still hauled by horses as they had been for centuries. The home lacked a flush toilet. The cuisine also took some getting used to, particularly the large amounts of fried food and horse meat. "A specialty of the house was cow udders dipped in grease," Heid recalled. "I got so I liked sandwiches made with cow udders."

He got around Belgium's cold, rainy winter by racing indoors on velodromes. On occasion he got into road races up to sixty-five miles long in Belgium and Holland. He improved and newspapers began calling him the Antwerp Yank. Sometimes he turned training rides into shopping trips; he would cycle to Holland twelve miles away, where he bought cold cuts, cheese, and smoked fish, which were cheaper there than in Antwerp. With the purchases in his knapsack, he would pedal home.

Back in America, the cycling community circulated news of Heid's accomplishments. Don Sheldon of Nutley liked what he heard. Sheldon had set national records at seventeen in 1947, won a national championship, and twice won the Tour of Somerville, a fifty-mile race in northern New Jersey on its way to being an American classic. Millions of Americans learned about Sheldon one Sunday morning from another of Ripley's "Believe It or Not!" cartoons, this one showing Sheldon in the national champion's jersey, and citing him for winning his second Tour of Somerville "from 134 crack riders, including Ted Smith, the national champ!" Sheldon followed Heid to Antwerp.

Early in the 1949 season, Heid and Sheldon traveled to England, where they raced regularly on the Herne Hill track, the Fallowfield track in Manchester, and Butts Stadium in Coventry. They lived strictly on what they made from the races. They sold merchandise certificates they won at a discount for cash. Heid supplemented his income by becoming an underground entrepreneur—he smuggled watches. Heid would buy a wristwatch for $5 in the Jewish quarter of Antwerp or Ghent and sell that watch in England for $25.

"England had a one hundred percent luxury tax," recalled Heid, "so this actually saved the English who bought from me twenty-five dollars. When I went from Belgium to England, I would take ten to fifteen watches with me. They would be good watches, shockproof, but not too expensive because nobody would buy an expensive watch."

He wrapped them in paper and put them in a dirty old tool pouch that he put on top of the knapsack he carried. Customs officials would push the tool pouch aside to look in his knapsack. "I was willing to risk a fine or jailing, or whatever it was they would have done if they had caught me, just to stay in Europe to race."

Heid also took derailleur gears or cycling jerseys and shorts, all of which were in short supply in England. "It was quite an adventure. I wasn't greedy. It was surviving."

In England during the outdoor track season, he beat so many national champions that the English press dubbed him the Yankee Clipper. One of Heid's major track wins came in July at the Manchester Wheelers Meet, an international competition. Sheldon, who found the races harder than races in America, was struggling to adapt, but he was a game competitor. He went with Heid to Denmark to race on the circuit of outdoor cement tracks.

"The Danes were very enthusiastic," Heid said. "We rode an international sprint, a handicap, a miss-and-out, and a Madison where two riders competed as a team. There was also tandem racing and motorpace. Professionals and amateurs raced separate events."

In Denmark, Heid discovered the Danes had pari-mutuel betting on cyclists. "If the people made money betting on you," he said, "they would take you out to eat."

When Heid and Sheldon went to the world championships in Copenhagen in late August 1949, Heid's performances proved a highlight of his career as well as a high spot in modern U.S. cycling for many years. Sheldon was eliminated early in the heats, but Heid got his momentum going when he quickly dispensed with two opponents to advance to the eighth-finals. There he came up against England's national amateur champion, Alan Bannister. On the bell lap, the Englishman led Heid up the 48-degree banking of the 370-meter (400-yard) cement track. Heid climbed higher, between Bannister and the outside fence, before suddenly dropping down as Bannister continued up. Heid gained six lengths before Bannister could react. The Englishman chased Heid until he saw it was hopeless and lifted his hands from the handlebars.

The quarterfinals pitted Heid against his nemesis, Danish champion Axel Schandorff, who had put him out of the Olympics and was now racing before a home audience. The preliminaries were over; qualifiers were competing in the best of three races. It was a different Heid racing against the Danish champion and he outsprinted Schandorff by three inches in their first match. Their second match was better—Heid won by a length and a half. He had come a long way.

Yet he still had lessons to learn. The following day in the semifinal, Jacques Bellanger of France beat him in two straight to put Heid in the runoff for the bronze medal, against another Frenchman, Emile Lognay, winner of the Grand Prix de Paris that season. This was high-stakes racing, but Heid was so fired up from his loss that he entered the two match races already a winner in his mind. The first he won decisively. The second turned into another photo finish that Heid won by the width of a tire.

Heid, America's premier sprinter, won the first world championship medal for the United States in thirty-seven years, and was the first American since Bobby Walthour, Iver Lawson, and Marcus Hurley in 1904 to win a world championship medal abroad.

Sid Patterson of Australia defeated Bellanger to win the world amateur crown. With Englishman Reg Harris dethroning Dutchman Arie Van Vliet to win the professional sprint championship, 1949 became the year of the English-speaking invasion in continental cycling.

Heid attracted a great deal of attention in the press in both England

and the United States. Souvenir programs at velodromes where Heid and Sheldon competed carried their photos on the covers.

Life as a top amateur in Europe, particularly after his third place in the worlds, had many advantages that weren't available in America. He could make a modest living as an amateur racer. Frequently he nego- tiated such perquisites as transportation, an appearance fee, and a carte blanche to sign for meals in restaurants. In Copenhagen, the Ordrupp Velodrome promoter allowed Heid's fiancée, Julia De Witte of Antwerp, to watch races from a private box.

After the worlds, Sheldon followed cycling's flow to warmer weather in Morocco, still a French colony, where the Italian, French, and Belgian cyclists had migrated.

Heid accepted an invitation to race in Paris where he won enough to afford to marry his fiancée. But before the wedding came a three-month racing trip to the Union of South Africa.

8
BLAZING THE EUROPEAN TRAIL

American racing after World War II offered nothing like the racing Heid and Sheldon found in Europe. A new group of promoters, however, headed by Jimmy (the Whale) Proscia, was trying to revive interest in six-day events. Jimmy the Whale held races in New York City's 168th Street Armory, and hoped to foster a return of the sixes to Madison Square Garden. He also put on other sixes in Chicago, Cleveland, Buffalo, Toronto, Montreal, and Minneapolis.

Ted Smith recalls being paid $25,000 to turn professional and ride in the six-days after he won his third national championship in 1948. "My first six-day was in Memorial Auditorium in Buffalo. I took one look at the velodrome and thought it was so small that for a moment I wondered if I was going to run around it or ride. It was a lot different racing than I thought it would be. Going around and around like that affected my stomach and I couldn't eat."

Smith competed in a dozen six-days, which brought some of Europe's best riders to the States that winter and spring. At the March 1949 six-day in New York's 168th Street Armory, Smith competed against Hugo Koblet, the Swiss star who went on to win the 1951 Tour de France by twenty-two minutes.

Outside of the winter six-days, there was very little professional racing in America. But Smith also earned money riding track events in eastern Canada. The promoter, Albert Schelstraete, was a Belgian who grew up in Canada, and he put on races in Ontario towns like Delhi, Simcoe, and Shawinigan Falls. Schelstraete had a portable velodrome, thirteen laps to the mile, and a flair for attracting audiences, especially the Belgian tobacco farm workers in the area.

"Schelstraete one time called me up and asked, 'Do you want to race a horse for two hundred and fifty dollars?' " Smith recounts. "So I went up there to Delhi for the race on a horse track against a sulky. The people there are Belgians and they bet on anything. They will bet on where a fly will land. Well, the race was the best two out of three matches, a mile each race. I rode behind the sulky. I had to be careful because the horse was kicking up a lot of dirt in my face. But I came around and beat the horse in two straight. The driver wanted me to ride in front of the horse. But I didn't want any of that. The horse would bite off my ear."

Another rider who competed in Schelstraete's races was Jim Lauf. To liven up a race program, Schelstraete persuaded Smith to lie down on the track and let Lauf jump over him on a bicycle. "I lay down on my face on the straightaway," Smith says. "Jimmy got speed up and jumped his bike over me. He touched me just a little."

Lauf, a dark-haired Marylander, succeeded Smith as national champion in 1949. Like Smith, he felt the rules that governed the sport in this country inhibited development.

"When I won the nationals in San Diego in 1949, a Schwinn Company vice-president offered me two Schwinn bicycles if I would come to Chicago," recounts Lauf. "I went out at my expense to the corporate headquarters, but the deal fell through because the ABL officials said they would turn me professional by taking the two bikes that were offered. That is how crazy things were in those days. If you took a bicycle, they turned you professional."

Schelstraete had a European approach in awarding prizes—cash to all, professional and amateur. Lauf saved his money in a Canadian bank, a compromise he made with ABL officials who threatened to declare him professional if he spent his winnings in the United States. At the end of the 1949 season, the twenty-two-year-old Lauf withdrew his savings and bought a ticket on the Queen Elizabeth bound for Antwerp and serious racing. He moved into the home where Heid and Sheldon had lived.

Smith, at the start of the 1950 season, went to Dienze, near Ghent. There he lived in the home of a Belgian coach, Jules Vershelden, a longtime friend of Schelstraete. When Smith arrived, he discovered that Belgian newspapers had published his photo in a story announcing his arrival. "People came up to me and said my name like they knew me all my life," Smith tells. "Then they would talk to me in Flemish, which I don't understand at all. I would shake their hand if they were a man, or kiss them on the cheek if they were a woman. It was a lot different than I thought it would be. In my day, our riders were scared to go to Europe because those European riders were so superior. When I got to Belgium I was treated nicely. The Belgian people were still grateful because the American soldiers had pushed the Germans out during the war."

After the limited professional program in America, he found he had all the races he wanted. While there were few races in the United States, in Belgium there were many. Every day offered a wide choice of professional races. No travel expenses were involved as Smith could usually ride to the races, compete, and then ride back home.

In Antwerp, Lauf could find ten to fifteen races every day within a thirty-mile radius. Like the other three Americans, he was well received and was offered contracts to ride track events as the incumbent national champion. Track events paid $20 to $30 a meet—as good as the top three professionals, enough to live on for a week or two. But he found he also had to get into road races to supplement his income.

While Belgium had an abundance of races, to the Americans the racing and living conditions were shocking. Smith was appalled by the roads. "They were terrible. I never saw roads like them in my life. They were all cobblestones and bricks. When you race seven hours at a time on them, that is tough. I'm not talking about just riding on those cobbles for seven hours. I'm talking about racing on them. Going hard. Your wrists, your back, your whole body takes a pounding."

There were 150 to 200 riders in the amateur races, all of them vying for the narrow cinder paths that bordered the cobblestone roads. Beyond the cinder paths were ditches in which open sewage flowed.

"The packs strung out for a kilometer on the sides of the cobblestones," Lauf recalls. "I'll never forget the first time I rode an open race. I tried to pass somebody on the cycle path and fell. I got dumped into the sewage beside the road."

Smith wanted to leave after the first week. But he had paid his own expenses to get to Belgium, and he didn't feel like just turning around and going back home. He also realized that staying and racing against other pros was part of paying his dues to become a champion.

The amenity he and Lauf missed most was a shower. Belgian riders sponged off. After a race, the manager of a local cafe would fill a tub with cold water in the back courtyard. Riders would then strip down and sponge off the sweat and grit.

"If you finished the race first, you got clean water," Smith says. "But it was strictly first come, first served. If you got there last, all you got was dirty water."

Smith found that the superman reputation of the European cyclists was overstated, but it was not without foundation. The races were longer and harder than those to which he was accustomed. The popular American road races were 50-milers around a circuit. In Belgium he was racing 60 to 100 miles a day every day until he got so tired he realized he was overdoing it and cut back. His Belgian competitors were strong and fast.

In the town of Waarschoot he scored a first for the Stars and Stripes when he won a 140-mile professional race. That was in June, and the victory got him several contracts to compete on the velodromes, which made for smoother riding, much to his relief.

In 1950 when Smith and Lauf were breaking into European racing in Belgium, Jack Heid was a married man and a veteran of international racing in Europe. He was the lone wolf blazing the European trail that was drawing other top Americans. When the weather warmed and the English outdoor track season opened, Heid and his bride moved from Belgium to England.

Heid earned a comfortable living in England where he could make more money as an amateur than a pro sprinter could on the Continent. He was earning about £15 a week when the average English worker was earning £5 to £7, then worth about $2.80 a pound. He had help with equipment from the Claude Butler Company, a bicycle manufacturer near London. They even produced a frame named after him—the Jack Heid Special.

Two factors helped endear him to the public of early postwar England: his keen competitive nature, and being an American. He also fit in with the best riders; his regular training partners were world champions Reg Harris and Sid Patterson. Harris's formal education ended after grammar school, and he went to work polishing cars. His athletic career was thus his fortune, and he selected training partners carefully. Harris's choice of Heid as a training partner indicated the latter's increased stature in cycling.

Harris, Patterson, and Heid had a standard regimen. They warmed up on a half-hour ride in the afternoon, with the pace getting progressively faster, followed by a light ride for a half-hour. Then they raced four sprints on the Fallowfield track, with each man taking a turn leading out.

Back in the United States, the surviving members of the Bicycle Racing Stars of the Nineteenth Century Association were counting on Heid to win the world amateur championship and show once again that the United States was a force in international bicycle racing. Their glory days were long past, and those who had been part of them had died. August Zimmerman and Major Taylor were gone. America's first national champion, George M. Hendee, died in 1943. Eddie (the Cannon) Bald, who won the first national professional title, died in 1946, a few months before cyclist/car racer Barney Oldfield. Mile-a-Minute Murphy died in February 1950. The members of the association were pensioners, yet they took up a collection and sent Heid $200 to help pay expenses.

It looked like Heid was going to fulfill their hopes as well as Frank Kramer's prescription for the "one good American rider" to help revive the sport in America. But Heid's idyllic life was upset in mid-May when he lost his balance on the fine line between amateur and professional. He was hit with a six-week suspension for an infraction involving expense money from a race promoter. His chance to win the world amateur championship was suddenly in jeopardy.

A representative of the Claude Butler Company offered Heid a covert stipend to help him through the suspension as he kept training. While he mulled this over, his wife heightened the dilemma when she announced that she was pregnant. Reg Harris told him that if he turned professional he would guarantee Heid £50 from race promoters every

time he raced. Heid began to give serious consideration to this possibility. He held Gerard Debaets in high esteem for being a good racer and
dutifully raising two sons when his wife took ill with tuberculosis.
Debaets raced as a professional. So did Harris. So did his earlier mentor
Jack Simes II.

The big problem with turning pro at the time was that there wasn't
much money in sports. A world champion did well. Harris, for example,
had his Raleigh sponsorship, which paid him a base salary, plus bonuses
for records he set, plus the appearance fees he negotiated, plus the
race prizes he won. But Harris was at the summit of a steep pyramid,
along with only a small number of other professionals who did well.
Most professionals didn't earn as much as Heid and the other top
amateurs.

Yet being a professional would put Heid at the top of the sport, free
to make his own deals. He felt responsibility for the hopes of the Bicycle
Racing Stars of the Nineteenth Century Association, but his family
responsibilities were more important. Heid decided to make the leap
and turn professional.

When the world cycling championships came up in late August 1950 in
Liege, Belgium, someone asked Ted Smith if he were riding in the
amateur road race. Smith replied, "Not me. I'm riding with the big
boys."

Smith became the first U.S. rider to compete in the world professional road race, 178 miles over a hilly course. Among the sixty-five
starters were such legends as Stan Ockers of Belgium, Louis Bobet of
France, Gino Bartali of Italy, and Hugo Koblet and Ferdi Kubler of
Switzerland.

The pace was hot from the start and never let up. After 100 miles,
a tire went on Smith's bike. In those days before support vehicles, road
racers wore a spare tire in a figure eight across their back and under
each arm. Smith got off his bike to change tires but discovered he had
forgotten his pump.

"I was glad to get that flat," he admits. He hitched a ride in the wagon
that followed the field of riders to pick up those who dropped out. Inside
was Swiss star Hugo Koblet.

Smith knew Koblet from riding in track races with him in the States.
Smith asked what was he doing there and Koblet said he "got tired."

The man who was to win the Tour de France by twenty-two minutes said he was tired. "No excuses," Smith says.

At the sprint matches on the velodrome in nearby Rocourt, promoters were hoping for a sentimental match, preferably in the final, between Belgian Jef Scherens and Frenchman Louis Gerardin, both heroes from the 1930s. Scherens and Gerardin had finished one-two at the world professional sprint championships in Paris in 1947.

Heid drew Scherens in his first match. "I had great respect for Scherens," Heid said. "He was fifteen times Belgian national sprint champion. Seven times world champion. He used to do a sprint with me when we trained on the same velodrome—a friendly sprint, the experienced pro helping to bring up a younger rider, because I was a friend of Debaets. But I could see that I was matched as a lightweight at the worlds against Scherens."

When Heid warmed up he found the banking so steep he had to cut his right pedal to keep the bottom from scraping against the concrete surface. Part of his pre-race warm-up consisted of imposing his opponent's style of racing on the course to work out details beforehand. Scherens had such sharp spring in his sprint that he was called the Cat. Audiences all around Europe were thrilled at how smartly he dashed from behind an opponent's rear wheel to a lead of two bike lengths. Heid figured out where Scherens would make his move in their match race.

In the race, Heid watched Scherens closely and jumped a little before him on the turn. They blasted for the line, one sprinter beginning his pro career, the other ending a distinguished one. The crowd that packed into the stadium raucously rose to its feet in excitement. Scherens started to come past Heid's rear wheel down the final straight. But Heid was prepared. He had another jump of his own and beat Scherens to the line by a wheel. Belgium's favorite sprinter was eliminated by the sprinter from the New World.

In the next round, Heid dispensed with Jacques Bellanger, who had used the silver medal from the previous amateur world championships to help launch a professional career. Next, the Antwerp Yank drew Arie Van Vliet, the Flying Dutchman. Van Vliet had established a reputation for being a tough opponent in 1936 when he won a gold medal in the kilometer and won the world amateur sprint championship. He also won the world professional title in 1938 and again in 1948, and he was still a serious contender in 1950.

Heid wasn't sure how to beat him. Belgian coach Aloise DeGraeve, in his fifties, had made a study of Van Vliet and told Heid to lead the Dutchman up and down the velodrome banking to tire his legs.

Unfortunately, DeGraeve knew Van Vliet better than he knew Heid. "I had never ridden like that," Heid recalled. "I was a pure sprinter. I depended on my jump. I would get in front and stall a long sprinter. But I tried running Van Vliet up and down the track. It really messed me up. I was too tired to sprint."

Heid wound up eighth in the world championships. Van Vliet went on to finish second to Harris. The Englishman kept his promise to Heid and made sure promoters paid him £50 a race in England, but when what was left of the summer was over the Heids moved back to Antwerp for the birth of their first child.

Sheldon traveled widely to races around Europe. About the time Heid turned professional, Sheldon moved to Paris where he used connections he had made in Morocco to negotiate a slot in the Velo Club Le'Veloise, supported by Peugeot Cycles. It was a big break, as riders were provided with food and lodging, road and track equipment, shoes, and Peugeot wearing apparel.

By the summer of 1950, the Korean War brought an abrupt halt to the migration of American cyclists to Europe. The draft was reinstated. In October, Smith returned to Buffalo where he was drafted into the Army Air Corps and sent for a year of duty in Korea.

Lauf also went back home after the worlds. He returned to America in time to ride in the Tour of Mexico stage race—1,200 miles in fourteen days—which drew teams from Europe and all over South America. Lauf captured the ninth stage, sprinting out of a small bunch of riders to cross the line first in Guadalajara.

He was thrilled with the race—a million and a half spectators lined the streets in Mexico City. The contingent of U.S. riders Lauf rode with found the race more than they could handle. After the third stage, his teammates went home. Following his win in the ninth stage, Lauf, misinformed about the next day's starting time, missed the start.

Lauf soon went back to Maryland, enlisted in the Coast Guard, and was stationed at a New Jersey supply depot. The base commander let him train during duty hours after Lauf assured him that he would make the Olympic team.

Sheldon, twenty-one, returned to Paris from the Centennial Games in Christ Church, New Zealand, where he had gone to escape the European winter. In May 1951 he enlisted at the U.S. embassy in London for four years in the air force. Because of his background, he was stationed in England where he was assigned to a Special Services athletics division. His main duty was to prepare for the Olympics.

After the 1950 worlds, Heid hustled to make a living. In Antwerp he competed in road races entirely different from those he had been in for more than a year. Riders in packs of 50 to 100 competed in professional events which paid down to thirty places.

In early September he pedaled twenty-two miles to a ninety-mile race in which he finished seventh and received $17—enough to live on for a week. His wife had borne a son, John, further boosting his need to earn money. When the weather turned bad he competed in the indoor track circuit in Belgium, Holland, France, Germany, and Switzerland. He found that the smaller velodromes favored his sprinting ability as the riders laid over on the steep turns and accelerated only on the short straights.

In late February he was back racing on the roads, frequently in the cold, numbing rain. Twelve months earlier the sun had been shining on his career. But 1951 was turning into a difficult year. For the first time, Heid began to get discouraged. He adapted to the long races and did as well as anybody else until the midpoint, when some riders began drinking out of a different bottle they carried. Then they got revved up, which made the races harder. Heid did not want to get into drugs like steroids or amphetamines.

"Van Vliet saw me riding and said, 'You've been racing on the roads. Your pedal action shows it.' He was right. I wasn't pedaling with the smoothness of a track rider."

While on a lead breakaway with another rider in a seventy-five-mile race in March, the frame of his bicycle, weakened by the constant pounding on coarse pavement of the road, cracked and broke in two, throwing Heid to the ground.

At the age of twenty-six, Heid was one of the top sprinters in the world. But there on the ground, dirty, grimy, scraped and bleeding, he felt it was time to quit. In late March Heid moved his family back home.

The Heids settled in Rockaway, in northern New Jersey. Heid hung up his bicycles and found full-time work as a maintenance man for a chemical company. He bought a house, and when another son, Rik, was born in 1953, Heid found a part-time maintenance job. Now his former northern New Jersey training partners would joke about him "painting a barn."

Heid had gone through a strenuous apprenticeship to become a professional racer, but there was nothing left for him in America. The six-day races that Ted Smith had competed in failed to spark a revival and were discontinued. Under ABL rules, he had to wait five years for reinstatement as an amateur to make a comeback.

"Jack Heid was a great bike rider," his mentor Jack Simes II said. "But he was born thirty-five years too late."

9
OUTSIDE NORMAL LIMITS

By the time eighteen-year-old Art Longsjo took off his shirt in October 1950 for the Selective Service physician to put a stethoscope against his sternum, he had developed into one of the outstanding junior speed skaters in the country. He swept his age-group division in major meets, set state records, and won a national championship race. Alex Goguen trained him in a series of sprints from 220 yards to 2 miles, over and over in a workout, on alternate days, a popular interval workout today but rare in the late 1940s. Years of these workouts sharpened Longsjo's speed while the repetitions gave him great stamina. When the Selective Service physician listened to his stethoscope, he heard an unusually slow heartbeat. Sports medicine was virtually unknown at the time. The physician thought he heard a heart murmur rather than the heart of an endurance athlete. Longsjo failed his draft physical and was classified 4-F.

As Longsjo's coach, Goguen saw him differently: "He could stay with you and stay with you, and then take off so fast that you would wonder what was wrong with you."

That is what he did in the national two-mile championship in late 1949 in St. Paul. Two days of events drew 4,000 spectators who bundled up

to withstand the frigid weather and watch the best skaters in the
country. Jack Heid's training partner Ray Blum won the men's open
national championship. In the juniors' two-mile race for sixteen- to
seventeen-year-olds, Longsjo forced the pace and broke away at the
mile. He won by a wide margin and chopped 9 seconds from the
Minnesota state record.

After his draft physical, Longsjo went back to Pittsfield to skate
another season with Goguen and work for the parks department. It was
his first year of open skating. He was good but just another one of the
bunch. Wanderlust had a better grip on him than anything else. At the
end of February, recalls Goguen, Longsjo and another young skater
picked up their final paycheck and hitchhiked south to Florida.

After Florida, his buddy went home and Longsjo hitchhiked west
alone. In Texas he spent a week picking cotton before moving on to San
Francisco where he stayed the summer. When he needed money he
waited on tables and worked odd jobs. Seeing a lot of Bay Area cyclists
influenced him to take up cycling, a sport many speed skaters did in
warm weather. Racing bicycles at the time meant track bikes, which
sold for $100. He called home for the money, which was more than his
parents had. But they had confidence in their son's athletic abilities and
took out a bank loan.

At the end of the summer, Longsjo returned home with his bike and
a repertoire of stories about his travels and life in California. He decided
to stay in Fitchburg rather than return to Pittsfield for the winter. For
fitness he rode twenty-five to forty miles a day when he wasn't working
at the United Farmers' Co-Op moving grain bags. When the weather
turned cold and a pond near his home froze, he switched to skating.

Longsjo went out to the Olympic skating trials in January 1951 in St.
Paul where he skated well enough that officials picked him as alternate
for the Olympic team. Speed skaters were selected for the Olympic
team a year early to give them time to adjust to the European-style
skating used in the Olympics. The type of races Longsjo grew up on
had massed starts, marked by pushing and shoving, and the first over
the finish line won. In European-style skating, two skaters at a time
compete individually on two concentric tracks. At the end of each
400-meter (437-yard) lap, the skaters switch tracks through an open
lane between them. They skate for the fastest time, but the judges also
note skating technique, which emphasizes a smoothness that was totally new to Longsjo.

Not making the team at nineteen didn't upset him. He was recognized wherever he went to meets, often with Goguen. Longsjo was winning big silver skates competitions from Chicago to Lake Placid to Boston. But when the next Olympic team was to be selected, he didn't want to be an alternate again. He returned in late 1951 to train under Goguen and work for the Pittsfield Parks Department.

Longsjo and Goguen planned a four-year program to get Longsjo ready for the Olympics. In January 1952 they started with the nationals in St. Paul. To be on the safe side, Goguen took Longsjo for a physical. The doctor took his heartbeat, said it was too slow, and told him to go home and rest, much to Longsjo's wry amusement. The next week at the nationals in St. Paul, he won three races.

But not without prodding. The first day he was not aggressive and Goguen asked him why they went all that way and spent the money to get there. The next day Longsjo won the one-mile, two-mile, and five-mile races. That got him runner-up in the nationals, which drew 15,500 spectators. Goguen was sixth overall.

In February they traveled to the North American outdoor championships for two days of racing in Alpena, Michigan, in the northeastern corner of the state, on Thunder Bay. On the first day of competition, after skating in races from 440 yards to 2 miles, Longsjo was tied in points with Ray Blum. The next day, the two skaters watched each other closely as a fierce snowstorm swept in from Lake Huron. Blum and other skaters had folded newspaper pages under their sweaters against their chests to cut down on the wind chill as they skated.

Terry Browne, a Detroit firefighter, broke away from the front of the three-mile race with a group of Detroit skaters to nearly lap the field and win the race. The points collected put him in a three-way tie for first.

After the competition concluded and the athletes were in a warm building for awards and photos, they heard over the radio that Don McDermott of the U.S. Olympic speed-skating team had won a silver medal in the 500-meter (550-yard) event at the Winter Games in Oslo, Norway.

McDermott had started out as a cyclist but changed to speed skating as his primary sport. He rode on Sunday mornings with his northern New Jersey cycling and skating buddies—Jack Heid, Don Sheldon, Ray Blum, Gerard Debaets, and others.

"I accidentally sprayed a shower of confetti in the air when we heard the news about McDermott's silver medal," Blum says. "I took off my sweater by crossing my arms over my chest and pulled the bottom of the sweater up. The newspaper under my sweater had become soaked with sweat, then dried and became brittle in the frigid air. The shower of confetti in the air was like a celebration of McDermott's Olympic medal."

On a blind date in 1952, Longsjo met Terry L'Ecuyer, a tall, attractive brunette from Fitchburg who was attending Becker Junior College in Worcester, where she was studying to be a medical secretary. It was the beginning of a five-year courtship that spanned three continents.

"He was my first love," she explains. "I went with him sometimes to watch his morning workouts. I helped him shovel snow off the ice. He was dedicated to sports, sometimes too dedicated. But he didn't sit around and talk about doing something he wasn't going to do. I knew he wasn't going to change and I was willing to help him excel."

Their romance kept him closer to Fitchburg. He worked as a file clerk at the Fitchburg General Electric plant and joined the Leominister Center skating club. In the next skating season, he pushed harder. Longsjo became a dominant skater in the Northeast, and was a strong contender for the next Olympic skating team.

As part of his training he took up cycling on a more ambitious level. Both sports use similar leg muscles—particularly those upper-leg muscles—in the same way. And both cycling and American-style speed skating use related tactics. In both sports, competitors are jostled in packs around turns and down straights. In both sports, drafting behind competitors, keeping presence of mind in a speeding pack, and timing a sprint under pressure require the same concentration and the same skill.

Longsjo's debut as a bicycle racer at the 1953 Massachusetts state championship is a familiar story in the Bay State. When the twenty-one-year-old Longsjo showed up at the Westboro Raceway, a banked cement track made for midget-car racing, he was obviously out of his league. Longsjo wore cutoff skating tights, a T-shirt, and brown moccasins—his standard cycling gear. People looked at him and rolled their eyes. All the bike racers wore bright-colored jerseys and black wool shorts imported from Europe, and bike shoes with a metal cleat on the sole to fasten over the pedal for better drive.

Art Longsjo with his fiancé Terry L'Ecuyer in July 1953 when Longsjo broke into bike racing at the Massachusetts state championships at the Westboro Raceway. (*Alex Goguen*)

He caught the looks and played along. He didn't have a car, so he rode his bike to the race, pedaling an hour and a half to get there, and stopped along the way to pump up his front tire, which had a leaky valve. What chance did he have against the better-rested riders? His bike wasn't shiny and new like the others, so he referred to it as "my truck." He didn't have a helmet, so he had to borrow one. He could get through the mile and three-mile races in the championship with the leaky valve in his front tire, but he would be at a disadvantage in the last race, the twenty-five-miler. How could he compete against these better-equipped riders?

It's a wonder that nobody picked up on the slight hustle in Longsjo's deadpan modesty. If they had, they might have realized that Longsjo's legs were muscular and strong and perfect for cycling. They might have noticed, too, that Longsjo's "truck" was really a Schwinn Paramount, one of the best bikes available. It needed cleaning, it needed oiling, and it needed new tires, but it was good.

So was Longsjo. In his first event, a qualifying heat for the mile, he won impressively. He then went on to win all three races.

But success didn't end there. Longsjo's state championship victory qualified him for the national ABL championship in St. Louis—and expense money as well. The ABL, kept together "with spit and Scotch Tape," could grant Longsjo only $60, which wouldn't begin to cover round-trip transportation, food, and three days of hotel costs. Moreover, for a national championship Longsjo needed proper cycling clothing and, some fans and friends believed, a better bicycle.

The *Fitchburg Sentinel* ran an article about his state championship victory and the financial predicament he faced for going to the nationals. The *Sentinel* announced a fund drive. Mayor Peter J. Levanti opened the campaign with a $5 donation, and Police Chief Carlisle F. Taylor served as fund treasurer.

A total of $97 was collected. All but $5 was spent to buy him a racing uniform. A veteran racer rebuilt Longsjo's "truck" for a nominal fee. A second fund drive raised $100 to provide expense money for St. Louis to supplement the ABL allowance.

At the nationals—races of one, three, five, and twenty-five miles— Longsjo the novice bike racer crashed twice. He suffered gouges and scrapes to his arms and legs. Yet he won points for third in the three-mile race to wind up in ninth overall in his first national championship.

Three weeks later, Longsjo rode in his third bike race—the New England track championships in Lonsdale, Rhode Island. He won all four events, from one to twenty-five miles. It was a short but brilliant cycling season. Nobody gave much thought to the possibility that he could make two Olympic teams in one year, but the potential existed.

In January 1954, Longsjo packed his skates, not his bicycle, and went to West Allis, Wisconsin, to compete in the Great Lakes Open. He was so popular that skating officials proposed he race instead at the Midwest Championship which the *Detroit Times* held at Belle Isle. To entice him, officials agreed to cover his expenses to the national championship coming up in St. Paul.

The switch had another payoff for Longsjo. In Detroit, he won four of the meet's seven races and earned the "Skater of the Day" award. The *Detroit Times* acclaimed him as one of the greatest skaters ever to race in the championship, which had attracted the top U.S. and Canadian skaters for thirty-two years.

At the nationals in St. Paul, Longsjo set a national record in the two-mile. He also won the five-mile, sprinting out of the lead pack after the final turn. However, falls in the 220-yard event and the mile cost him potential points. He finished second overall in the national championship.

Next came the North American outdoor championship in February in Pittsfield. The city's common was flooded to create an ice rink with a track measuring six laps to the mile. Pittsfield's Winter Carnival put on eighty races for men and women in assorted age groups. The most thrilling race was the men's open two-mile in which Goguen led until two laps before the finish. Then Longsjo flashed past his mentor, followed closely by Olympic silver medalist Don McDermott. Goguen gave chase, with the pack strung out behind like a game of crack the whip. McDermott and Longsjo, the same size, skated stroke for stroke around the final turn. In the final straight, Longsjo opened up two strides on McDermott to win. Then he went on to take the 880-yard event and to capture the North American outdoor championship.

Longsjo's triumph duplicated Carmelita Landry's 1941 victory— which was fitting, because her victory had inspired him to become a speed skater. Yet he felt he hadn't peaked, and he set his sights on the North American indoor championship in four weeks in Lake Placid. No male skater had ever won both indoor and outdoor championships in the same season. Longsjo decided to try for the North American double.

More than 300 skaters from the United States and Canada, ranging from seven to fifty-six years old, entered the two-day North American indoor championship in Lake Placid. Longsjo skated to first in four races from the half-mile to five miles. He also scored second in two others to amass an overwhelming number of points and win by a wide margin to clinch both North American titles.

Longsjo's versatility in two sports helped attract press attention to the bike races he entered in 1954. Newspaper coverage of the races mentioned that Longsjo was two-time winner of the North American speed-skating championships. Sports pages proclaimed "Skater Cycles to Victory" and "Champ Skater Shows Heels to Cyclists." The publicity helped bring new attention to the sport. More and more, he appeared to be that "one good American rider" Frank Kramer had prescribed to bring back spectator interest in cycling.

The coverage no doubt enhanced his personal satisfaction, but it gave him little else, as there was not much to gain. Sometimes he won wristwatches, cycling equipment, and an occasional piece of luggage. In the 1950s, amateur athletes were expected to be gentleman amateurs. International Olympic Committee president Avery Brundage liked to say that amateur sports would remain unchanged because they were only for those who didn't have to work a regular job to support themselves. Athletes like cyclists and skaters grumbled in frustration as Brundage ignored their pleas to permit better prizes and more travel expenses so they could devote more time to training.

Longsjo, the son of a lathe operator, didn't come from the affluent background that Brundage seemed to suggest was necessary, yet he was determined to compete and to be the best. His pursuit of excellence in two sports that bound him to a year-round regimen gave him a reputation around Fitchburg as an eccentric.

People used to say he was an outsider. Fitchburg is a city where people work, get married, and raise a family. Longsjo did not adhere to that mold. He shaved his legs, which men just did not do, and trained constantly, before exercise was popular. Sometimes motorists drove past him when he was on his bike and threw soft-drink bottles out the window at him. Any job he had was secondary to making the Olympic team. He had no hesitation about taking leave from his job without pay to drive in someone else's car to a race that would take him out of town for days.

One of Longsjo's regular training rides took him 180 miles, starting west across Massachusetts, up along the Mohawk Valley in New York, then north and east over mountains in southeastern Vermont to Keene, New Hampshire, before curving south into Massachusetts and back to Fitchburg. He concluded with a final climb up Mount Wachusett, a popular local ski resort, and did it all on a bike with a fixed gear so he wouldn't coast.

In the summer of 1954, as his final preparations for the Olympic skating trials, Longsjo raced in all the major cycling events he could get to. The fifty-mile Tour of Somerville in northern New Jersey had become an American classic, the Kentucky Derby of American bicycle racing, and drew the best from the United States and Canada. Longsjo finished fourth. He also won his second Massachusetts state championship by sweeping all four events from the half-mile to ten miles.

As state cycling champion, he again went to the nationals, in Minneapolis. He finished third in the twelve-mile and second in the ten-mile. In the one-mile, he swept around the final turn in a good position in the pack when his bike went out from under him. He fell and skidded on the asphalt. When he got back to his feet, both elbows and one knee bloodied, he discovered the real damage—both tires were ripped from the rims. He grabbed his bike and ran 150 yards to the finish and still came in fifth. That gave him enough points for fourth overall.

His never-say-die performance in Minneapolis contributed to his popularity, but the legend of Longsjo really began to take shape in mid-September in Canada. One of the most prestigious races on the continent began in front of the Hotel Frontenac in Quebec and finished 170 miles later, in front of the city hall in Montreal. Montreal's *La Presse* sponsored the race, the longest one-day event for amateurs in the world, and ebulliently compared it to the Stanley Cup in hockey. Only two U.S. riders had won it since 1931.

Ninety racers lined up for the 6:30 A.M. Sunday start. The pace was lively from the beginning and a group of eight broke away after only a few miles.

"I drove my Plymouth in a caravan of vehicles that followed the riders," Goguen remembers. "We passed a Catholic church on the way and I stopped in to attend mass. When I got back out and caught the caravan, I decided to go on past the pack where Art was and check on the breakaway. I kept driving and driving. I was surprised to see the breakaway had a lead of two miles, so I pulled over to the side of the road and waited for the pack to pass. When I spotted Art, I shouted, 'Hey! You better get somebody to work with you to catch the breakaway. Otherwise, you're racing for ninth place!' "

Only Pat Murphy, a Canadian national champion, was interested in going with Longsjo in pursuit of the breakaway. They worked in a relay, taking turns drafting behind each other for twenty miles until Murphy's rear tire went flat.

Goguen drove up and saw the two of them stopped to change the tire. Goguen pulled his bike from the car and gave it to Murphy. It was a little small, but the two riders resumed their chase. They caught the breakaway over the next twenty miles while Murphy's support crew made a wheel change and got him back on his own bike again. About fifty miles then remained in the race.

Several of the original breakaway riders were tired—they had been out in front for 120 miles—and were reluctant to keep up the record pace they were setting. The pack behind them started to organize a chase and sped up. Longsjo took long pulls at the front of the breakaway to keep up the tempo.

Goguen was concerned that Longsjo didn't know just where the finish was in Montreal. So many spectators lined the roads that the landmarks Longsjo had identified earlier were hidden. When Goguen saw Gothic church spires on the city's skyline, he drove his car one last time to the breakaway and signaled Longsjo that he would drive ahead and stand on the side of the road 300 yards from the finish.

The outcome of the 170-mile ride came down to a ten-man sprint. From Montreal's city limits all the way into the city, spectators were packed ten deep on each side of the road. In the last mile, one rider after another tried to charge away, attempting to capitalize on the other riders' fatigue after 7 hours 22 minutes of nonstop racing. Longsjo caught them, drafted, and waited. The pace got faster. The spectators got louder.

Finally, he spotted Goguen waving both arms at the side of the road. Longsjo took a deep breath, got out of the saddle, and sprinted with all he had. He won by five lengths over Murphy and shattered the course record by 7 minutes.

Nearly 4 minutes behind came the pack, reduced to only thirty-one riders. Longsjo's cheerful manner as he signed autographs and answered reporters' questions helped make him a new hero. The Association des Cyclistes du Canada named him Canadian cyclist of 1954.

The race was among the Canadian events that paid modest sums of cash, something that ABL officials publicly spoke out against. But ABL officials did not press the issue too hard. The U.S. and Canadian governing bodies agreed not to tell each other how to conduct their own affairs. For winning the race, Longsjo was quietly presented with an envelope containing $300, although the prize he posed with was his trophy with a cyclist mounted on top. He also received a new road-racing bicycle.

When the Olympic skating trials were scheduled for early February 1955 on Lake Como in St. Paul, Longsjo was twenty-three and a definite Olympic contender. Hedley Bray, the new mayor of Fitchburg, helped raise $300 so Longsjo could go a few weeks early and train where he would skate in the Olympic trials. Two other skaters accompanied Longsjo—his boyhood friend, Dick Ring, who financed his trip to the trials by spending money he had set aside to buy furniture for his upcoming marriage, and Arnold Uhrlass of Yonkers, New York, a skating rival of Longsjo's. Soon after they arrived, Longsjo's hopes were nearly dashed during a hard workout on Lake Como. His right skate blade caught a crack in the ice, causing him to trip and fall. He wrenched the knee.

Longsjo was made to rest and take daily whirlpools at the University of Minnesota's physical education facility. The treatment kept him out of the Eastern States qualifier in mid-January. He applied for a waiver and submitted a complete medical report to the Olympic Committee. The Committee granted him an automatic qualifier based on his winning nine of eleven major national-level meets in 1954.

Longsjo had spent a week in whirlpool treatments when a professor who had watched him approached and asked him to follow.

As Ring tells the story, Longsjo figured that as a guest using the facilities he should follow. "He had only a towel wrapped around his waist, and the professor led him down some hallways. Pretty soon the professor stops and opens a door. Suddenly, Art is staring at a whole classroom of students. He's embarrassed. He's standing there in front of them with only a towel around his waist and everybody's staring at his legs. They were art students and they couldn't believe the definition in his legs. They had never seen an athlete's legs like Art's before."

Longsjo was still pampering his swollen knee when it came time to skate in the 5,000-meter (3.1-mile) time trial, the event he trained for to make the Olympic team.

Ring recalls the momentous occasion in vivid detail. "Art began slow. He had a talent for winding up easy. He got very low on the ice and built his speed up. He was like a symphony in motion, moving low and fast. Faster and faster. And then he exploded all the way to the finish line. He just croaked everybody. He won the five-thousand meter. That put him on the team."

The records show he skated the distance in 8 minutes 56.4 seconds to beat twenty-five other finalists. Uhrlass was second, 6 seconds behind; Ring was fifteenth.

Under an idiosyncratic rule of the U.S. Olympic Committee, Longsjo—and the other skating Olympians—were kept out of skating competitions for the rest of the season to prepare on their own for the European-style skating used in the Olympics. (This rule has been abandoned.) He let his swollen knee recover and prepared for a rigorous cycling season. Not until May was his knee completely healed, just in time for the Tour of Somerville on Memorial Day, where he finished second to Pat Murphy of Canada.

Longsjo won or placed well up in whatever bike races he entered. He won his third consecutive Massachusetts state championship, which qualified him for the nationals in Flushing Meadows, where Shea Stadium is today. On a half-mile cement oval track, he won the national ten-mile, was second in the five-mile, but failed to place in the mile and half-mile races. His tally at the 1955 ABL nationals put him second overall.

Making the Olympic speed-skating team and looking like a contender for the Olympic cycling team made him a cult hero in both sports, but still he only scraped by financially. The *Fitchburg Sentinel* published a letter, written by someone identified only as a local businessman, that touched on Longsjo's predicament: "It is indeed unfortunate that Art's greatness is achieved in a sport as little supported as speed skating or bicycle racing, for the result is complete lack of support and interest in his achievement. Were he a track and field man, a football, baseball or basketball player, his name would be heard the world over and the city of Fitchburg would proudly claim him as one of her own."

The letter writer noted that Longsjo was overlooked in his hometown, "a city which he, alone, today is putting on the map," and said: "I remember the celebration in honor of Miss Carmelita Landry when she won the North American outdoor speed skating championship, a feat well deserving of the tribute bestowed. Yet my memory fails to recall any similar celebration in honor of the man who brought that same crown in the men's division, plus the indoor championship, to Fitchburg, and then to really top it off with a berth on the Olympic speed skating team."

From time to time Longsjo told friends he felt he should give up amateur athletics and work for a professional ice show "to earn a little money for a change." Other times he wistfully said he would like to go to France and ride on a professional cycling team "for the experience," Goguen recalls.

Yet he never complained about lacking money. He scraped along and said the traveling he did and the friends he made compensated for the economic difficulties.

Occasionally, Longsjo received financial support, but in unexpected ways. In early January 1956 he was in a Fitchburg department store when the owner—Lester Kimball—asked him why he wasn't in Norway with Olympic skating team members who went there early to train. Longsjo said he couldn't afford to go until the U.S. Olympic Committee gave him plane fare. Kimball promptly wrote Longsjo a personal check which enabled him to fly there ten days earlier than the USOC would have sent him.

Skating in Norway was like entering a new world for Longsjo. Skaters were popular, well-known athletes. People in the stands timed the skaters with their own stopwatches, and paid attention to subtleties in the styles of the skaters. Longsjo studied the way skating meets were conducted, as well as the European form of skating which stresses technique.

From Norway the team flew to Davos, Switzerland, for pre-Olympic international competition, which put the skaters against their rivals before the official races for the medals.

Longsjo was enjoying himself. Yet he could be stubborn. He and coach Del Lamb, a veteran of the 1948 Olympic skating team, argued about training methods. Lamb wanted Longsjo to skate an all-out effort every day, which Longsjo disagreed with because he said he needed some recovery time. After Lamb reprimanded Longsjo at the end of one session, Longsjo told teammates that if Lamb thought he skated slowly that day, the next day in a 500-meter (550-yard) race, which was not his event, he would skate even slower. Longsjo finished seventy-fourth out of seventy-five. He told friends the competition was so hard he could only manage seventy-fourth place.

The cold war between the East and West was sometimes fought in athletic events on ice rinks, running tracks, and boxing rings. In 1951 Russia applied to the International Olympic Committee to participate in the Olympics. Their application came too late for the Winter Olympics, but they were able to send athletes to the 1952 Summer Games. The 1956 Winter Olympics in Cortina d'Ampezzo, high up in the Italian Dolomites in northeastern Italy, were the first for Russia, and their skaters were well prepared. Russian coaching was the world's best. The Russians were the only coaches taking motion pictures of their skaters, who wore bright buttons on the hips, knees, ankles, and arms of their uniforms so that skating techniques could be analyzed and improved. This intimidated many of the other athletes, including Longsjo, who knew they lacked the support the Russians had.

A few days before Longsjo was to compete in the Olympics, he was stricken with the flu and lost seven pounds from his usual weight of 160. He finished fortieth in the 5,000-meter (3.1-mile) race won by Boris Skilkov of Russia. If he hadn't become ill, Longsjo said he still would have done no better than twenty-fifth place. The Russians were good. Longsjo noted in an interview that three U.S. skaters set new national records in four events, and still the team went home empty-handed.

Russian athletes held a dark fascination for the American public. When Longsjo returned home, a *Fitchburg Sentinel* reporter immediately asked him what the Russians were like. The story ran over the Associated Press wire. "The Russians are terrific, both from a personal and a competitive standpoint," said Longsjo. He said the Russian skaters were like anybody else and won by training hard. The Russian athletes were the least argumentative and the most subdued athletes, he continued, unlike athletes from other iron curtain countries like Poland and Czechoslovakia who "scrapped constantly."

The interview gave him a forum to speak out on two issues that put him years ahead of his time. "I think we will eventually have to resort to government sponsorship of our teams," he said. "Especially in a sport like speed skating, where there is such a demand on training to produce stamina and endurance. I feel that the amateur must be given a break. He must be given the time and opportunity to get himself in as good shape as his fellow contestants. Almost every European country does it, why can't we?"

He also attributed the poor showing of U.S. speed skaters in the

Olympics primarily to the different style of competition. He called for adopting the European style used in the Olympics.

More than twenty years would pass before anything like that happened. In the meantime, Longsjo began training for the Olympic cycling trials. They were to be held in mid-September in San Francisco to determine who made the team bound for the Summer Olympics in Melbourne, Australia. No one had ever competed in two separate U.S. Olympic teams in the same year.

10
NANCY NEIMAN BARANET, AMERICA'S PIONEER STAGE RACER IN EUROPE

In all this time, bicycle racing was principally a man's sport. Before the turn of the century when cycling was a craze, women had taken to cycling and this had influenced women's fashions, such as divided skirts, or short capes that were removed from the shoulders after a ride and fastened around the waist to cover the divided skirts. Around 1850, Amelia Bloomer of New York had introduced athletic apparel with a short skirt extending to the knees, below which were loose trousers fastened about the ankles. Bloomers, as they became known, were popular with women cyclists. Women who rode, however, were subject to sharp criticism from newspaper editorials and the pulpit.

Social pressures and lack of opportunity kept women from making an impression on the sport. But the 1950s turned into a landmark decade for women cyclists, as a woman led the way as the first U.S. rider, man or woman, to compete in a European stage race. She was Nancy Neiman Baranet of Detroit, and she first made her mark on the sport by getting ABL officials to recognize her as the national women's champion, not girls' champion.

"When I started, national championship divisions were men's open, juniors, which referred to boys fourteen to sixteen, and the girls' division," she recalls. "I said, 'Enough of this.' When I won the national girls' championship for the second time in 1954, I told the ABL officials that I was twenty-one and was no longer a girl. I said I wanted the name of the division switched to women's, and it was."

Baranet, a small brunette, was one of about a hundred women racing cyclists in the 1950s, compared with about a thousand men. Her mother didn't think racing was ladylike. "Her main objection was not the consequences of a spill," Baranet said, "but what the neighbors would think."

Recognition has come slowly for women athletes, including women bicycle racers. Women cyclists were not included in any national cycling championship until the ABL nationals in 1937. Doris Kopsky of Jersey City, New Jersey, daughter of 1912 Olympic bronze medalist Joe Kopsky, won the first ABL (women's) championship.

Women entered the sport either through their families, like Doris Kopsky, or, like Baranet, by joining local clubs. Baranet began cycling as a tourist in 1951 when she took an American Youth Hostel trip that toured Cape Cod and Martha's Vineyard. When she returned home to Detroit she joined a local club that offered the best coaching around, from an Italian named Gene Portuesi, whose strictness matched the name of the club, Spartan Cycling Club. Their training began as soon as the mercury rose above five degrees Fahrenheit, and they rode in small groups. Baranet worked out with the men. By April they were riding about 300 miles a week, and they began sprint training in May, when they had about 2,000 miles under their legs.

"The level of women's racing in this country in the 1950s was as good as we could get," Baranet points out. "The drive was there, but we had no facilities to take advantage of like there are today. We worked regular jobs from nine to five, and trained after work. I was a secretary. We lived for the sport, but we had to put food on the table. Nobody took care of that for us."

Baranet followed Jack Heid's example and went to Europe, where she achieved several firsts. In 1955 she went to Europe to race for the summer because she felt that was "the thing to do." She wrote to Eileen Gray of the British Cycling Federation, who set up racing engagements for her in England and France.

Baranet paid her own way from savings and couldn't expect any reimbursement. "Absolutely nobody even *breathed* the word money in those days," she says. "You didn't want to lose your amateur status."

Nancy Neiman Baranet in action on the Municipal Track in
Paris, 1955, the year before she returned to France to
become the first U.S. rider to compete in a stage race in
Europe. (*Nancy Baranet*)

She discovered how sensitive amateur status was when her plane first landed in London. The flight's 180 passengers remained seated as she was called to the front cabin to meet Eileen Gray, who had boarded the plane with special permission. Gray told Baranet that a Claude Butler Cycles representative was waiting in the airport to give Baranet a new frame which she could accept as long as she quickly covered up the name and never mentioned anything about it. After Gray briefed Baranet, the rest of the passengers were free to leave their seats.

The highlight of her three months of racing in Europe came in August when she tied the world record for 200 meters (220 yards) at the Paddington track in Leicester. Baranet went 14.4 seconds to equal the mark that Daisy Franks of England had set. Baranet also went to Paris and raced on the Parc des Princes Velodrome where other Americans like Walthour, Taylor, and Heid had competed.

In 1956 she returned to France to compete in the Criterium Cycliste Féminin Lyonnaise-Auvergne, billed as the women's Tour de France, an eight-day stage race in late July on narrow secondary roads in central France.

"I had some amusing problems with the French language," she recalls with a laugh. "I was trying to introduce myself as America's woman champion, but I said the French word *champignon,* which means mushroom, so it came out that I was introducing myself as a mushroom. My French got along very well with kids five and under."

Baranet was the sole U.S. entrant in a field of eighty-seven starters from England, France, Belgium, Switzerland, and Luxembourg. Her previous racing had been limited to weekend events of no more than ten miles each, but in France she had eight straight days of competing up to fifty miles a day.

"Did I ever suffer!" she moans. "I was a trackie. I had absolutely no experience in road racing and mountain climbing. At the base of the climbs, I started at the front of the pack and then lost places as we went. The longer the hill, the more I lost on the leaders. But once I got to the end of the stage, my track experience helped me sprint for a good place."

The race officials wouldn't let Baranet wear a silk jersey for the twenty-mile time trial stage. The reduced wind resistance of the silk jersey gave her an unfair advantage, the officials said. (What would they have thought about today's teardrop helmets and skintight Lycra body suits?) She had to borrow a wool jersey.

At the end of some stages her legs felt like rubber bands, and her hands were so tired from gripping the handlebars that she was unable to close them for hours. Yet as the race went on, she got stronger. In the seventh stage she finished second, losing the sprint in the final fifteen yards.

America's first stage racer in Europe ended up fourteenth out of forty finishers. She followed the race up with more events around France before heading to England for ten days—where her races were rained out every day. Baranet went back to the United States in time to win her third national championship, in Orlando.

In early 1956, the ABL reinstated Jack Heid and Ted Smith as amateurs. Heid resumed the Sunday morning rides with his northern New Jersey friends, who didn't mind that he had been away painting a barn. Smith, nervous about the new talent that was coming up, trained for three years to get competitive. The big change in American racing while they were gone was that European road bicycles with derailleurs had finally taken over from the track bikes and fixed gears. Derailleurs had been refined to enable riders to use ten speeds, a vast improvement over fixed gears on the hills.

While the two former professionals returned to the pack, former expatriates Jim Lauf and Don Sheldon had retired. Both had competed in the 1952 Olympics in Helsinki, Finland. Lauf was dismayed when ABL officials shifted him from the kilometer, the event he won in the trials, to the 4,000-meter (2.5 miles) team pursuit, which also included Sheldon. They didn't get past the first round. Sheldon doubled in the 112-mile road race where he finished twenty-second. After the Olympics, both retired, as Lauf put it, "to get on with life."

For Heid and Smith, reinstatement meant they could compete in all amateur events except the ABL national championships, but the de facto national championship was the fifty-mile Tour of Somerville on Memorial Day. After the war when races resumed, the Tour of Somerville took on added importance because the velodromes in Nutley and Coney Island were gone. Racers had nothing left but road events and the Tour of Somerville became the premier race. It was such a classic that the town's 10,000 population tripled on race day to watch the riders charge around the two-mile course that wound through closed downtown streets. The Tour of Somerville was begun in 1940 and had become to bicycle racing what the Boston Marathon is to running and the Indianapolis 500 is to car racing.

At the 1956 event, 130 riders from around the United States, Canada, and Mexico lined up for the start. Winners of the last six classics were there, plus six Olympians. Beyond the glory, they were competing for a prize list starting at $500 in merchandise plus a racing bicycle valued at $200 for the winner, descending to $100 in merchandise and a trophy to tenth place. To heat up the pace were premes plus $150 in merchandise for the rider who led the largest number of laps. Frank Kramer was in charge of handing out the prizes.

A new Ford Thunderbird with its lights on led as pace car. Shortly after the racers blasted away, Heid shot to the front of the pack. Over the fifty-mile course, racers negotiated 174 street corners. Thirty-two-year-old Heid had enough experience to know that he avoided many crashes around the turns by being in front. He was also able to chase down breakaway attempts by sprinting up to them with the entire pack in tow.

With a half-mile remaining, the lead pack was down to seventeen. They rounded the final turn and surged down the last stretch, where asphalt covered trolley rails which were bordered by bricks. Racers scattered from curb to curb, bent low over their bikes as they wound up the sprint.

Smith recounts drafting behind Heid's rear wheel somewhere in the middle of the pack with 300 yards left. Then Heid swiftly led him up the middle of the road, to the left of the tracks. Smith was getting knocked on the elbows by riders who challenged him for Heid's rear wheel. But he held his place as they sped past everybody until they were in the clear at the finish line. Smith tried unsuccessfully to move up on Heid. Three lengths back was Longsjo, in third.

"When we hit that line," Smith continues, "I shouted, 'I got second, buddy! You won. I got second!'"

After they coasted past the finish of their first race in five years, Heid put his hand on Smith's shoulders, leaned over, and kissed him on the cheek.

———————————

Photos show Longsjo sprinting with his elbows bent slightly, pulling at the handlebars like a weight lifter seizing a bar of weights. He was a rider that Heid and others paid close attention to. "Longsjo's form was good," Heid said. "He used a more European approach to bicycle racing. He attacked more frequently during the races. In the 1950s, most of the races had bunch finishes, and the sprints at the end were shorter than now. Longsjo was a long sprinter. He improved later on because he rode those long races in Canada."

That season, Longsjo won nearly every race he entered. In a 62-mile race in Valleyfield, Quebec, he crashed on a turn, got up, chased on his own to catch the field of 100 riders, and still won. Afterward, he had to be treated for cuts and bruises to his left leg.

He won another Massachusetts state championship, but passed up the ABL national championship to compete in the Canadian national road race instead. It ran 110 miles, from Montreal north over the Laurentian Mountains to St. Agathe and back. The Laurentian Mountains are famous for winter skiing and include a particularly steep and long ascent appropriately called Mount Savage.

Guy Morin of Montreal was a top rider who competed on the Canadian national team in the British Commonwealth Games in Perth, Australia, in 1954 and the Pan American Games in Vancouver the next year. The way he tells the story, Longsjo wasn't intimidated by Mount Savage. "Art got out of his saddle and began sprinting as though the finish was only two hundred meters away. We had more than eighty miles left. And he's sprinting madly down the road. I began yelling, 'You crazy American! It's too early!' He didn't listen. All the rest of us decided, What the hell, let him go. He'll run out of steam. His lead got bigger and then we lost sight of him.

"Up at the top of Mount Savage was my trainer, Fioro Baggio. He was a retired Italian professional who raced sixty-eight six-days in Europe. He moved to Montreal and has a bicycle store. Baggio watched Art climb up Mount Savage all alone. Then, that crazy American, you know what he does? He takes his feet off his pedals, lets his legs hang, and coasts. Then he gets off his bike, walks over to Baggio. 'Excuse me,' he says to Baggio. Not hurried. Like he's sightseeing. 'I'm looking for Mount Savage. Can you tell me where it is?' Baggio just looked at him for a moment. Nobody in the race was in sight. Baggio smiled. He said, 'I think you just passed it.' "

Longsjo won the race.

Morin continued: "I tried to figure out Art's riding, to beat him. I forced him into a long sprint, but that was a mistake. He beat me easily. I stalled him to a short sprint near the finish of a race with thirty others. But he nipped me a few yards from the finish and won. Finally, I thought I had him when we went into the final turn of a race. I'm much shorter than Art. I used my lower center of gravity to take the turn tight and get the inside, open a gap. Ah, I thought, I've got him now. I got twenty lengths on him. Then with fifty meters left, he went by me. I yelled at him, 'You crazy American!' "

Baggio was the Canadian distributor for Torpado Bicycles of Italy and sponsored a team, Baggio-Torpado. Morin couldn't beat Longsjo, so he got him on the team. Each member got two road-racing frames and two track frames every year, a big deal in those days.

On Labor Day, Longsjo entered the fifty-mile race in Hartford's Colt Park, a major Northeast race, with a string of fifteen consecutive victories. In the last half-mile, he was in a group of six that included Smith. As the riders flashed down the descent of a short hill that led to the finish, Smith broke his steel toe clip.

"I overreacted and pulled the toe strap so tight it broke, too," Smith recalls. "All I had left was the cleat on the bottom of my shoe. We were flying down that hill, I want you to know. I had to concentrate on riding as smoothly as I could and manage to beat Longsjo. I did. I just beat him out in the sprint. When we coasted past the finish, he congratulated me and said, 'I'd like to see what you could do with both legs.' "

The Olympic cycling trials consisted of two road races of 116 miles each, on a 6-mile course around Lake Merced, three days apart. On the first day, ABL officials selected the top three finishers for the Olympic road team. Then the first two riders from the second. In the intervening days sprint events were held in San Jose on a velodrome built in 1950.

Longsjo's bid to make his second Olympic team appeared to end with a loud bang when his rear tire burst a short distance from the starting line of the first early-morning race. His rear derailleur was also acting up, so he pulled out and returned to the starting line in time to go to breakfast with the race officials.

Three days later, for the second road race, Longsjo had his derailleur working and new tires on his rims. He and Ring succeeded in going with the breakaway of twenty from the pack of a hundred. The leaders were fighting for the last two spots on the Olympic team. They were so aggressive that the pace was ten minutes faster than the first road race.

At the end of 4 hours 51 minutes of racing, twenty riders fought for two places. Dave Rhoads of San Jose, a veteran of the 1952 Olympic cycling team and national ABL champion, streaked to the lead with 220 yards left. Longsjo finished half a bike length down on Rhoads to secure a second Olympic team berth.

The U.S. Olympic Cycling Committee officials, however, assigned him to ride the 4,000-meter (2.5-mile) team pursuit race on the velodrome. The Olympic cycling team was considerably smaller than current teams. Selection of the four-rider pursuit team was up to officials, who picked two road and two track cyclists on the basis of speed and power. (The practice was soon abandoned when the Olympic cycling trials were expanded to hold designated races to determine the selection of the pursuit team.) Longsjo was disappointed at the assignment, as the road race was the event for which he had qualified.

After Longsjo was told to ride the team pursuit, he commuted to Montreal where he stayed at the home of his friend Guy Morin, and trained on a new velodrome that had opened there.

The XVI Olympiad, held in Melbourne from November 22 to December 8, was noted for its pageantry. The Australians were so enthusiastic over the Games that they lined both sides of the road to watch Olympic athletes ride buses five miles from the Olympic Village to the competition sites. Spectators paid an admission fee of twenty-five cents to watch the athletes work out, and besieged the athletes with requests for autographs.

The Melbourne Games were also the first time the Russian athletes stayed in the Olympic Village, which generated even more international excitement. But the Olympics were not the media events they are today. Television was just coming into homes, and the number of programs was limited. The amount of coverage in newspapers and on radio and television was substantially less than what we are accustomed to today. One improvement over the past, however, was that U.S. amateur rules had eased slightly to permit the Schwinn Bicycle Company to supply bicycles to our Olympic cyclists.

In the Olympic cycling team pursuit, riders work a close-order drill that begins with the lead rider pedaling about 220 yards with the other three tucked behind in a tight file. The leader swings out slightly to let the other three pass through as the leader catches the end and the new leader pulls another 220 yards. Only the first three are timed in the race for the fastest time. Longsjo rode with Dave Rhoads and sprinters Alan Bell of Somerville, New Jersey, and Dick Cortright of Buffalo. Unlike the European squads, Longsjo's pursuit team spent little time together because after the trials they were on their own until they arrived in Melbourne for the Olympics. Predictably, they didn't get past the preliminary heats.

The year 1956 is remembered for two achievements in sports. Rocky Marciano became the only world boxing heavyweight champion to retire without losing a professional fight (his 49-0 record remains undisturbed today). Don Larsen of the New York Yankees pitched the only perfect game—no opposing batter reached base—in a World Series, Game 5 against the Brooklyn Dodgers, a record that still stands.

But Longsjo's feat—making two separate Olympic teams in the same year—went generally overlooked. He finished out of the medals in both Olympics, as did his teammates. But he was remarkable for being among the best in each of two sports that lacked the support they have today.

Twenty-eight years later, many in the media forgot Longsjo's accomplishment when another athlete—Dave Gilman—made the 1984 U.S. Olympic team in the winter luge event and the summer kayak event. Gilman was credited with being the first such athlete.

Longsjo's only recognition came from promoters of a new six-day circuit. Shortly after he returned home from Australia, Belgian promoters offered him a contract paying $500 a day for six of their six-days scheduled in America. He readily acknowledged to reporters that he could use the $3,000 a race. But he said he wanted to remain an amateur to make the 1960 Olympics, and he thought the six-day races were a gamble.

Instead, he took a job teaching skating for the Fitchburg Parks Department. Because his job could be seen as a violation of amateur rules, he worked for free. In a Sunday skating session, he slipped and slammed full speed into the wooden border of a rink. He broke a leg and was sidelined for months.

Jack Heid heard—and heeded—the siren song of the six-days. The

After that, the other races on the schedule were scuttled. Heid finished the Chicago event with his legs, neck, wrists, and back aching, and all for nothing. He got in his car and drove back home to retirement.

In August 1957, Nancy Baranet sprinted to her fourth national ABL championship, in Kenosha, Wisconsin. She posed for photos with the men's national champion, Jack Disney of Pasadena, California, whose national title was his fourth as well. Both were familiar faces in their national championship jerseys, but the rider next to them was not only a new face but also the first black rider to win the national amateur championship, and the first black national champion since Major Taylor. He was sixteen-year-old Perry Metzler of Brooklyn.

Metzler and his twin brother, Jerry, got into cycling with several other black youths in 1953 as members of the Crusaders Club of Brooklyn. They couldn't afford fancy equipment; they rode used bicycles and did their own repairs. They wore blue-and-white jerseys with a cross on the front.

The Crusaders rode in local races. In May 1954, Jerry was the first of the Crusaders to win a race, capturing the junior division in a twenty-five-mile time trial in Westbury, Long Island; Perry was second.

The twins took to racing. Amos Ottley of St. Albans, another black rider then in his early thirties, informally coached them and served as a father figure as the twins' parents had broken up after the family moved from Mississippi to Brooklyn.

In mid-1954, the Crusaders disbanded when the club treasurer split with the modest treasury. Many of the area's cycling clubs, including the Century Road Club Association, one of the oldest and biggest in the country, had bylaws that barred blacks. That left the Metzler twins and others few alternatives when the club broke up. Many of the other kids quit cycling.

The Metzlers, however, kept riding with Ottley. In the 1955 ABL state championship, Perry finished third to qualify for the ABL national championship on the half-mile oval not far away in Flushing Meadows. The nationals that year were a matter of local pride because of nostalgia associated with the sport's heyday. ABL officials got Jimmy Walthour, Jr., to act as official starter for some of the races, which drew more than 200 riders from around the country.

For the event, Flushing Meadows took on the atmosphere of the gayest years of six-day history in the Garden. Each state represented had its flags flying in the area set aside for its contestants and their equipment. The Department of Parks set up long lines of bleachers which were filled at the start and finish lines. Attendance was estimated at 10,000 daily over the late-August weekend.

Metzler rode his bike from home—a high-rise public housing project in Bedford-Stuyvesant—to the races in Flushing Meadows for the nationals. He finished out of the points in the first day's races, but on the second day snatched fifth in the five-mile to earn a point, which placed him ninth overall. At the age of fourteen, he showed he had what it took, and by age sixteen he had become national champion.

The twins grew to a well-proportioned 5 feet 9 inches. Their bodies matured early, with long thin faces and deep chests. The Metzler twins raced often and began collecting a mass of trophies.

In 1956, the twins went one-two in the state ABL championship, with Jerry winning, so that they both qualified for the nationals, in Orlando. They both sought to win a national ABL medal, but instead came up against a bigger obstacle than the poverty they lived with, and the sport was never again the same for Jerry.

Florida was still racially segregated. Two years earlier, the Supreme Court had ruled unanimously in *Brown* v. *Board of Education of Topeka* that racial segregation in the classroom was against the Constitution, but segregation remained the order of the day in Florida—in the schoolrooms, hotels, and restaurants. Throughout the South, newspapers had separate obituary sections according to race. It was not unusual for police in the South to arrest blacks just for being out on the street after sundown.

"I told them not to make the trip down there," Ottley remembers. "I had places in Brooklyn that I couldn't get into. Things were different then."

Segregation was not something new to the twins. They had lived in Mississippi for nearly ten years before their family moved to New York. They went to Orlando anyway, taking a bus. They were thrown out of the city and had to turn right around and go back home. Jerry, always outgoing and quick-tempered, became disgusted and quit riding.

Although Perry Metzler was kept out of the national championship, he gave another indication of his talent in 1956 when he won the junior Best All Round trophy, based on points awarded to top finishers in five designated ten-mile races in Northeast and Middle Atlantic cities.

The black rider Metzler looked up to was Ken Farnum, a sprinter who migrated to Manhattan after competing for his native Barbados in the 1952 Olympics. He stood a little over six feet and weighed a trim 180. A smart tactician who had been in the sport since he was ten, Farnum also had power to pedal big gears and wind them up fast. He was a minor legend in the West Indies for winning their sprint title eight times. In 1955 he had established himself as a force to reckon with in New York by winning the state ABL championship.

He usually trained alone, but sometimes he worked out with Metzler, Ottley, and two other black teenage talents—Jeff Wood of St. Albans and Herb Francis of Harlem. At the 1957 New York ABL championship, Ottley's friends were the talk of the sprints. Farnum again won the men's open, against competition that included Arnold Uhrlass, the champion speed skater.

Wood and Metzler finished one-two in the junior boys' race. Wood, who was Metzler's age and size, specialized in the fast-paced yet tactical half-mile. At sixteen, Wood looked like a likely prospect to win the national ABL championship. He was second in the Tour of Somerville juniors' ten-mile race to Metzler's fourth. The two racers often battled each other for first, and their sprint for the finish quickly left the others to fight for third.

The ABL awarded expenses for the national championship only to the state champion, which left Metzler on his own. He had struggled to buy tires; he certainly couldn't afford to travel nearly halfway across the country.

Al Toefield, a New York City police sergeant, was an ABL district representative. He saw Metzler in a parking lot a few days before the 1957 national championship. "I asked him why he wasn't in Kenosha," Toefield says. "He said he didn't have any way to get there. So I said he could ride with me in my car."

At the national championship in Kenosha, on the shore of Lake Michigan in southeast Wisconsin, the pre-start favorites in the junior boys' race were Wood and Ed Reusing, the blond Missouri champion. Reusing had won the junior race at Somerville on Memorial Day, and was third in the 1956 national championship. Seven thousand spectators filled the bleachers of Kenosha's Washington Park asphalt velodrome to watch.

Juniors competed for points in the half-, one-, two-, and five-mile races. The first race was Wood's specialty, the half-mile. Fifty of the country's fastest fourteen- to sixteen-year-olds set a brisk tempo around the tight, steeply banked turns and down the straights.

"Metzler was the kind of guy who could rise to any occasion," Toefield contends. "He could find a hole and ride through it. He had no fear."

Metzler rode with his back straight and flat, close to the frame and parallel to the ground. In a sprint, his chin dropped low over the handlebars, his neck arched back, and his face turned up like a headlight focused on the finish. He was so admired for his uncanny ability to stay upright when others crashed that he was called the Magician.

Metzler stole the spotlight with a magnificent ride in the half-mile event, which he won from Larry Hartman of Washington State with Reusing coming in third. In the five-mile, Reusing watched the field carefully and won the race from Metzler and Wood, who finished second

Perry Metzler of Brooklyn, first black to win the national amateur cycling championship, in 1957 for junior boys, ages 14–16, takes a seat with men's national champion Jack Disney and women's national champion Nancy Neiman Baranet. (*Nancy Neiman Baranet*)

and third, respectively. This made the standings twelve points for Metzler and ten for Reusing. On Sunday, Reusing refused to ride in the rain, which practically assured Metzler the championship.

Rain forced officials to move races to the street. Metzler was shut out of points in the mile, in which Wood was second. But Metzler came back in the final event, the two-mile, for fifth place and one more point for a total of thirteen to Reusing's ten. Wood's eight got him fourth in the nationals. In the men's open, Farnum finished tenth.

Metzler's victory marked the first time that a black rider had won a national title medal. He was awarded the national champion's red, white, and blue cycling jersey, a hefty trophy to add to his burgeoning collection, and an even larger and grander one, the Grenda-Heit Memorial Junior Trophy, for display by his school. "It took up half the back seat on the drive back home," Toefield says. "The memorial trophy was for Perry's high school, Boys' High in Brooklyn, a major force in area sports, to display for a year in the school's showcase."

The national champion's jersey was as good as a jacket and tie for Metzler, who posed with friends after he returned to Brooklyn from the nationals in Kenosha, Wisconsin. Seated from the left are Sam Herzberg, Lou Maltese, and Al Toefield. Standing from the left are Ken Farnum, Jeff Wood, Metzler, and Harold Ott. (*Amos Ottley*)

Patricia Assam, who married Metzler in 1960, said that Metzler wore his national champion's jersey around the streets of Bedford-Stuyvesant for others to see. "Perry was so proud of wearing that national champion's jersey," she remembers. "When he got home he wore it to stand around on the corner with. The word went around the neighborhood what Perry did in winning the nationals. I went by and saw him. He was standing there, practically glowing, he was so proud."

As Metzler's riding career was getting started, Nancy Baranet decided to retire after winning her fourth national championship. In recognition of her accomplishments, the Detroit City Council passed a testimonial resolution that named her Sports Woman of the Year. She married her weight-training coach, and served as the only woman ABL officer and as a board member for twenty-seven years, from 1956 to 1983. In that time, American women cyclists were the first to achieve international recognition.

11
PEDALI ALPINI

Art Longsjo recovered from his broken leg to make 1958 one of American cycling's most phenomenal seasons—he won every race he started during an active season in the United States and Canada.

"He was really starting to enjoy life," Goguen said. "He was married and things were falling into place. When I was in Fitchburg visiting relatives, he would call me up and ask me to come over to fix his wheels. Said they were all banged up. When I went to his home I could see that just some spokes were loose. Two or three. He just wanted to see me. And he would give me a saddle or some other piece of equipment he had won in a race. He would say, 'Here, take this. I've got too many of them.' "

On Memorial Day in Somerville, a breakaway of four looked like they had the race won. "They had about a half-mile on us when Longsjo started to chase," Ted Smith recalls. "I went with him. After we got out alone, he swung out for me to come through so he could draft behind me. But he was much bigger than me and gave me a great wind break. I didn't want to give that up, so I swung out with him. 'No, thanks,' I told him. 'I don't work on holidays.' "

Longsjo towed Smith up to the breakaway. "Then when we wound up for the sprint, it was his race. Ah, Longsjo was a true champion. I couldn't beat him if I had four legs that day." Smith finished second, tucked behind Longsjo's rear wheel.

As Longsjo continued to win race after race, he tugged at many hearts and imaginations. He drew many spectators to the races and inspired much interest for being what sportswriters called "a two-sport Olympian." At twenty-six, he was in his prime and the greatest American cycling talent since Frank Kramer.

In July Longsjo won his sixth straight Massachusetts state championship. Rather than race the ABL nationals in late August, he took on the biggest challenge of his career—the Tour du St. Laurent stage race, a grueling four-day event in eastern Canada, styled after the Tour de France. The race had stages of at least 100 miles in the morning and another 25 to 40 in the evening. It drew the best on the continent for the ultimate test of speed and endurance. Those who competed had a reputation for being hardy. One fell off a cliff, climbed back to the road, and still finished.

Art Longsjo bursts across the finish to capture the 1958 Tour of Somerville, with Ted Smith snugly on his rear wheel for second. (*Terry Longsjo)*

Longsjo rode for the Baggio-Torpado team which Guy Morin captained. The defending champion, Rene Grossi of Montreal, was their teammate. The six-member team was working for Grossi to win again: Grossi's teammates would chase after breakaway riders and pull the rest of the field up to the break. They would also ride to protect Grossi from the wind, leaving him rested for the final sprint. The group had to win the team prize, which was a thousand dollars, a lot of money then, to cover expenses such as their hotel rooms, meals, and gas for the support car.

Morin prides himself on getting Grossi to first place by the second day, with the team also in first. The next day, Morin and Grossi initiated a breakaway with two others in a 110-mile stage. Fioro Baggio drove up in the team car and told Morin they were 7 minutes ahead of the pack.

"At first, I thought that was real success," Morin recounts. "Then I realized Art was in the pack, and that could cost us the team prize because it was three who scored. So I immediately pulled out of the breakaway, turned around, and tore back down the road. I was real mad that Art had allowed himself to fall so far behind. I turned around when the pack came up and really gave Art a scolding. 'You crazy American,' I told him. 'The race is going on and here you are sleeping in the pack.' "

They sprinted away together. But after a few miles, Morin was too tired to work in a relay with Longsjo and just drafted behind. "I began to regret that I spoke so harshly to him," Morin said. "Then he wouldn't be pedaling so hard. And I didn't dare fall behind after what I said. By the end, we closed to within two minutes of the breakaway. That kept our team in first."

The final stage was a 30-mile time trial. Grossi had a lead of 2 minutes 24 seconds over Longsjo in second. Morin told Grossi to "go out there and really open up." Grossi had such a big lead that it seemed impossible that anyone would get near him.

Grossi tried. But his legs were tired after more than 500 miles in four days. He lost 2 minutes 35 seconds to Longsjo, who won the race by 11 seconds. Longsjo led the team to victory and became the first U.S. rider to win the Tour du St. Laurent.

His record for the Quebec-to-Montreal race still stood when he was invited back for the twenty-fifth edition of the race on Sunday, September 15. He decided to return for another attempt at winning it.

Race day was hot. After ninety miles, the course left the town of Three Rivers and yawned in a straight, flat expanse for thirty miles. Riders disliked it because they were totally exposed to the wind and glaring sun, and the road stretched to infinity. That was where Longsjo attacked. Six others saw it was a strategic point—where many riders lost their concentration in the monotony of the stretch—and went with him. After that portion of the race, the roads wound through villages and curved to make the riding more scenic and lively. The breakaway gained a 6-minute lead by the time they got into Montreal.

When Longsjo saw Goguen standing near the finish, he sprinted. The others watched him closely and responded with him. They were out of their saddles, spread across the road, giving it all they had. Longsjo won by 3 seconds over Roland Williot of Montreal.

Only nineteen of the nearly one hundred starters finished. Longsjo garnered more headlines and press interest. He was invited for an interview on a local television station, so he decided to spend the night at Morin's home. Goguen drove back to Pittsfield after the race.

Longsjo had been driven to the race by a friend—a twenty-year-old former Fitchburg High School track and football star. "I didn't notice much about the fellow who drove Art," Morin said. "He was kind of shy around the riders and stayed out of the way. The next morning, we discussed the possibility of Art going to Europe to ride for a professional team. Baggio said he could fix it up and Art said he was interested. Art and I shook hands good-bye about ten o'clock. He got in the car and left. I was the last one to speak with him."

Longsjo was asleep in the passenger seat with his head resting against the passenger window when they traveled south through Vermont. The winding road they took as a shortcut was wet after a rain. At about 11:15, a bee in the car distracted the driver. He made a swipe at the bee as the car approached a curve near North Hero and lost control of the vehicle. The car veered into a utility pole and crashed with such force that the pole was imbedded in the passenger's side of the demolished car. Rescue workers had to cut Longsjo out of the vehicle to get to him. He was unconscious and suffered a fractured skull and internal injuries. The driver's back was broken. Longsjo died that evening.

———————————

Longsjo's death stunned the cycling and skating communities. More than 1,000 people attended his funeral, many comprising a Who's Who of the two sports in the United States and Canada. Three Olympic speed skaters and three Olympic cyclists served as pallbearers.

A movement was organized to create a memorial, and suggestions ranged from renaming Mirror Lake the Arthur Longsjo Mirror Lake, in honor of his start in athletics, to naming a city park after him. Morin visited Fitchburg mayor George Bourke to recommend that a bicycle race be started to commemorate him. Morin helped organize the race, and he spread the word through the cycling community to get top riders from both countries there. Another committee was organized to create a marble memorial to Longsjo and his accomplishments.

On Memorial Day America's best cycling talents line up for the start of the Tour of Somerville. In 1960, southern Californian Mike Hiltner ignited the season and ushered in a new era of American cycling when he roared across the finish to a new national fifty-mile record.

Another rider who influenced cycling in the next decade also established his reputation at Somerville the previous year. In the ten-mile junior boys' race, sixteen-year-old Jack Simes III thought his race was blown when a tire burst. He got off his bike and looked up to spot a teenager standing on the side of the curb with a balloon-tired bicycle. It had a seat jacked up two feet and stylish, long-horned handlebars. Simes dropped his racing bike to the street, grabbed the other kid's bike, and gave chase, although the metal cleats of his cycling shoes caused his feet to slip off the rubber pedals.

Thousands of spectators watched the pack of juniors whiz past, followed by Simes pedaling furiously on a bicycle with handlebars that put his hands up high, like he was a gopher standing back on his haunches. On the next lap, his father stood on the edge of the street with a spare racing bicycle. Simes traded bikes again, regained the pack, and won.

Simes and Hiltner, nearly the same age but vastly different in personality, faced the same difficulties as aspiring American cyclists. They both set national records in winning the Tour of Somerville and won national championships in the 1960s—Simes on the track, Hiltner on the road—and made determined efforts competing in Europe.

Simes was a third-generation rider who grew up in northern New Jersey with an inherent sense of the sport's heritage. He heard stories from his father and grandfather, both of whom had raced professionally in this country, and he learned about foreign racing experiences from Jack Heid. As a youngster, Simes learned from his father the basics of how to ride and draft, and how to time coming off an opponent's wheel to dash for the finish. "I grew up thinking that sprinting was the class act of cycling," he says.

His father introduced him to Frank Kramer in 1958, a few months before Kramer died of a heart ailment that October, at the age of seventy-seven. "Kramer came to a bike race at Weequahic Park, near Newark," Simes recalls. "He was a white-haired man in a dark suit, very quiet and standing all alone. My father was the only one who recognized him. Cycling was such an underground sport then. We walked over to him and he said hello. My father told me he was the greatest bike rider of all time. That meant something. It sunk in. I hoped what he had would rub off on me."

Hiltner was a West Coast phenomenon. When he grew up in a Los Angeles suburb, teenagers drank beer, hung around the beach, surfed, or worked on cars for show or drag racing. In the popular American mind—and especially in southern California—bicycles were for children. Bicycle manufacturers aimed their advertising at the postwar baby boomers. Bicycles had balloon tires for a cushy ride, upright handlebars, chrome fenders and trim, and often had a headlight and a horn that worked until the batteries died and corroded. Bicycle racing was distinctly European, like soccer. A neighbor introduced Hiltner to cycling. He entered his first race, a twenty-miler against eleven others, in Santa Barbara on July 4, 1957. He finished last, but enjoyed the race so much he decided he wanted to take part in all Olympics until he was at least forty.

Most of California's bicycle racing was in the northern part of the state. A typical race today with events for various divisions will draw at least 400 riders. Bill Best of San Francisco, one of the top riders, estimates that in the late 1950s the entire state only had about 200 racers registered with the ABL.

"Races were mostly informal affairs on the West Coast then," Best says. "A big event might draw as many as fifty riders. A standard practice was for twenty to thirty riders to get together in a town where we would select a long flat stretch with good pavement and hold five to ten sprints up the street to a finish we agreed on, like the end of a block. We lined up across the road and took off together. We bumped elbows, shoved one another out of the way, and learned how to stay up while we went hell for leather.

"The winner got a pat on the back, or sometimes a trophy. A pair of tires was considered a valuable prize. A race was considered big time if the organizers managed to give the winner a black-and-white television set."

Simes grew up under the influence of his father, who stressed pedaling briskly and smoothly. Hiltner was self-coached and followed his intuition. He sat low in the saddle and favored big gears that moved his legs more slowly than Simes would pedal at the same speed.

In 1959 Hiltner won the Tour du St. Laurent at age eighteen. Suddenly, everybody was talking about a short, quiet Californian in a burr haircut who became the youngest to win the race. If somebody excitedly asked him what he did to get so good, he was known to blush in modesty and mumble a self-deprecating reply.

The next year he moved to northern California to train with a group of San Francisco Bay Area riders who lived for the sport. Several of them had raced in Europe—some while in the army, like Bill Best, who was stationed in Germany, or Dave Staub, 1956 national ABL junior champion, who went to Europe to race for fourteen months with Steve Pfeifer in England, Germany, Belgium, and Italy. Rick Bronson and George Koenig spent enough time in Italy in 1956 to fall under its spell. They returned to San Francisco speaking flowery Italian and whimsically putting *i*'s and *o*'s at the ends of English words. They formed a new cycling club—Pedali Alpini—whose members included most of northern California's best, including Hiltner.

All it took to get along with Pedali Alpini was to race bicycles. Italy was their Mecca. Italian cycling greats such as Ercole Baldini, Alfredo Binda, and Gino Bartali were their heroes. The greatest was Fausto Coppi, the raven-haired, hawk-nosed climber who won all the major races in Europe. When they were in Italy, Staub and Pfeifer shook the hand of *Il Championissimo* (Champion of Champions). Coppi was such an inspiration to the Pedali Alpini that his name was painted in large letters on a boulder near the peak of a long and arduous climb in the Bay Area. When a rider felt his muscles burning and he had endured all he could take, he would look up to read "COPPI" and renew his efforts to charge to the top.

Hiltner was drawn to Lars Zebroski, a small-framed man of Hiltner's age, with a narrow face tapering to a small chin. They rented a small shack on the southern part of the San Francisco peninsula, on Tunitas Creek Road, an old road with switchbacks that hugged the curves of the mountainous coast laden with redwood, pines, and oak trees. In this idyllic setting, they trained with Peter Rich of Berkeley and others. They went hard up the hills and, to sharpen their speed, every time they came to a city or town boundary sign, like Half Moon Bay or La Honda, they got out of the saddle to sprint as though they were going for a valuable premium. They wanted their races to be a cakewalk by comparison.

Pedali Alpini riders were so enthusiastic about cycling that they drove 16,000 miles in one six-week stretch in 1959, going from race to race from California to Chicago to eastern Canada. When Memorial Day approached, they piled in cars to drive cross-country to New Jersey where Hiltner won the 1960 Tour of Somerville.

It was only appropriate for Pedali Alpini riders that the 1960 Summer Olympics were going to be held in Rome. At the road racing Olympic trials in July in New York City's Central Park, Hiltner and Zebroski made the team on the first day, with the club's founding member, George Koenig, racing to a spot the following day. They were not just going to the Olympics in the Eternal City. They were going to the homeland of Fausto Coppi and cycling. They saved what little money they earned from jobs that fit into their training and racing schedules and planned to stay in Italy and race with the masters.

Jack Simes III was seventeen when he went to the Olympic cycling trials in New York. The track events were held on the half-mile oval in Flushing Meadows, and there he rode one of the most unusual match-race finals in American Olympic cycling trials. He progressed through the qualifying heats until at last he rode in the deciding match for a berth on the team against Ed Lynch, of Compton, California, who had ridden in the London Olympics with Jack Heid.

Lynch was part of a group of West Coast riders who experimented with unusual equipment. He attracted attention with the enormous gear he rode. It was 30 percent bigger than normal, giving him 129 inches of forward motion with each pedal revolution; his front chain ring looked like a steel wheel. Lynch also pedaled with crank arms that were half-again longer than usual to give him greater leverage. He was easily spotted at the track because even on hot summer days he wore dark tights to protect his skin, which had been badly burned years earlier in a kerosene fire.

His experimentation didn't end with equipment. Lynch set up a pup tent in the track infield where he kept a tank of oxygen. A lungful of oxygen before each of his match races seemed to give him a temporary physical boost that helped raise his confidence. (This practice speeds recovery after an effort but has more mental than physical value before a race.)

When the Olympic veteran and the high school student rode their match, Lynch didn't mind when Simes perched on his rear wheel around the last turn for the finish. Simes had developed what he called a snap—the explosion of speed for the finish. In both match races, Simes edged Lynch by six inches to ride his way to the Olympic cycling team at age seventeen. The high school student, whose grandfather took his father to Newark to see Frank Kramer's final ride in 1922, became the family's first Olympian.

In a departure from the usual custom of limiting each country to one match-race sprinter in the Olympics, countries at the 1960 Rome Olympics were permitted to send two, a practice not repeated until the 1984 Los Angeles Olympics. Simes's match-race partner was Herb Francis of Harlem, the country's first black Olympic cyclist.

The twenty-year-old Francis was big and muscular, but amazingly catlike and quick. He would rise slightly from his saddle and rely on his powerful quadriceps to accelerate sharply. Francis was considered one of the fastest one-sprint cyclists on the racing circuit.

Perry Metzler had been a likely prospect to make the team. After high school, he went to work in the garment district of New York and trained after work. His old rival Jeff Wood dropped out of the sport, but Metzler made the transition from junior racing to the open division at seventeen and started winning big regional races in the Northeast and Middle Atlantic states.

Herb Francis of Harlem made the 1960 Olympic cycling team
to become the country's first black Olympic cyclist. On his
left is fellow Olympic team sprinter Jack Simes III. (Jack
Simes III photo)

The Century Road Club Association, New York's biggest cycling
club, wanted Metzler to join, but somebody pointed out that bylaws
specifically prohibited blacks. They got around this by having Metzler
write on the application form that he was Mexican. From then on, he
rode for the CRCA.

Metzler's riding was part of the mystique that grew around him.
Another part was that he commuted to races in a shiny red and green
Ferrari. The long and low Italian racing car was at the other end of the
spectrum from the boatlike, chrome-laden Fords and Chevrolets that
everybody else drove at the time. The Ferrari belonged to Bill Wilson,
an older black man with salt-and-pepper hair who smoked a meer-

schaum pipe and generally stayed in the background during races. Wilson worked at the Warwick Boys Training School and became a "big brother" to Metzler, who was never close to his father after the family broke up.

In January 1960, Metzler was drafted into the army. After basic training he was stationed at Fort Jackson, South Carolina. Al Toefield, then a member of the U.S. Olympic Cycling Committee, tried repeatedly to get Metzler assigned to the army's Special Services so he could train for the Olympic trials the way Don Sheldon and Jim Lauf had. Although the armed forces had been integrated in 1952, blacks were not openly received. Toefield later discovered that a colonel from one of the southern states kept blocking Perry's transfer to Special Services.

The 1960 Summer Olympic Games were called the Grand Olympics because of Rome's classical background. They were the Olympics in which Abebe Bakila of Ethiopia ran barefoot through the streets to win the marathon, Mohammed Ali—then known as Cassius Clay—won the light heavyweight boxing gold medal, and Italian cyclists won five of six Olympic gold medals.

Hiltner raced with three others in the 100-kilometer (62.5-mile) team time trial to eleventh of thirty teams—the best U.S. cycling performance of the Games. He also doubled in the 109-mile road race that lasted 4 hours 20 minutes through a Roman heat wave. At 85 miles, a Russian and Italian broke away, causing the pack of 140 to split apart in its pursuit. Hiltner was the only American to go with the lead group of 31 riders. He wound up engulfed in that pack, which finished in a tight bunch in a fight for the bronze medal. Hiltner was awarded twenty-third place; his next teammate, Zebroski, was fifty-third, 8 minutes behind. In the match races on the velodrome, Simes and Francis were eliminated early.

When the Olympics concluded, the Pedali Alpini members stayed behind just as Jack Heid and Al Stiller had before them. Peter Rich, a cherub-faced rider called Cannonball for the swift way he descended hills, accompanied the club members to the Olympics and stayed, too.

"Our object was to get to Italy and live in cheap digs, eat as inexpensively as we could, and do what we had to get by," Rich explains. "Dave Staub and Steve Pfeifer had met the Cinelli family earlier, and they knew we were coming. So the first thing we did was head north to Milan and get outfitted with new Cinelli bicycles. The Cinelli family welcomed us like we were old friends and invited us to dinner. They gave us a feast, with silver on the table and maid service. We hardly knew where our next meal was coming from, or how long we would be able to last overseas. But at last we were in Italy, and we had new Cinellis. That counted for something."

Afterward, the Pedali Alpini shifted their base to Florence where they had a big selection of races. Hiltner won a hefty gold medal and made headlines in the local newspaper for being the first non-Italian finisher in an international race of more than 100 miles. He came in twentieth of a field of some 200.

They spent the winter in Florence where they bundled up and trained as best they could. Rich left in early 1961 to explore conditions in Belgium, Holland, and Denmark for what turned into a fourteen-month sojourn.

Hiltner drew considerable attention when he won the first race of the season, a fifty-mile event in Florence. He was so excited at being in the race that he let himself go after twenty-five miles and sprinted from the pack of 150. Three others went with him and they established a breakaway. When Hiltner saw the finish 275 yards away, he put his head down and went for it. They were fanned out shoulder to shoulder at the finish line. It was so close, the judges deliberated for a half-hour. But they gave it to Hiltner.

As the weeks went on, the Americans found the racing was far harder than they were accustomed to. "The Italians were so fast, and there was far more depth in the quality of the fields," Hiltner said. "Those guys were machines."

In April, he was in an eight-man breakaway in a 120-mile road race. Near the finish, the others began watching one another closely to see who would make the first move. He jumped ahead and won clean.

Hiltner was being written up in local newspapers, but success eluded his partner Zebroski. He suffered several crashes, and left after the middle of the season.

Hiltner joined a local club, Groupe Sportif Lastrense-Gizac, which provided him with a new bicycle, all the tires he needed, and transportation to events. In July and August he won two more races. He won small amounts of prize money, distributed to fifteenth place, and the club paid small bonuses when he won or placed well.

But Hiltner also discovered that the ride to the top is fraught with diversions, and he encountered one he had never been exposed to before: drugs. Drug use among international cyclists was widespread but unchecked. During the Rome Olympics, a Danish cyclist collapsed in the 100-kilometer (62.5-mile) team time trial and died. The twenty-three-year-old cyclist's death was attributed to an overdose of a stimulant. But his death did not deter drug use among riders, including Hiltner.

"Mostly we were burning uppers—amphetamines," he said. "We would get wired for the end of a race. What we called *La Bomba,* the bomb bottle, we usually carried in the hip pocket of our shorts. Basically, it was strong coffee, espresso, and guys would doctor it with amphetamines. Guys would start sipping on this after the halfway point in the race, and if you were doing well, then you would take a whole bunch of it.

"A couple of times I got injections from my coach before the start of the race. The coach would say, 'This is new stuff from Switzerland,' and give me an injection in the rear. But I grew fearful. Once I made such a fuss that the coach threw away the needle and syringe with stuff in it. There were nights when I had taken large doses before the race and I would stay wired into the night. Once I went around a turn too fast in a race and crashed into a wall. When they carried me away, I was whistling. But sometimes I burned out my energy supply of the drugs before the finish and had a real hard time getting to the finish. Well, it was my first contact with dope and I didn't use it wisely."

By the end of the season, he was the only American competing abroad. For the following season, he joined another team, Associatione Sportif Alfa-Cure, backed by physicians who didn't permit their riders to use stimulants. He managed second places, but no wins. "I think all the dope I took had blown my body," he said. "I just didn't have any poop left." He went back to California to rest.

While Hiltner was racing in Europe, Ted Smith turned professional for the first six-day race to be held in Madison Square Garden in twenty-two years. The organizers—again Jimmy the Whale—lined up a roster of fifteen teams from all over Europe and South America. They had a difficult time getting U.S. riders, but Smith, at thirty-three, was ready for one last shot at the big time before retiring.

There was plenty of pre-race publicity. *Variety,* the show-business weekly, and New York's newspapers ran features and editorials leading up to the September 22, 1961, start. For the Garden's seventy-fifth international six-day, the slate of riders was arguably as good as in the sport's best days. Alf Goullet was the race's chief referee. World track champions Oscar Plattner of Switzerland and Rudi Altig of West Germany lined up with Smith for the 9 P.M. Friday start.

Yet the race was plagued with difficulties right from the start. A new pine velodrome was constructed in sections in the Garden's basement, but when the workers brought it up to put it together, they discovered the blueprint had been misread. The pieces failed to fit.

As a result, the start was delayed for six hours while an army of sixty-two carpenters were paid time and a half to correct the problem. Ticket refunds and carpentry costs put the race $20,000 in the red before the starting pistol went off at 3 A.M. The pre-race publicity didn't pay off. As the days passed, the soft rumble of bicycle tires on the boards was rarely overcome by applause from the spectators. *Variety* had touted the race for "recalling Prohibition's razzle-dazzle," but the song of the wheels did not entice the younger generation.

Red Smith of the *New York Herald-Tribune* attended the Garden's six-day to look for material for his syndicated sports column. The most widely read sportswriter in the country took advantage of a lull in the afternoon's action to scan the roster and he seized on Ted Smith's name with an exclamation. Red Smith skipped over names like Wout Wagtmans, Tonino Domenicali, Aves Barbosa, Bruno Sivilotti, Anselmo Zarlenga, Enzo Sacchi, and Nando Terruzzi. When chance permitted, Smith interviewed the tired Smith.

The columnist went back to his office with an idea that excited him. His column went over the newspaper wires with a heading that read "Smith Is a Rare Name for Cyclist." He wrote about the Smiths in his native Wisconsin, where some family members were given to eccentric and stubborn behavior, but none in his branch was a six-day cyclist.

"Under every family tree," he noted, "some shells are found." His column discussed "how a Smith ever got into this dodge," reviewed highlights of the cyclist's past, and told readers that the three-time national champion and Olympian was retiring after the Garden's six-day to embark on a new career as a barber in Buffalo.

By the time the six-day was over, a committee in Fitchburg was planning the third annual Arthur M. Longsjo, Jr., Memorial Race, a fifty-mile event held on a circuit of streets in downtown Fitchburg. The race had become a major event in New England.

In the inaugural race on the first Sunday in July 1960, about 200 riders converged on Fitchburg in cars with license plates from twenty states and Canadian provinces. Oom-pah-pah bands played with abandon on two ends of the course that was to be traversed thirty-seven times. People went downtown to see what it was, and were amazed to discover the sport of bicycle racing.

Guy Morin was instrumental in setting up the race. He was still riding well, and he had represented Canada in the Pan American Games the year before in Chicago. In the inaugural race, he had it in his heart to win. He broke away with another of Longsjo's good friends, Arnold Uhrlass, and they lapped the field. When it came to the end, Morin blasted to the finish and won.

The inaugural race was also the day of the unveiling of the Longsjo Memorial, a marble slab seven feet tall bearing the name of the athlete and an engraving of the Olympic torch. The slab is flanked on either side by two smaller stones—one depicting a cyclist, the other depicting a speed skater. The stone memorial is one of the few for an athlete in the nation and is inscribed "Honored, admired, and respected for his character, ability, and sportsmanship."

The following year, Uhrlass came back to win. Morin had retired from competition to become president of the Quebec Cycling Association. Yet Morin did not forget Longsjo and was back to supervise the race and drive the pace car, something he continued for twenty-five years.

By the first Sunday in July 1962, Don McDermott, the three-time Olympian, was a married man, the last to marry of the northern New Jersey group who trained together on Sunday mornings when there was no race. He drove from his home in Englewood Cliffs, New Jersey, to Fitchburg. During the third annual race, he located Ray Blum's parked car, forced open the wing window, and left a big used paintbrush on the driver's seat. Then McDermott drove back home. It was a long way to go just to plant the paintbrush on Blum, but he felt that Longsjo would have done the same thing.

12
THE RAINBOW AT THE END OF THE CRASH

Going to the Rome Olympics as a high schooler and seeing the Games as an insider stoked Jack Simes's ambition to move up in the sport. Two years and many races later, he wanted to go to Europe to find out what made Europeans so superior to contemporary American riders.

He went to see Jack Heid. Heid told him about adapting to what life was like in Europe, what the racing was like. It was important because Simes had no idea. Heid also gave him a letter of introduction to Jorgen Beyerholm, promoter of the Ordrupp Velodrome in Copenhagen. There were no tracks at that time and Heid's letter of introduction helped pave the way.

Simes's 1962 overseas foray ended after six weeks. On June 25 he suffered a broken nose, a concussion, a broken shoulder, and numerous cuts, abrasions, and bruises after a nasty fall in a match race against an Italian rider. The Italian swerved sharply in front of Simes, his right pedal catching Simes's front wheel and tearing out all the spokes. The wheel collapsed and Simes landed face first on the cement.

It was another hard lesson in the big leagues of European racing. He returned home to recover. But in 1963 he was ready again. That year he made the Pan American cycling team that went to São Paulo, Brazil.

Two northern Californians—Dave Staub, who rode the kilometer on the velodrome, and Mike Hiltner—also made the team. After the Games, the team went on a tour of the West Indies, but Hiltner—who finished eleventh in the 100-mile road race—stayed behind to marry Adelina Neide Marchena, whom he had met in São Paulo. He learned to speak Portuguese, which he found similar to the Italian he knew. The Brazilian bureaucracy was slow in approving the marriage, and as the weeks went by he became active in local races. Six months later, the couple married and moved to Santa Monica, California. He got a job as a postman and trained after work to make his second Olympic cycling team.

Simes also had his sights set on making the Olympic team. After the Pan American Games, he went back to Europe to race and performed so well that sportswriters began touting him as a possible medal winner in the upcoming Tokyo Olympics. On his second stint in Denmark, he finished second to Belgium's Patrick Sercu—known as the Flemish Arrow—at the Danish Grand Prix. Simes beat Danish champion Neils Fredborg in the Dane's hometown of Aarhus. And Simes outclassed France's Pierre Trentin, who twice finished third in the world championships.

Sports Illustrated featured Simes in a four-page article that described him as "America's foremost hope for a medal," although he was warned that the prospect for an Olympic cycling medal "has a touch of Walter Mitty in it."

Walter Mitty was an uncomfortably appropriate image for American cyclists at the 1964 Olympics. More than a half-century had passed since 1912 when American riders took home two bronze medals, both in torturous 320-kilometer (200-mile) races (individual and four-man team) that were held concurrently on a course around Lake Malmar and finished in the Olympic Stadium in Stockholm.

Joe Kopsky of Jersey City rode in the team time trial, winning a bronze medal. He used to tell friends he finished the race on his wooden rims after the rough roads shredded his tires. Carl O. Schutte of Kansas City placed third in the individual road race to win the other bronze medal.

(America swept the cycling events at the 1904 Olympics in St. Louis, but the International Olympic Committee doesn't recognize the medals won because only Americans competed. Perhaps the most remarkable medal tally was taken in by Hardy Downing's younger brother, Burton, who collected two golds, three silvers, and a bronze.)

By the 1960s, the U.S. Olympic Committee saw cyclists as "a questionable group." Although the Olympic Committee never directly indicated that cycling would be dropped, the intention was made through innuendo. The USOC had a limited number of sports, usually around twenty-seven, for both the Winter and Summer Olympics. Sports like downhill skiing, equestrian, swimming, wrestling, and track and field were high up on the Olympic Committee's list. But because the Europeans dominated Olympic cycling, and the sport had decreased to minor status in America, cycling was twenty-fourth or twenty-fifth on the Olympic Committee's list. When another sport came along for international competition, like archery, ABL officials had to fight to keep cycling in those twenty-seven sports.

What helped keep cycling on the USOC roster was, ironically, the strength of the iron curtain countries in the sport. The Russians, Poles, East Germans, and Czechs were strong cycling countries. American cycling had lost the audience it had had in this country, but it was politically important to keep sending cyclists to the Olympics, even though U.S. riders tended to get lost in the pack. In the 122-mile individual road race at the Tokyo Olympics, our top finisher was John Allis, in seventy-fifth place, about halfway from the top.

Even Simes, despite his European racing experience, was eliminated early in the Tokyo Olympics match-race sprints. But another Olympic team member—Oliver Martin, Jr., of Manhattan—was hooked and wanted to see how far he could go. He realized that meant going to Europe for a prolonged stay, which meant he was the first American black rider in Europe since Major Taylor. Martin developed under the tutelage of Perry Metzler and Herb Francis.

Martin was about Metzler's height, but slighter of build, with a slim torso that is the ideal cyclist's build—light yet strong. In 1963, he burst on the national scene at the juniors' ten-mile race in Somerville where he beat a field of ninety. Francis got sixteen-year-old Martin into the club he rode for, the Union Sportif Italiano.

Martin, the son of an Italian mother who met his dad, a G.I., during World War II, was born in Harlem and grew up in Manhattan. Martin lived near the George Washington Bridge, which he rode across to gain access to lightly traveled roads in New Jersey. He also rode thousands of miles in Central Park.

In 1964 Martin turned seventeen and entered the men's open division. He and Metzler finished near each other in many races. At the

Jack Simes III, a third-generation racer, was versatile and won short races on the track as well as long races on the road. At one time he held concurrent national records for 200 meters and 50 miles. (*Robert F. George*)

Oliver Martin, Jr. of Manhattan received guidance early in his career from Perry Metzler and Herb Francis, which helped him make the Olympic cycling teams in 1964 and 1968. (*Robert F. George*)

Fitchburg-Longsjo Memorial, Metzler was fifth, one place ahead of Martin. Then it was Martin who beat Metzler at the fifty-mile Tour of Flemington, in New Jersey. Martin kept developing and surpassed his mentors to make the next Olympic cycling team in the 4,000-meter (2.5-mile) team pursuit.

The pursuit team was eliminated early in the Olympics, but Martin's appetite to succeed was whetted. He returned home but vowed to do better in the next Olympics, and he knew that meant going overseas to race. Martin had his mother's family to help provide him with connections in Italy. In January 1965 he left for northern Italy.

In 1965, the ABL tried to improve its limited program by changing the national championships format from the four-race series to individual events, like the national sprint championship, which Simes won. The ABL also introduced the national road-racing championship with a 100-mile race, which Hiltner won. His prize was a plane ticket to the worlds in San Sebastian, Spain. The airline ticket was also his incentive to make another attempt at racing professionally in Europe.

Although Hiltner, now twenty-four, finished far out of the medals at the world championship race, he and his wife bought a Volkswagen and moved to Ghent, Belgium, for the remainder of the racing season. He made some money placing in races and did well enough to be offered contracts for events in the Ghent Velodrome. That led to a contract for a month-long series of velodrome races in Meunster, West Germany, in January 1966. In the Meunster city championship, he placed third. He and his wife then drove south to Florence for the start of the Italian racing season. By the time they arrived, however, they were living on the last of their savings.

He had a fair season, with two victories and another half-dozen second places, but that wasn't enough to attract a pro sponsor. He was not making much money racing and occasionally had to write home for money during the season. His wife, meanwhile, was getting tired of the itinerant life of a bicycle racer. The couple lived in an apartment with no furniture. They slept on the bare floor. They cooked on a hot plate. Hiltner was doing his best, but that didn't compare with some of the top amateurs who were winning twenty or more races, which got them offers for professional contracts.

His final big chance came at the world championships in early September in Nurburgring, West Germany, over the diabolically hilly, twisty circuit designed for grand prix car racing. Disappointingly, he did not finish. It seems he had burned himself out with his rigorous racing schedule that year.

After he returned to Florence, Hiltner finished the season in local races as he pondered his next move. The main course of his life was still racing, which made Brazil seem more attractive because it had a structure for bike racing that didn't exist in the United States. The draft back home also gave him some concern. At the end of 1966, Hiltner and his wife packed up and went to Brazil.

After they got settled with his wife's family in São Paulo, Hiltner rode for a team that Pirelli, the Italian car tire company, sponsored. But his riding was winding down. At the end of the season, he was competing in the Tour of São Paulo when he fell ill. Hiltner's racing career ended when he pulled out of the race.

While Hiltner raced in central Italy, Oliver Martin lived in Milan and raced in northern Italy as a member of the Societa Ciclistica Corsico team. For twenty-three months, Martin competed in a variety of road and track races. He rode on the Vigorelli Velodrome in the winter track-racing season of 1965–1966, which helped sharpen his speed. He won five road races, and got eleven second places. On the track, he rode some pro-am team races with the pros.

By 1966, Martin, like Hiltner, was looking to turn professional. The problem was Vietnam. With the escalation of the war effort, the draft was going after men Martin's age. He returned to New York about the time Hiltner went to São Paulo.

Martin got a draft deferment when he enrolled in City College of New York. He took light course loads while he kept training. At the 1967 Tour of Somerville, he helped force the pace at the head of a 150-rider pack that sped around the course to a new national fifty-mile record. When they sprinted for the finish, he narrowly lost to Jack Simes.

Traveling abroad every season for international competition sharpened Simes's riding and helped him with big domestic races like the Tour of

Somerville, but his overseas travel puzzled the FBI. By 1967, nearly a half-million U.S. troops were in Vietnam, and the draft was pulling in young men like twenty-four-year-old Simes. He had no deferment, was single, did not have a full-time job, occasionally took evening classes at a local community college, and had no apparent way to fund his numerous trips to Europe, South America, and Japan.

He went home one day to find an FBI agent waiting to interview him about what he did. When Simes told the agent that he was a bicycle racer, the agent frowned and asked for a fuller explanation. Simes invited him inside the house, showed him assorted racing bicycles, and told him about speed skating in the winter and then resuming cycling when the weather improved. By late spring Simes usually quit whatever job he had to train and race full time.

Simes took the agent on a tour of the house. There were trophies and silver cups on all the mantels, crammed in bookcases, the china cabinet, some stashed in cupboards, some in boxes. They were in the living room, dining room, bedrooms, hallway, and kitchen. Plaques filled the walls. A couple of drawers were filled with medals. There still were some trophies and cups in boxes in the basement because there was no where else to put them. The agent took notes and left to file his report.

That autumn Simes was drafted. After basic training in Fort Dix, he was held over for two months. He couldn't get a security clearance because of all the trips he had taken out of the country.

Simes was assigned as a physical activities specialist and wound up managing a base gymnasium at Fort MacArthur, near Los Angeles. He rode for the army cycling team, which was in essence the first national cycling team. Oliver Martin, who lost his college deferment and was drafted about the same time as Simes, soon joined him at Fort MacArthur.

Both riders made the next Olympic team, bound for Mexico City. Improvements were apparent in the Olympic cycling team. Members were doing their homework, not just the riders but also management and administration.

Martin, afflicted with an intestinal ailment, wasn't up to his full strength in his road event. Simes had better luck with the food and felt sure he was ready to win a medal in the kilometer (two-thirds of a mile) event, a lung-bursting individual time trial on the velodrome, which he had been specializing in. The previous year in the Pan American Games' kilometer in Winnipeg, Canada, he had won a silver medal. But Simes didn't perform at his best. He also went out early in the match-race sprints. He admits to beginning to get discouraged. He had always wanted to turn professional. But if he couldn't beat the top amateurs, there was no reason to turn professional. Two weeks later, he had another chance—at the world track cycling championships in Montevideo, Uruguay. The 1968 world championships were spread out on two continents—the amateur velodrome events were in Montevideo while all the road races were in Rome. The worlds in Montevideo were Simes's last chance to show he could make the grade.

The trip from Mexico City to Uruguay had been long and arduous. Yet it was worth it for one more kilometer ride in world competition. In the lottery for the order of the ride, he drew number one, ordinarily considered a handicap because everyone else has a mark to chase.

Simes did not mind. The pressure of the Olympics was off. As he warmed up, the other riders were called off the track. This was his last chance to show he had what it took. He realized he had come a long way for that chance, and this fueled his determination. Alone on the track, he thought of all the trips he had taken abroad, the Olympic teams he had made, the support he had along the way from family and friends. He thought about all the American cyclists who would give anything to have what he had, to be where he was. He got more psyched. By the time the gun went off, nothing was going to stop him. When he finished, he felt completely spent. Then rider after rider chased his time. For a while, Januscz Kierzkowski of Poland, the Olympic bronze medalist in the kilometer, looked like he would beat Simes's time, but didn't. As more and more finished behind him, it looked like he would become the world champion. Finally, Neils Fredborg, the last rider and Olympic silver medalist in the kilometer, who at 5 feet 9 inches and 165 pounds was slightly bigger than Simes, sped around the track to win by three-tenths of a second.

Simes was disappointed, yet he realized Fredborg's greatness. And he now knew he could carry on and turn professional—an opportunity he hadn't had when he left Mexico City.

Simes's silver medal ended the seventeen-year drought since Jack Heid's bronze medal at the world championships. The next year marked an even bigger moment in American cycling when Audrey Phleger McElmury of La Jolla, California, won the women's world road-racing championship in the rain at Brno, Czechoslovakia.

McElmury got up after falling to regain the pack and win by more than a minute. Not since 1912, when Frank Kramer won the professional sprint championship, had a U.S. rider won a world title. Her victory was so unexpected that officials had to hunt for thirty minutes to find a recording of the national anthem of the United States.

McElmury was among those who helped give women's racing credibility. Not until 1958 were women cyclists included in the world championships. McElmury, fifteen at the time, was an avid surfer. She started cycling after she broke a leg while skate boarding in the early 1960s. In 1964 she won the California women's state championship.

She began with track racing because that was all women had. What she preferred was road racing, which was exclusive to men, so she trained with the men. She joined their workouts, took her share of pulls at the front while others drafted behind, and gained acceptance on her own. Occasionally, being the only woman among the men subjected her to hoaxes, such as being told that a women's six-day circuit was starting in Europe. The harassment she took pointed to the lack of opportunities for women, yet she never let disappointments get to her.

(Another who believed in integrating the sexes in the sport was Nancy Neiman Baranet. In 1965 she wrote in *American Cycling Newsletter,* "Training with women is a waste of time." She said that women didn't exert themselves the way men did. She advocated the same training program for both genders: "Naturally, the best woman athlete will never be able to defeat the best male athlete, but she can uncompromisingly defeat one-half of the country's senior men's champions." *American Cycling Newsletter* has since become *Bicycling* magazine, the biggest of all U.S. cycling periodicals.)

McElmury speaks with confidence and with a forcefulness that reflects the way she trained and competed. She worked out diligently with weights, which cyclists didn't indulge in at the time. The 5 feet 8 inch McElmury was known for doing 135-pound leg squats, 5 pounds more than she weighed. Her training got her up as early as 4:30 A.M. for the first of two daily rides. It was a strict regimen which she admits was so single-minded that she subsequently rode her way out of her marriage with Scott McElmury, a racer she had married after she received a zoology degree from the University of California at San Diego.

Audrey McElmury won national championship jerseys in the United States, then went to the 1969 world championships in Brno, Czechoslovakia, where she became the first American—man or woman—to win the world road title. (*Sandra Sutherland*)

In 1967 she had a son, Ian. The following year, she was back racing and went to Rome to compete in the women's world championship road race which ended in a group sprint. She finished fifth.

That made her a contender for the world championship road race in 1969 in Brno, Czechoslovakia. She went there with three other women and eight men on the ABL team. The ABL was not able to provide full funding for the trip. McElmury had to work a full-time job to support her racing.

Czechoslovakia's world championships coincided with the first anniversary of the Russian invasion. Tanks were everywhere, up and down every street, and soldiers were armed with machine guns. The Czechs were anti-Communist and pro-American; they cheered the U.S. riders wildly in the races and booed the Russians. When the Russians won, the Czechs even walked out on the medal ceremonies.

McElmury had won the national women's track championship to represent the United States in the women's 3,000-meter (almost 2-mile) track pursuit event. She finished seventh, but it was a good event to ride in so as to release some of the tension that had built up in anticipation of the road race.

The 43-mile race consisted of five laps on a hilly course. "The pavement was somewhat chewed up from the tank treads," she said. "The course was one that suited my riding. I was good in the hills, and I time-trialed well. On about the third lap, it started pouring buckets. On the fourth lap, I got away on the hill by about fifteen seconds, but I fell down while putting on the brakes in a corner on the descent.

"The pack caught me as I got up. The rain was chilly enough that I didn't feel the full effect of my bruised hip, and the rain exaggerated the amount of blood from a cut on my elbows. I chased the pack with an ambulance following me to see if I was all right. After I caught the pack for the last lap, I got away again on the final hill. On the descent, I refrained from using my brakes around the turn where I crashed. On the finishing stretch, I confess I kept looking around, because I couldn't believe I was out in front."

She won with 1 minute 10 seconds over Bernadette Swinnerton of England. Her triumph was the first world road-racing championship for any U.S. rider—man or woman. She became the first American to don the rainbow jersey, awarded since the early 1920s to world champions. The last American to win the championship—Kramer, in track racing—did so in 1912, before jerseys were given out. Across the chest and back of the white jersey is a band of colors derived from those of the five Olympic rings. At least one appears on the national flag of every country.

Reaction in America to her victory was relatively limited. Cycling did not receive much media coverage, and women's cycling got even less. When McElmury arrived back home in San Diego, a local television news reporter interviewed her at the airport. He didn't care much about the worlds, but wanted to know about the first anniversary of the Russian invasion.

Though her world championship victory was virtually overlooked in her own country, it was not in Europe. In France, *Miroir du Cyclisme* prophetically wrote that American women were the future of American cycling. The magazine published a cartoon depicting a woman cyclist revising popular graffiti that read "US Go Home" to "US Go *Femme.*"

McElmury's gold medal and Simes's silver in two world championships helped Al Toefield, ABL president and chairman of the U.S. Olympic Cycling Committee, use contacts in the Pentagon to organize the first fully supported army cycling team. The army was willing to go along for the public relations benefit. Vietnam was an unpopular war, with antiwar activists doing their best to make the army look bad. What Toefield offered the army was a public relations opportunity to develop members of the next Olympic cycling team.

The army had created Special Services for athletes many years before. Its advantages were chiefly limited to providing time to train, but left athletes like cyclists isolated on different bases around the country and on their own for transportation to races. Under Toefield's stewardship, the army cycling team was consolidated first at Fort MacArthur in California and then at Fort Wadsworth on Staten Island, New York, where the team had army vehicles at their disposal to drive to better training areas and commute to races.

The formation of the team was not without its problems, however, as two Olympians from the Mexico City Games found out. Dave Chauner, from suburban Philadelphia, dropped out of Upsala College to get drafted in November 1970. He figured he would go into the army in late 1970 and finish up basic training in early 1971, receive orders for the team, and train in plenty of time to get ready for the Pan Am trials. But after basic training he was sent to Fort Polk for nine weeks of field maneuvers simulating combat. When Chauner told his company commander at Fort Polk that there had been some mistake and that he should be on the army cycling team, he learned that he was soon headed for Vietnam.

Chauner, a six-footer with curly brown hair, had raced in Holland during the 1969 season. After a few weeks in Fort Polk, he sent for his Cinelli racing bicycle. He kept it in a storage area at one end of the barracks. When maneuvers were over for the day, he went out for a ride to maintain his physical shape and stamina.

On the other side of the base, John Howard, a strong-willed 6 foot

3 inch rider from Springfield, Missouri, trained all day instead of going out on maneuvers. His company commander had competed in the Little 500 bicycle race at Indiana University and knew what bicycle racing was. He had heard of Howard as an Olympic cyclist who competed in the Mexico City Olympics and let Howard ride his bike instead of going out with the rest of the company on maneuvers. But then Howard received orders to report to Officer Candidate School in Fort Benning, Georgia. For a while, it didn't look like the army cycling team was going to happen.

Chauner had the same doubts until he caught a glimpse of Howard riding by in the national team jersey. Chauner was on a bus going out on a bivouac, sitting with his M-14 rifle resting on the floor between his feet, when he looked out the window in time to see Howard ride over the brow of a hill and disappear. That was all Chauner needed. He told his company commander that he was going to get orders soon for the army cycling team, but once again he heard, "Vietnam."

When Chauner returned to the barracks he was told to report to the company commander. When he reported in, the company commander was shaking his head and holding some papers. There was a look of disbelief on his face. He said that Chauner's orders had come in commanding him to report to the army cycling team at Fort Wadsworth on Staten Island.

About a dozen national-class riders were stationed at Fort Wadsworth, with time to train and army vehicles at their disposal for going to races. Howard and Chauner were among the army cycling team riders bound for Cali, Colombia, for the 1971 Pan American Games that gave U.S. cycling a big boost.

The Sixth Pan American Games that August were memorable for having a contingent of 138 U.S. officials—more officials than the number of athletes any other nation sent. Frank Shorter of Boulder, credited with starting the running boom in America, won gold medals in both the 42-kilometer (26.2-mile) marathon and the 10-kilometer (6.2-mile) event. Chauner rode in the 4,000-meter (2.5-mile) team pursuit, which won a bronze medal.

But the final event of the Games was the 200-kilometer (125-mile) road race. Howard stole the show. After the pack caught a two-rider breakaway at 100 kilometers, Howard attacked. Brazilian Luis Carlos Florez sprinted away with him and the two worked harmoniously together, relaying each other to keep their breakaway going.

They never got much of a lead. But cycling is the national sport in Colombia, and more than a million spectators lined the road to cheer, which kept Howard and Florez working well together. During the last mile, Howard's rear wheel broke a spoke, causing the rim to rub against the brake block every revolution, but that didn't bother him. Florez began to sprint when they saw the finish a short distance ahead. With 55 yards left, Howard flashed past and won by four lengths.

It was the United States' 105th gold medal of the week-long Games,

John Howard raises his arms in triumph as he captures the 1971 Pan American road race in Cali, Colombia. His victory resulted in a great deal of favorable publicity for the sport and helped renew interest in cycling in the United States. The man in the white short-sleeved shirt and tie in the street is Howard's father, Harry. (*John Howard*)

but coming as the final event, Howard's win drew more media attention than it might otherwise have received. Newspapers across the United States carried wire-service photos of Howard crossing the line a champion. The *New York Times* headed its story "U.S. Wins Cycling Breakthrough."

The U.S. Olympic Committee had a new look at cycling with Howard's gold medal at Cali. It came right after the world championship medals that Simes and McElmury won. The USOC began to realize that cycling was an emerging sport. With the Army Special Services cycling team, the USOC began to see cyclists as a disciplined group.

The 1960s ended with two world cycling championship medals. John Howard kept the momentum rolling at the start of the 1970s with his gold medal in the Pan American Games. Jack Simes III went to race in Europe as the first professional since Jack Heid. And while an Olympic cycling medal continued to be a fantasy through the decade, American women cyclists followed Audrey McElmury's example and won world championship medals with regularity. Race officials learned to keep a recording of "The Star Spangled Banner" on hand.

THREE

"One Good American Rider"

13
THE AWAKENING

The new era in American cycling dawned in the early 1970s with the fitness explosion. The recession in the national economy was not reflected in bicycle sales. Health-conscious baby boomers were buying bicycles in unprecedented numbers. In 1971, 8.5 million bicycles were sold, more than double the 3.7 million sold in 1960. What distinguished the new sales was the shift in riders: one-third of the bicycles sold in 1971 were for adults. As children in the 1950s, they rode balloon-tired bikes that were the bicycle industry's equivalent of Detroit iron. Now, as adults, they bought lightweight, ten-speed bicycles with derailleurs for exercise and for nonpolluting transportation. All over the country, abandoned railroad beds were converted into paved bike paths. The new cyclists were not just riding their bikes; they were racing them. ABL membership, about 1,000 when Jack Simes III made his first Olympic team, tripled to 3,000 by 1968 and nearly tripled again by 1973 to 8,600.

Although membership growth brought in more revenue for the ABL, the organization still relied totally on volunteers. By 1971 the annual budget had more than doubled since Audrey McElmury won the world championship, but it had only risen to $25,000. Two new developments helped improve the sport's conditions: the ABL board of directors approved sponsorship for the riders, and the U.S. Olympic Committee started to grant Olympic development funds, enabling ABL officials to introduce racing programs that better prepared riders for Olympic competition. Top riders started getting more financial support, although there still was more glory than money, as riders had no guarantee that their race expenses would be paid.

None of these problems concerned McElmury and Simes, both of whom were racing full time in Europe in 1971. The Italians were extremely supportive of women's bicycle racing. By the time McElmury had set twenty-five national records in the United States, she accepted an invitation to race in northern Italy for Groupo Sportivo CBM. The club provided her with a racing bicycle, clothing, accommodations, and a stipend, along with a team car, mechanics, and a coach.

McElmury's husband, Michael Levonas of New York, also rode in Italy that season and made the 1971 Pan American cycling team. Before each Italian race, they scrutinized the preme prizes to decide which she would sprint for—like a case of wine or a brace of pheasants.

The Italian Cycling Federation paid cash to McElmury and the other women riders, based on how they placed, what their appearance fee was, and what their sponsors paid them. This money created problems for her back home. The ABL tried to kick her out because they said she was not an amateur. "What I was getting was nice, but we were just getting by," she says. "I just ignored the ABL."

At the world cycling championships that year in Gap, France, McElmury was in the lead group at the end of the women's road race and finished fourth. The following year, she moved to Boulder, Colorado. She continued to race and took up coaching, but a serious crash in 1976 gave her a concussion that resulted in a permanent loss of smell. The crash effectively ended her career.

"Frankly, I didn't have the nerve to race any more after so many accidents," she says. "You have to be fearless." She retired after eighteen years of competition to spend more time with her family and take up backpacking and running.

While McElmury raced in Italy as an amateur, Jack Simes competed on the Continent as a professional. After his release from the army, he went to Europe in early 1970. He broke into professional racing on the Antwerp Velodrome, a 275-yard tobacco-stained indoor board track.

In February, he got into his first big pro event there, a six-day with three-man teams. The race got off to a roaring start with derny racing, where riders pace behind motorcycles. "I was pedaling so fast that my legs were like the blades of a fan. The opening chase was an hour and forty-five minutes, and I lost five laps on the leaders.

"I was really moving," he stressed. "But I never hurt like that before. Everything hurt from going so fast—my stomach, legs, everything. And I felt terrible that I lost five laps. After I got off the track, I saw that other guys in the race had lost twenty to twenty-five laps. Suddenly, my performance wasn't so bad, put in that perspective. You have to learn those things. I was thrown into brutal racing. Those guys were flying! Their season began in late September and they were in terrific shape by February. I was just out of the army. It was such an experience."

The following September, he signed a contract for the start of the six-day season for the Skol Six in London, a major league race. There he made international sporting news, but not the way he intended. On the Skol Six's opening day, Simes and Dutchman Post (the same Peter Post who fifteen years earlier had competed against Jack Heid in the six-days in Cleveland, Louisville, and Chicago) collided and fell to the boards. English rider Tony Gowland crashed into Post's back. No rider was badly hurt, but Post was fuming. He accused Simes of deliberately causing the accident. The two men soon wound up on the track infield. When Simes threw a punch at Post, he also threw away his race. Simes did not start the second day. It was a serious incident that resulted in his getting blackballed from further race engagements that season. Soon after he returned to the United States.

When Simes arrived home in 1971, American cycling was improving in many ways. The Olympic development funds were clearing the way for such projects as the Tour of Florida, an early spring race that helped riders get in shape. The money was meager, but college students then flew for half-price plane tickets. Some races were designated as Olympic development events. That enabled ABL officials to prevail on promoters to provide low-cost housing; in exchange, promoters got a better quality field.

In international competition, American women gave the men something to look up to. In 1972, Sheila Young of Detroit made big news when she won a bronze medal at the world cycling match-race championships in Marseilles, France. The following year she made headlines at the world championships in San Sebastian, Spain, where she became the second American to don the rainbow jersey.

She got off to a nearly disastrous start, and made an inspiring comeback. In the first match race, she and Iva Zajickova of Czechoslovakia were winding up their sprint when Zajickova suddenly swerved in front of Young, causing the American to hit Zajickova's back wheel, flip through the air, and land on her head. She suffered a gash on her head, and her bike frame was twisted.

The judges ordered Young and Zajickova to re-ride the race after an intermission of twenty minutes. Young had a cut a couple of inches long on the top of her head and needed stitches, which she didn't have time for. A Dutch doctor at trackside closed the wound with two staples that cut into unanesthetized flesh because novocaine is considered a contraband drug in world competition. Meanwhile, teammates fixed her bike by removing the fork and replacing it with the fork from another bike. Twenty minutes after the crash, Young was back on her bike. She felt a little dizzy, but her adrenaline was pumping. She won her next two races.

Young was introduced to cycling by her father, Clair, who was Michigan state champion for more than ten years. Her first bicycle race in 1965, at age fifteen, almost ended her career when she fell and broke her arm. At that point, speed skating, which was her primary sport, became both more important and more realistic.

She told me, "My dad used to say that if you want to be number one, you have to suffer. When I was an adolescent, I thought I was working hard and suffering. I kind of got a sweat going once in a while. I didn't know what he was talking about. I began to realize what he meant in the summer of 1972, when I was twenty-one. I got into cycling then to help me for skating, and I still remember distinctly when I realized the difference between sort of suffering and really suffering. But it paid off. One of the reasons I liked cycling was because of the travel. And when I got better, I did a lot of traveling."

Sheila Young-Ochowicz became a world champion cyclist and Olympic gold medalist speed skater. (*Robert F. George*)

Sue Novara-Reber competed against Sheila Young-Ochowicz
to raise her fitness level and improve her tactics and became
a world champion cyclist herself. (*Robert F. George*)

In 1974, aficionados were surprised when eighteen-year-old Sue
Novara broke Young's domination and beat her in the Michigan state
championship, and then again at the nationals. Novara raced to a silver
medal in the world match-sprint championships that year in Montreal,
where she lost in a photo finish to a Soviet rider.

Novara, who lived in Flint, an hour's drive from Detroit, began as a
speed skater and started cycling at the age of thirteen to keep in shape
in the warm weather. A little taller and more lithe than Young, Novara

was known as Navajo Sue for the long ponytail she wore down the middle of her back.

It was remarkable that the two Michigan cyclists were so fast and lived near each other. They took their rivalry overseas to the 1975 world championships in Liege, Belgium, where Novara won the women's sprint championship and Young finished third.

"We influenced each other by being good competitors," Young says. "We drove each other to win. You are only as good as your competition. We helped each other out competitively."

The following year, Young made world sporting news when she speed-skated at the Winter Olympics in Innsbruck, Austria, to gold, silver, and bronze medals. She returned to cycling and led Novara to a one-two finish at the world sprint championships in Mendrisio, Italy.

Racing against one another was not as beneficial for American men, however, as it was for American women. By 1973, sponsorship had improved substantially and Raleigh Bicycles sponsored the first national ABL team, which comprised many of the previous army cycling team who had stayed together when their enlistments were up. The new national team in 1974 started making trips abroad to big international races, like the two-week Tour of Britain. The experience left three-time national champion John Howard with no illusion about the state of American racing. When he returned home, he declared, "Compared to Europe, we are infantile."

Over the next couple of years, the sport's organization made substantial changes modeled after European cycling. A category system was introduced for riders, based on their race performances. The four-category system helped make races more competitive and reduce the size of packs. The entry age in men's open racing was raised from seventeen to eighteen.

In 1976, the sport's governing body changed its name from the Amateur Bicycle League of America to the U.S. Cycling Federation to resolve long-standing friction with Latin American cycling organizations that complained the United States was not all of America.

Much of the action at the time was in northern California. Some races had distinct San Francisco Bay Area flourishes. One race was kicked off by a Grateful Dead rock concert, a parade of Playboy bunnies, and a bumper-to-bumper procession of high-powered, metal-flaked Shelby Mustang GT 350s.

Riders like Peter Rich, who had gone with Pedali Alpini members to race in Europe, came back to pass along some of what they learned. He opened a bike shop, Velo-Sport, in Berkeley that sold the latest European equipment and put on local races. In 1971, he put on the seven-day Tour of California stage race, the first major stage race in the country. The budget was $50,000. Regional U.S. teams competed against teams from Germany, Canada, and Mexico.

Two of the Bay Area riders he sponsored and encouraged became national forces in the early 1970s and then rose to international class: Mike Neel and George Mount. Both were dedicated to cycling, which meant they lived the nomadic life of a bike bum, often sleeping in Rich's bike shop.

In 1972, Neel went on his own to race the season in France where he won club races and started to make a name for himself abroad. He came back to the States at the end of the season, but subsequently returned to Europe with John Howard and the national ABL team when their expenses were paid. The team gained respect in the 1975 Tour of Britain when Dave Chauner won a stage and the team finished fifth. Neel also made racing trips to Italy where he did well.

Neel and Mount made the 1976 Olympic cycling team that went to Montreal. Rain on race day made road conditions slick; a pileup in the 110-mile event eliminated Neel. But Mount rode at the front of the pack and finished sixth—the best American performance since 1912. For the first time in memory, Mount made the prospect of an Olympic cycling medal a distinct possibility.

Most important, Italian professional teams were taking a different look at U.S. cycling. American women were winning world championships, the ABL was sending a national team on racing trips, and George Mount finished two bike lengths from a bronze medal in the Olympic road race. American cyclists in the 1970s were gaining the respectability they hadn't received in the 1960s when Mike Hiltner raced in Italy.

After the Olympics, twenty-four-year-old Neel went to Italy and turned professional to race in the world championships, where he finished tenth in the 180-mile professional road race. He ended the season with a contract to ride for the Italian team Magniflex. A U.S. rider had finally broken into the professional big leagues of European racing.

George Mount threw himself into cycling and in 1976 showed that an Olympic cycling medal for the United States was not far away. At the Montreal Olympics that year, he finished sixth in the road race and went on to join a professional team in Italy. (*Tom Moran*)

The performances of Young, Novara, and Neel at the world championships, Mount's sixth place in the Olympics road race, and the new name for the sport's governing body were outward signs that 1976 was

Mike Neel dedicated himself to cycling and after the 1976
Olympics turned professional in time to compete in the world
professional championship road race for a remarkable tenth
place. (*Robert F. George*)

American cycling's pivotal year. But there were other developments that didn't become apparent until later which also helped America's international image as a nation of champion bicycle racers.

By 1976, mounting concern for disadvantages that American athletes had in Olympic competition against state-supported Eastern-bloc athletes prompted the President's Commission on Olympic Sports to begin a comprehensive two-year study of the U.S. Olympic movement. The entire U.S. Olympic program was examined to see what reforms—which many observers felt were already overdue—were needed to restructure amateur sports.

When the President's Commission examined bicycle racing, it noted that the sport was growing in popularity but that lack of money and bad administration hindered the full development of U.S. riders as compared to cyclists in other countries. The Commission recognized the fact that until the sport overcame deficiencies in its organization, attracted more U.S. cyclists to Europe, hired a permanent staff, and upgraded programs of development at the school and college levels, U.S. competitive cycling would fail to reach its full potential.

The Commission's findings and recommendations led to House and Senate passage in 1978 of Public Law 95-606, which President Carter signed into law. Called the Amateur Sports Act of 1978, it made sweeping changes in the U.S. Olympic Committee. The Amateur Sports Act included giving each sport a national governing body, and made corporate funding available for development and training grants, a key to relieving the athletes of the intense pressure to support themselves while training all day.

As the President's Commission noted, cycling was continuing to gain popularity. Membership in the U.S. Cycling Federation topped 10,000 in 1976. Its budget had shot up tenfold in five years—increased corporate involvement and more money from the U.S. Olympic Committee helped pump the Federation's budget to $235,000. Corporations like Exxon, Miller, Smirnoff, Pepsi, and Yamaha were sponsoring clubs.

Conditions were improving rapidly for American bicycle racing, but an essential ingredient was still missing—a salaried full-time national coach. USCF board members felt that our own former bike racers were not working out as coaches.

After the Montreal Olympics, Eddie Borysewicz went to New Jersey to visit friends he had raced with years earlier on the Polish national team. He met Mike Fraysee of Ridgefield Park, New Jersey, who was USCF competition committee chairman. Fraysee recommended him to the Federation's board, which hired Borysewicz the next year as the United States' first full-time national cycling coach. He then took the necessary steps to become a U.S. citizen.

Borysewicz spoke French with Fraysee, who speaks it fluently, but he had to learn English to communicate with those he had to coach. Americans called him Eddie B., which was easier for them than pronouncing his surname. When he began as the full-time national cycling coach at the Olympic Training Center in Squaw Valley, in northern California, he relied on his translator, the twelve-year-old son of a former Polish teammate. "It really cuts your authority," Borysewicz later said, "when you want to be commanding and you have to speak through a twelve-year-old."

Borysewicz found that American racers didn't sit on their bikes properly (their saddles were too low or too high, or more forward or back than they should be) and that they were not physically fit. He complained that America was "a land of fat people," and told the national team members that only one of them was not overweight.

"American cycling was incredibly empty," he observes. His approach was like that of a baseball or football manager who takes over a major league team and builds the future around youth. Veterans, like twenty-eight-year-old John Howard, found they were history. Many suddenly former national team members became outspoken critics of the new national coach, claiming that he didn't understand the philosophy of U.S. riders.

Borysewicz's lack of English helped him miss much of the criticism as he introduced the concept that the team, not the individual, is what counts in racing. American racing over the years was marked by individuals going for the win rather than team tactics.

One way to look at bicycle racing is that it is an individual sport done by a team. Riders in the pack can block for a teammate on a breakaway by going to the front and slowing the pace, and a rider can foil a breakaway by refusing to take a turn at the front in draft relays to interrupt the rhythm until the pack with its greater resources reels them in.

Such tactics enable a team to best use an array of talents, from helping the team climber to ride away alone on a hill, to discouraging breakaway attempts by chasing from the front of the field and bringing everybody up to the breakaway, to positioning the team's best sprinter behind one or two teammates who lead him out at the end of a mass finish. All of this means that the particular talents of individuals contribute toward improving the performance of the entire team.

At Squaw Valley not long after he became national cycling coach, Borysewicz spotted a junior rider named Greg LeMond from Carson City, Nevada. LeMond had started racing in 1976 at age fourteen and felt bike racing was a cross between running and car racing. He rode exuberantly, won races easily, and quickly made vivid impressions wherever he went. At sixteen, LeMond sought a big challenge in the three-day Tour of Fresno for Category I men—top riders only. LeMond got special permission to enter the race. He finished second, 6 seconds down on John Howard.

At the 1977 Squaw Valley training camp, Borysewicz watched LeMond ride. LeMond won two of the three qualifier races to determine selection of the junior riders going to the junior world road-racing championships. Although LeMond rode well enough to make first spot on the team, he was ineligible to go because he was underage.

At 5 feet 10 inches and 150 pounds, the blond, tanned, blue-eyed LeMond had an all-American look. When Borysewicz was asked what he saw, he overlooked the pigeon-toed way LeMond's feet sat on the pedals. That was easily corrected. Borysewicz saw a youth who loved the sport, had quick recovery, and was ready to work extremely hard. In addition, the coach saw immediately that LeMond was in a special class as a young athlete. Borysewicz replied, "A diamond, a clear diamond."

LeMond didn't make the trip to the 1977 world juniors' championships. At these world championships in San Cristobal, Venezuela, U.S. women continued to show the men how it was done. Sue Novara won a silver medal in the match-race sprints, and another speed skater turned cyclist, Connie Carpenter of Madison, Wisconsin, won a silver medal in the women's road race. By the time the team returned home, Eddie B. was planning his campaign for the next season and working to get his athletes ready for the 1980 Summer Olympics in Moscow. American cycling was awakening in time for the Olympics.

14 BREAKING AWAY

By the late 1970s, American racing was becoming more sophisticated, reflecting the changes in the sport. American cycling was starting to develop a system that nurtured a better group of riders instead of relying on cyclists operating individually.

The Amateur Sports Act of 1978 benefited all the Olympic sports, including cycling. F. Don Miller, executive director of the U.S. Olympic Committee from 1973 to 1985, said that through the late 1970s the Olympic Committee was limited to being a travel agency. It brought together the athletes and sent them to the Pan American Games one year, then the Olympic Games the next year, and that was it for another two years.

National governing bodies of the various sports—like the ABL and then the USCF in cycling—were what he described as "kitchen table operations." The officials of the national governing bodies were volunteers who donated their time and resources. National cycling records were written on index cards kept in shoe boxes that were passed from officer to officer over the years.

Under Miller's stewardship, the Olympic Committee moved from New York to a decommissioned air force base in Colorado Springs shortly after passage of the Amateur Sports Act. One of the first sport governing bodies to move into the new Olympic Training Center was the USCF. The USCF had rooms and buildings at its disposal for conducting classes, and it could house athletes in dormitories in converted barracks. Revenue generated from corporate sponsorship, U.S. Olympic Committee support, membership dues, and other related incomes by 1980 gave the Federation a budget of nearly $500,000, a considerable jump from $38,500 in 1973. Staff were hired to develop, coach, train, and select amateur riders to compete on national teams.

One of the first coaches hired after Borysewicz was Mike Neel, who ended his professional career on an Italian team when the 1977 season concluded. That year, Neel became the first American to ride in a major professional stage race, the 2,000-mile Veulta d'España, the Tour of Spain, the third most prestigious professional stage race. He finished in the top four in two stages, but fell ill on the thirteenth of the nineteen daily stages and had to drop out. He found the life of a professional bicycle racer—competing up to seven hours a day through rain and sun from early spring to mid-autumn—a hard life. Neel decided to stay with the sport in a support position.

As preparations for the 1980 Olympics stepped up, it began to seem likely that, after so many years without, the United States could win an Olympic cycling medal. Beginning in 1978, the Federation sent teams to Europe for extended, ambitious racing programs. Our top amateurs kept going back to Europe each season to learn the hard lessons of the sport and continue to get into better shape. Two riders who had earned international respect were George Mount and always-improving Greg LeMond.

In major amateur European events, the powerful Mount was often at the head of the pack. Mount won two races in Italy and finished fourth in the Tour of Britain. He won a stage of France's pro-am Circuit de la Sarthe and finished first in the Tour d'Auvergne. Under revised rules governing amateurs, he won $4,000 when he captured the Apple Lap, the seventy-five-mile race through New York City's five boroughs, and set a national record for seventy-five miles on the way. At the 1979 Pan American Games in Puerto Rico, he helped power the four-man team in the 100-kilometer (62.5-mile) time trial to a gold medal. Shortly afterward, he went to Italy to race for the rest of the season.

LeMond won his first world championship medal in 1978 when he helped lead the junior world championship team to a bronze medal in the 70-kilometer (44-mile) four-man team time trial, held in Washington, D.C. The next year at the junior world championships in Buenos Aires, eighteen-year-old LeMond became the first road racer to win three medals at the world championships. He won a bronze in the team 70-kilometer time trial, a silver in the individual 3,000-meter (1.9-mile) pursuit race on the velodrome, and a gold in the 120-kilometer (75-mile) road race.

Just when it appeared that the long gap since the last Olympic cycling medals was to end for U.S. cyclists, international politics intervened. In late 1979, the Soviet invasion of Afghanistan stirred world protests. Shortly after the 1980 Winter Olympics in Lake Placid, New York, President Carter announced a U.S. boycott of the Moscow Summer Olympics.

President Carter's boycott kept American cyclists out of the Olympics. Meanwhile, the biggest sporting event on the globe, the seventy-seven-year-old Tour de France, was still untouched by American wheels. The 2,500-mile, three-week stage race that navigates the inside circumference of France was still something that Americans only dreamed of competing in. Every July, through steamy summer weather and pouring rain, 150 professional cyclists set out to conquer the Gallic landscape on twenty-pound bicycles. They pedal up snowcapped mountain ranges in the Alps and Pyrenees and plunge down them at 65 miles an hour on twisting, narrow roads.

An American finally broke into the Tour *peloton* (French for pack of riders) in 1981 when Jonathan Boyer of Carmel, California, rode on the ten-member Renault-Gitane French professional team. His debut as first U.S. rider was so special in the sixty-eighth Tour that race organizers let him wear a red, white, and blue racing jersey with stars on it rather than his team's yellow, black, and white team jersey.

It took Boyer seven years to ride his way into the Tour. In 1973, when he was eighteen, Boyer made the first U.S. juniors team that went to Europe for the junior world championships. He had started in the sport around 1970 and realized that all roads to the top of the sport led to Europe. He made his mind up early that he was going to live in France, progress through the amateur ranks there, and turn professional.

With money he earned from waiting on tables in high school, he went to Paris in 1973 and joined the Athletic Club Boulogne-Billancourt. He went completely all out for bicycle racing while in France. The racing was a lot faster in France than what he was used to in the States. Riders had a lot more experience, and they were out to make $20 to $50 a race. Boyer earned his way up in the peloton and started to win races and premes.

After three years with the ACBB, Boyer became a top amateur and turned professional in 1977 to ride with the Lejeune-BP team. Its coach was former French champion Henri Anglade, who once finished second in the Tour de France. One of Boyer's teammates was Lucien Van Impe, the Belgian who won the 1976 Tour de France.

Boyer's first-year pro contract paid about $650 a month. Although the season began with promise, it ended with biting disappointments. He was scheduled to ride as a member of the Lejeune-BP team in the Tour that year with the defending champion, but a bad race crash days before the start deprived him of his chance. At the end of the season at the world championships in Venezuela, he contracted an intestinal virus. The lingering virus forced him to miss the 1978 Tour. Boyer, a wiry 5 feet 11 inches at 150 pounds, was positively emaciated at 125 pounds. His performances that year were erratic. By the end of the season he returned home and competed in local races.

In 1980, his health and fitness restored, he returned to France and joined the Puch-Campagnolo team. That got him back into action. He rode well in the mountainous, eleven-stage Tour of Switzerland. At the world championships in Sallanches, France, Boyer finished fifth in the professional 168-mile road race. Cyrille Guimard, team director of the Renault-Gitane team, signed Boyer up to ride the next season for his team. Captain of the team was Bernard Hinault, winner of the world championship road race that year, and a major force in cycling, with victories in the 1978 and 1979 Tours de France.

When Boyer started the 1981 Tour de France, he was already well known in France. The French press called him Jacques. Sometimes they called him *Le Cowboy* for the Wyoming license plate with the bucking bronco on his car.

Boyer's role on the team was to help support Hinault, and he subordinated his performances to Hinault's. That meant chasing after breakaways with team members, including Hinault, who was sheltered from the wind by his teammates. When the breakaways were caught, Hinault

was fresh to sprint away. Boyer's best performance during the 1981
Tour was ninth in the longest stage, 160 miles.

After three weeks and 2,500 miles that wound around France and
included stages in Switzerland and Belgium, Boyer raced up the
Champs-Elysees in Paris to a respectable thirty-second-place finish in
front of the Arc de Triomphe. The twenty-five-year-old Boyer, and
American cycling in general, had come a long way.

While Boyer's fifth place at the 1980 world professional road-racing
championship demonstrated that he was indeed a racer to contend with,
two American women continued to give the men something to look up
to.

Sue Novara won her second gold medal in the women's match-race
sprints. And Beth Heiden, who won a bronze medal in the 1980 Winter
Olympics as a speed skater, won a gold medal by sprinting away from
the lead pack of four at the finish of the thirty-six-mile race.

Europeans could see that the Americans were coming. The one who
was quickest to act was Cyrille Guimard, team manager of Renault-
Gitane. A former professional himself, Guimard was an innovative man
in a sport bound to tradition. He was the first to have his riders convert
from wool jerseys and shorts to slicker Lycra outfits to cut down wind
resistance.

In 1980, Guimard, among others, spotted LeMond when he won the
Circuit de la Sarthe in western France. A little later, LeMond showed
Guimard the fiery temperament the Frenchman liked to see paired with
such talent. It happened after a team of Soviets broke away in a French
race and LeMond chased alone, between the breakaway and the peloton, until a tire punctured. He had to wait five minutes for the American
support car to arrive and give him a wheel replacement. By the time
his support car arrived, LeMond was so angry and disgusted that he
picked up his bike and threw it at the car. Guimard admired that. At the
end of the summer, he and world champion and Tour de France winner
Bernard Hinault went to America to recruit LeMond to ride for Renault-
Gitane.

LeMond's home lies on the outskirts of Carson City, between Reno
and Lake Tahoe, at 4,500 feet altitude in the high desert that leads to
the Sierra Nevadas. In 1975, the LeMond family was introduced to the

Beth Heiden speed-skated in the 1980 Winter Olympics and later that summer won the world championship road race for women in Sallanches, France. (*Robert F. George*)

Jonathan Boyer left California for France, and in 1980 became the first American to ride in the Tour de France. His success in Europe helped lead the way for the modern invasion of Americans. (*Tom Moran*) sport when a race went past their home. The northern California district championship—which includes Nevada—had a road-race circuit that included Franktown Road, the two-lane country road where the Le-Mond family lives. Greg and his father, Bob, stood out on the front lawn of their two-story house and watched their first race.

Greg and Bob LeMond were skiers, but they became cycling converts right away. Bob LeMond was thirty-eight when he started riding. He soon became a strong racer who got better as the races became longer. He passed up veterans races (for those over thirty-five) and worked his way up from Category IV to Category I. Bob LeMond took on all races and competed in the Red Zinger Colorado Classic, the stage race designated as America's national tour and now called the Coors Classic.

Greg LeMond is easygoing and spontaneous off the bike; on it he is fierce, "a cold killer in a race," according to Jack Simes III. His aggression is relentless. Bernard Hinault saw him race and right away liked what he saw. The Frenchman's own reputation for relentlessness earned him the sobriquet *Le Blaireau,* the Badger, known for never giving in. He and Guimard traveled to Carson City to sign up LeMond, where Hinault told reporters, "Greg will be the next champion after me."

The blond, latter-day Bobby Walthour was still nineteen in May 1981 when he scored his first professional victory for the Renault-Gitane team. He won the sixty-five-mile stage of the Tour de l'Oise in France. LeMond earned his place in the peloton.

LeMond's team director, Guimard, kept him on a light racing schedule in his first year as a pro. When Boyer raced the Tour de France, LeMond returned to the States to compete against a strong Soviet team at the Coors Classic stage race. The nine-stage event that year came to a showdown between LeMond and the top Soviets, with LeMond coming in on top.

At summer's end, LeMond and Boyer went to the world championships in Prague, Czechoslovakia, for the professional road race. George Mount joined them, making three American pros in the race.

Since turning professional in May 1980 after President Carter's boycott kept Americans out of the Olympics, Mount had been racing in Italy on the Benotto racing team. In 1981, he entered the Italian big time when he competed in the Giro d'Italia, the country's three-week stage race that ranks second only to the Tour de France. Mount finished a respectable twenty-fifth place after working for his team leader.

The three Americans rode well in the 175-mile world championship road race but finished in the back of the field. They were upstaged at the worlds by Shiela Young-Ochowicz. Back in 1976, she had married Jim Ochowicz, retired from competition after winning the world sprint championship, and had a daughter. When her daughter Kate began nursery school, the athlete in Young-Ochowicz hungered for a new challenge. She got back into shape, won the national women's sprint championship, and made headlines again when she won her third gold medal in the women's match-race championship.

It was LeMond, however, who rode to a height that no American would soon follow. In 1983 at the 169-mile world championship road race in Berne, Switzerland, he launched a solo that established him as one of the world's major contenders. For fifteen laps over a hilly 9.4-mile circuit, racing against the best professionals in the world, LeMond was always near the front of the pack. After 140 miles, only forty-six were left when Robert Millar, the small Scotsman, attacked up the long hill that reduced the field each lap. LeMond counterattacked immediately, out of the saddle and dancing powerfully on his pedals up the grade, and escaped. Only Italy's Moreno Argentin and Spain's Faustino Ruperez could go with him.

Three hundred thousand spectators lined the course and cheered as twenty-two-year-old LeMond kept on the pressure. Behind the trio, Belgians like Claude Criquielion and Lucien Van Impe sped to the head of the peloton to reel back LeMond and his two partners while the strong Italian team tried to interfere to protect the interest of their rider in the breakaway.

LeMond's companions dashed over the top and shot down the descent. LeMond continued forcing the pace on the flat stretch that took them to the finish area to start the last two laps. Thousands of spectators roared their approval at the audacity of the American who had taken over the race. The peloton charged through the finish area 29 seconds later.

Up a short climb before the big hill where the breakaway was born, Argentin faded off the back, taking with him Italy's chance of winning.

As a professional cyclist, LeMond knows the value of avoiding dehydration during a race under the summer sun. (*Michael Furman*)

OPPOSITE. When the dynamic Greg LeMond entered the sport, American cycling caught fire again. He leans through a turn in his amateur days in the late 1970s. (*Tom Moran*)

Spectators went wild in excitement as they saw that the rest of the Italian team continued to stall the peloton and protect their rider, who actually was no longer in the breakaway. By the time the Italians caught on to LeMond's strategy, it was too late for a successful chase.

LeMond kept forcing the tempo up the big climb and dropped the Spaniard. That left LeMond free to ride the last lap alone. For the first time ever, the red, white, and blue U.S. team jersey of stars and stripes was out alone in the grueling professional road race. LeMond's tactics and execution were appreciated by the spectators. LeMond had orchestrated a breakaway that took advantage of team rivalries while, unlike the Italians, French, Belgians, and other Europeans, he raced without the aid of a team.

Now, riding alone on the last lap of the 1983 world championship road race, LeMond was clearly America's cycling superstar. The entire last lap was his. And he rode it faster than any previous lap, increasing his lead to 1 minute 11 seconds.

Tens of thousands of spectators were so excited when he crossed the finish line that they swarmed over the road. The rest of the riders, sprinting for their places, were rushing headlong toward a wall of humanity. At the end of a seven-hour ordeal, America, in the figure of Greg LeMond, had reigned supreme in the professional world championship road race.

15 THE DROUGHT ENDS

The 1984 Summer Olympic Games in Los Angeles opened with the first-ever women's cycling event—a 49.9-mile road race. Under a searing July sun and over a hilly and rigorous 9.4-mile course in Mission Viejo, the race for medals became highly tactical. On the fifth and final lap, two U.S. riders—Connie Carpenter and Rebecca Twigg—had broken away with four others from West Germany, France, Norway, and Italy.

Two hundred thousand spectators cheered them around the course. The odds against both Americans winning medals seemed great. The tactical object would be for one to help the other rather than blow the chance altogether for America to place in the top three.

Carpenter has won national titles as a speed skater, rower, and cyclist. At fourteen, she competed as a speed skater in the 1972 Winter Olympics in Sapporo, Japan. In 1976, she won the women's national outdoor title. While training that year for the Olympic skating trials, she injured an ankle. A friend suggested that she take up cycling, a sport she immediately enjoyed.

Carpenter won national championships in her first season—in the women's road race and on the track in the 3,000-meter (1.9-mile) pursuit event. More national titles followed as she dominated women's racing in 1977, a year she capped with a silver medal at the world road-racing championship in Venezuela.

But early in the 1978 season she fell from her bicycle and suffered a concussion. She quit cycling to resume her studies at the University of California at Berkeley. There she branched out to rowing on the crew team. At 5 feet 10 inches and 130 pounds, Carpenter was well suited to rowing: her long torso gave her great reach for longer rowing strokes. She made the women's varsity shell the first year. In 1980 she rowed on the varsity women's coxed four shell which won the national collegiate championship in Oak Ridge, Tennessee.

Carpenter might have stayed away from cycling altogether if she hadn't met her future husband, Davis Phinney, a Boulder, Colorado, rider who was winning so many races he was called the Cash Register. Phinney convinced Carpenter that she had not realized her full potential in the sport.

Women's sponsorship had improved by 1981 when she resumed cycling. She received a sponsorship with Puch bicycles which included a stipend to help meet living expenses, an important factor because cycling at the national level requires traveling 150 to 200 days a year.

By then she had graduated with a degree in physical education, which she was putting to good use. Her return to cycling started successfully, but her domination was thwarted by a new star—Rebecca Twigg of Seattle. Twigg, shorter by four inches, lighter by five pounds, and younger by six years, was the only one who could beat Carpenter. At the 1982 world championships in England, Twigg and Carpenter competed against each other in the final of the pursuit event, the timed velodrome event where riders race at opposite ends of the track for 3,000 meters (1.9 miles). Twigg beat Carpenter for the gold medal.

Twigg's fast rise in cycling paralleled her academic performances. At age fourteen, she enrolled at the University of Washington. She wound up postponing the completion of her degree in biology to train full time for the Olympics and became a permanent resident at the Olympic Training Center in Colorado Springs.

In the Olympics road race, both Carpenter and Twigg were buoyed by 200,000 enthusiastic spectators lining the course that wound through suburban Los Angeles. Many set up camps the day before and held overnight barbecue parties to keep their places. Some climbed trees for a better view, and a few climbed streetlights. Crowds waved flags and chanted "U!S!A! U!S!A!"

Spectators easily recognized both women. Carpenter's angular face framed by long, curly, strawberry-blond hair and Twigg's cherubic one had accompanied pre-Olympic newspaper and magazine articles. Thousands of fans called out their names as they rode by.

"It definitely made a big difference," Carpenter points out. "What made the Olympics special was that a number of us had raced in the world championships several times where the support wasn't there, so we appreciated the support in the Olympics."

The pack of fifteen riders trailing the breakaway on the final lap included two of Carpenter and Twigg's teammates. They chased down any rider attempting to charge away to bridge the gap, and occasionally got to the front and held the pace in check.

Carpenter and Twigg looked in control during the final lap. Their movements were sure and efficient, even when they drank from the plastic water bottles they carried. Twigg had had the edge five weeks before when the team was selected at the Olympic cycling trials. Since then, however, Carpenter had focused her training to sharpen her sprint.

After riding up the last major climb, a steep slope in Vista del Lago, and swooping swiftly down the other side, the six leaders began eyeing one another closely to detect signs of the next breakaway. Over the final mile, thousands of spectators on the course and millions watching the television broadcast were wondering whether it would be Carpenter or Twigg to break the seventy-two-year dry spell for U.S. cyclists in the Olympics.

With 500 yards left, Maria Canins of Italy got out of her saddle and began to sprint. It was still too far from the finish to expect her to sustain the effort, but it made the others scramble in pursuit. They immediately strung out behind Canins, content to find a rear wheel to draft behind as the speed built for determining whose names would go in the record books as the first Olympic women's cycling medalists.

In the final 200 yards, Twigg dashed to the front. With each pedal stroke carrying her closer to the gold medal, she rode confidently, with poise, her legs churning faster and faster until her legs and feet became a blur.

Yet Carpenter was coming up fast on her right. With 3 yards left,

Twigg was leading. Both had their heads down, and their elbows were bent from pulling on the handlebars as they squeezed the last juices of strength from their legs. Behind them, the others were racing for the bronze medal.

A yard from the finish, Carpenter drew even with Twigg. Then Carpenter, the seasoned veteran of twelve years of international competition, eased up off her saddle and straightened her arms in front to throw her bike forward over the line—a cyclist's burst for the finish the way a runner leans at the tape. She closed her eyes at the line, then opened them and looked to Twigg at her left. As they coasted past the finish, they came together and Carpenter kissed Twigg on the cheek. They had clinched the top two medals in the Olympics. They were so

Connie Carpenter, left, and Rebecca Twigg radiate the thrill of winning gold and silver medals, respectively, in the inaugural women's cycling road race at the 1984 Olympics in Los Angeles. (*Michael Furman*)

close at the finish that the judges had to examine photos before they ruled Carpenter the winner.

Nobody could take anything away from the American victory, even though the Communist countries boycotted the Los Angeles Olympics in retaliation for President Carter's boycott of the Moscow Games four years earlier. The women's cycling race was unaffected by the boycott: Eastern-bloc countries did not excel in women's road races the way they did in track and field. In Los Angeles on a late-July morning, women cyclists rode into the Olympics and the United States rode out of cycling medal poverty.

Less than seven miles remained in the men's Olympic road race when the lead rider, Alexi Grewal of Aspen, Colorado, seemed shattered. Six miles earlier he had burst brilliantly from the breakaway of seven to build up a twenty-three-second lead, pedaling strongly like a sure winner. Now, however, after 111 miles of racing under a burning July sun, his energy was flagging. When he hit the steep slope of Vista del Lago, the last major climb which took the riders to 920 feet above sea level before the finish, he suddenly looked awful. The gangly 6 foot 2 inch, twenty-three-year-old who had earned his reputation by riding fast up hills was so fatigued that he had to zigzag up the grade.

His chance for a gold medal appeared all but over. If Grewal could get to the top before the others got him in sight, there was the outside possibility that he could recover on the descent. But once his competition saw the way he struggled, they would close in for the kill, and his race for any Olympic medal would be over.

The cheering for Grewal seemed forlorn as he fought his way up the steep slope. Guts and determination he had in abundance, but they might not be enough. As he zigged and zagged, it seemed he had spent his energy too soon, just as he had done at the amateur world championship road race the previous September, where he had finished fourteenth.

Suddenly from behind came Canadian Steve Bauer. Bauer, a more sturdily built athlete, caught Grewal on the hill and flashed past. Still out of sight but moving quickly to catch up were the remaining five leaders and behind them was the chasing pack of Olympic cyclists from more than two dozen countries.

Spectators on the course and the tens of millions watching television—most of them seeing bicycle races for the first time—wanted Grewal to hang in with Bauer as long as he could. Much to everyone's surprise, and perhaps to his own, Grewal rallied. He managed to catch Bauer's rear wheel and draft. That reduced his wind resistance, but it didn't make the hill any less steep. Yet every pedal stroke Grewal took with the seemingly fresh Canadian meant their pursuers were held at bay that much longer. Grewal still had a chance for an Olympic medal if he could be pulled by Bauer long enough.

Bauer led Grewal over the crest of the hill and the two riders barreled down the other side. Bauer's explosive finishing sprint was well known, and he appeared headed for Canada's first cycling medal. The blond, powerfully built Bauer had won many races, but was occasionally beaten. Two years earlier, he had been edged out at the finish of the Commonwealth Games road race in Australia.

Grewal was one of the country's most flamboyant, if not erratic, riders. The year before, he won a demanding ninety-two-mile race in Colorado's Rocky Mountains all alone, carrying his bike over the finish line, then collapsing with leg cramps. He was also emotional and had once left his team on a European tour. Until just before the Olympics, no one was sure he would even compete. The U.S. Cycling Federation disqualified him from leading a Colorado stage race when he tested positive for traces of ephedrine, an alkaloid found in many over-the-counter cold remedies as well as in Dr. Pepper and herbal tea. He was given a thirty-day suspension that included the Olympics. Just days before the Olympic torch was lit for the Summer Games the test was ruled to have been administered improperly and he was reinstated. Grewal vowed to win the Olympic gold medal.

Late afternoon shadows fell over the final mile of the course. Bauer steadily picked up the pace while Grewal remained close behind. At one point, the two riders looked over their shoulders—not at each other but to see that they still had a comfortable margin over their pursuers. Two Norwegian cyclists had broken away from the breakaway to chase after Grewal and Bauer.

With 300 yards to go, Grewal and Bauer were far enough ahead so that they had a match race. Bauer had always beaten Grewal in the past, and he made the first move now. Grewal rode snugly behind, as Bauer pedaled faster and faster. With less than 100 yards left, Grewal got out of his saddle and unleashed everything he had. Bauer dug down and worked harder, but it wasn't enough. Grewal out-accelerated him and burst past to beat him to the line by a wheel.

It was a stunning victory. Here was another gold for the United States on the opening day of the Olympic Summer Games.

At the end of the Games the United States had won nine medals—including four golds. The seventy-two-year dry spell was over. Although the Eastern bloc boycotted the Games, fifty-two nations participated, including those European countries that had been the dominant force in the sport for so long.

While American cyclists took turns going to the Olympic awards podium, an American woman continued to lead the men to the top of the sport in Europe. Just as Audrey McElmury was the first to wear the rainbow jersey and Connie Carpenter the first to win an Olympic gold medal, Marianne Martin of Boulder in 1984 became the first American to wear the yellow jersey that designates race leader of the Tour de France.

The tradition of wearing the *maillot jaune* began when the Tour was resumed shortly after World War I. Henri Desgrange, the newspaper publisher who had created the Tour, came up with the idea to enable spectators to pick out the race leader as the peloton swarmed past. The color was inspired by the yellow pages of Desgrange's publication, *L'Auto,* predecessor to *L'Equipe,* the French newspaper devoted to sports.

Today the 2,500-mile Tour is an international spectacle that draws an estimated thirty million spectators. More than 450 journalists report on the race, and 500 million people worldwide avidly follow it. Every day for three weeks in July the race tours the country, following a different route each year. Most stages typically last four to seven hours, and each ends in a different designated city or village. A fleet of about 800 vehicles—a mobile caravan more than nine miles long including journalists, visiting dignitaries, and support vehicles for the riders—follows the race.

So strong is the hold of the Tour on the French that sports columnist Red Smith explained it to American readers thus: "There is a saying here that an army from Mars could invade France, that the government could fall, and even the recipe for sauce bernaise could be lost, but if it happened during the Tour de France, nobody would notice."

In 1984 Tour organizers introduced the inaugural Tour for women, the Tour du France Féminin. The United States nearly went unrepresented. The U.S. Cycling Federation announced that because the best women riders were participating in the Olympics, it would not send a team to the Tour as well. The North Jersey Women's Bicycle Club sent a six-rider team, but its members wore jerseys supplied by a French company because they could not wear U.S. national team jerseys, and a French company supplied them with bicycles. Final selection of the team was not determined until two weeks before the riders boarded their Air France jet. The last rider picked was Marianne Martin.

"I begged and pleaded to get on the team," she said. "I hadn't been riding all that well in February and March. I was overtrained and anemic. It was April before I could really train to turn my condition around. I got back into form in early June. I knew I was a good climber. I really do like to climb. I just made it on the team."

She and five others lined up for the start of the eighteen-stage race against teams from Holland, England, Canada, and two from France. Women were to race the last thirty-five to fifty miles of the men's stages, finishing about two hours before the men.

From the start near Paris in northwestern France, the Dutch women dominated the early flat stages. Martin hung in with the peloton for the group sprints at the end of each stage.

One of her teammates was Betsy King, who had moved to France four years earlier to train with the Paris amateur club, Antony Berny Cycliste. She also had the distinction a month before the Tour of being the first woman to complete the 365-mile Bordeaux-Paris race, a one-day event held every year since the Victorian era. Martin expected to ride as support for King.

The extreme competitiveness of the race wore mentally and physically on the American team. Their lack of a coach led to a loss of cohesion after the race started. Each member had an opinion on how to do the race, which led to infighting. Martin found she was ignored when it came time to plan how they were going to race. After four stages, she felt that she wanted to go home but was encouraged by her teammate, Patty Peoples, an upbeat rider who didn't let infighting bother her.

Martin raced into shape, and by the time they got to the Alps she was strong, unlike King, who was still recovering from her Bordeaux-Paris

Marianne Martin, who was the last member chosen for the
inaugural Tour de France Feminin in 1984, raced into shape
as the three-week race went on and won by a wide margin.
(*Graham Watson*)

effort. The fourteenth stage was only 20 miles long but climbed nearly a mile in altitude to La Plagne, one of France's most popular ski resorts. Martin rode away from the front and went on to win by nearly four minutes, a decisive victory that changed the race completely. Martin was the first U.S. rider to win a stage of the Tour and to wear the *maillot jaune.* (Greg LeMond was riding his first Tour that year and went on to win the white jersey, the *maillot blanc,* as top rookie in the Tour, finishing third overall.)

Martin's teammates began to ride for her as they took over the team competition. Martin wore the yellow jersey into the final stage in Paris, despite strong opposition from the Dutch team, which ultimately won fifteen of the eighteen stages over the 620-mile race.

The final stage was fifty miles long and finished in Paris after eight laps on a circuit up and down the tree-lined Champs-Elysees. Two million spectators turned out for the final day's action. As the pack of racers sped around in a tight bunch, Martin was surprised to hear a familiar voice call her name from behind a street barricade.

On the next lap, she looked at the place where she had heard her name and saw her dad, who had flown in from his home in Fenton, Michigan, to watch his daughter win the inaugural Tour du France Féminin.

16 THE AMERICANS ARE COMING, THE AMERICANS ARE COMING

For the first time since the days of John M. Chapman, bicycle racing in America has matured enough to lure European riders here to compete. Greater American public interest in the sport has attracted more attention from major corporations and the rules governing amateurs have been made less strict. Amateurs are now permitted to win as much as $2,000 a day without jeopardizing their standing with the U.S. Cycling Federation; any amount over $2,000 goes into an individual trust fund that athletes can draw from upon retirement. Corporations as diverse as Pepsi, Ore-Ida Potatoes, Prince Spaghetti, and Subaru as well as breweries such as Coors, Molson, Budweiser, and Miller sponsor races here with better budgets than many in Europe. Companies that sponsor teams with substantial budgets include the 7-Eleven food-store chain, Alfa Romeo and Plymouth cars, Campbell Soup, Lowrey's Seasonings, Weight Watchers, and numerous bicycle makers in the United States, Japan, and Europe.

The growth of cycling is reflected in the Federation's budget and membership. Its budget tripled from 1980 to 1984, reaching nearly $1.5 million. About 40 percent of the revenue comes from membership dues, with about the same amount coming from a combination of corporate contributions and U.S. Olympic Committee support. Membership doubled in five years to more than 23,000 in 1986, then jumped 20 percent more in 1987 to top 28,000. There is now a full-time staff of about twenty who coach, administer records, conduct training camps, help members, and carry out other support work.

Home-grown talent is nurtured at the Federation's headquarters at the Olympic Training Center in Colorado Springs, on the site of the decommissioned air force base. There all athletes of all disciplines take advantage of the latest in sports medicine, physiology testing, and biomechanical data. USCF officials liken the organization's structure to a broad-based pyramid, with the best amateur riders, in Category I, at the top of an expanding number of lower categories. Development camps for road and track racing, aimed at developing varying levels of ability, are held regularly at the OTC in Colorado Springs, Lake Placid, and Squaw Valley, depending on the time of year. The Colorado Springs training center is where the sprinters go to use the 333-meter (365-yard) cement velodrome, where several world records have been set. Riders train in groups with on-bike coaching, and attend classes on tactics, nutrition, and training techniques. The three-week training camps are free and typically start each day at 8:30 in the morning and continue to 9 P.M.

"Anyone who attends a camp improves at least twenty-five percent," four-time national champion Nancy Baranet contends. "They learn more at the camp than they would on their own, and they go back home to pass on what they've learned. That helps raise the standards for everybody."

The Olympic Training Center can accommodate more than 500 athletes. Mealtime often looks like an international conference of athletes and coaches discussing their sports—gymnastics, boxing, basketball, weight lifting, and, of course, bicycle racing.

Membership of the national bicycle team fluctuates, but usually there are forty men on the A and B road teams, another twenty men on the track team, twenty women road riders, and ten women track cyclists.

All national team members are provided with clothing and equipment. The A team riders receive a stipend as well. Each year, national team members travel to twenty-five international amateur events in Europe, Latin America, Australia, and Japan. In the late 1980s, top amateurs have their expenses covered and earn modest but comfortable incomes that can top $20,000. The days when riders trained after putting in a day on a job are long gone.

With competitive standards rising and better races proliferating, more riders are able to make a living as racers. USCF officials complain, understandably, that their best riders leave to become professional, although they concede that many riders still enter the sport, and thus join the USCF, to emulate the professionals. American professional racing took a great leap upward after Greg LeMond won the world road-racing championship and signed a three-year contract with the French team La Vie Claire paying him a million dollars, plus lucrative product endorsements.

With more corporations backing races under the now-liberal rules governing amateurs, professionals and top amateurs compete against one another in many of the same domestic events. In 1985, ten members of the 7-Eleven team—one of the top U.S. professional cycling teams—made a six-week racing tour that included the first organized American effort in the Italian tour, the three-week Giro d'Italia.

Jonathan Boyer was hired to ride with the team to share his continental experience. "It was great," Boyer exclaims. "It was something I always dreamed of—riding in Europe with an American team."

Most stages—of three to six hours each—ended in mass sprints. Nearly every day for three weeks, more than a hundred riders formed a hydra-headed pack barreling down the final stretch at speeds of 45 miles an hour and faster. These finishes favored Davis Phinney, who eight times finished in the top ten. His Boulder, Colorado, teammates Andy Hampsten and Ron Kiefel won stages after breaking away in the mountains. Eric Heiden, best known for sweeping all five 1980 speedskating gold medals, was another 7-Eleven team surprise when he won the "catch sprints" prize for designated sprints within certain stages along the way.

For the first time ever, an American professional cycling team made its presence felt in Europe.

American riders, like those on the 7-Eleven team, go to Europe for crucial experience and ultimate conditioning, and European riders come here for prize lists far superior to those in Europe.

One of the races that attracts European professionals is the Core-States Championship, the 156-mile U.S. professional road race championship in mid-June in Philadelphia. The $20,000 first prize, more than most European professionals earn in a year, was at the top of the $105,000 prize list, greater than any sum for a one-day race in Europe. (Paris-Roubaix, the greatest one-day classic in northern France, had a prize list in 1987 of $43,000.)

Behind the CoreStates race, which began in 1985, is Olympian Dave Chauner, who traded his racing uniform for a three-piece suit to begin promoting races with Jack Simes III. They started holding race programs in the late 1970s at the Lehigh County Velodrome near Allen-

Eric Heiden is best remembered for sweeping five gold medals in speed skating at the 1980 Winter Olympics in Lake Placid, but he also made his mark in bicycle racing, including winning the 1985 national championship road race in Philadelphia. (*Michael Furman*)

town, Pennsylvania, and headed PRO, the Professional Racing Organization, which controls U.S. professional cycling. Simes became executive director of PRO in 1980.

Chauner subsequently branched out to form International Cycling Productions which organizes professional bicycle races with PRO. His CoreStates race is a bold enterprise that quickly beat many of the odds it faced. Chauner convinced Philadelphia city officials to close down for seven hours on Sunday afternoon fifteen miles of major streets for the course that starts and finishes on the Benjamin Franklin Parkway near the Philadelphia Art Museum. He also raised six-digit funding from the CoreStates Financial Corporation, parent company of the Philadelphia

Eddy Borysewicz gave American riders the support and guidance they needed to win nine medals in the 1984 Olympics. Here he holds up Leonard (Harvey) Nitz for the start of the 1986 world championships in Colorado Springs where Nitz won a bronze medal in the 31-mile points race on the velodrome. (Michael Furman)

National Bank. KLM Royal Dutch Airlines joined as a sponsor to fly riders in from Europe. Another two dozen companies joined up as sponsors supplying everything from mineral water to portable telephones. The Union Cycliste Internationale was so impressed with the presentation Simes made to their governing body in Rome that they put the event on the international race schedule, and professional teams in turn put the race on their itinerary.

The world cycling championships were held in Colorado Springs late in the summer of 1986—the first world championship program held in the United States since the 1912 worlds in Newark. More than 700 riders came from fifty-five countries. Big things were expected for the Colorado Springs world championships—they marked the first time since 1980 that Russian and American athletes competed against one another in a major international sporting event. Expectations were that U.S. riders would repeat their medal haul from the Los Angeles Olympics, spectators would flock to the races, and the eleven days of events would generate major media coverage. Instead, no U.S. rider won any of the sixteen events, attendance was surprisingly light, and the worlds did not become the media event that was expected.

U.S. riders were not without scintillating performances, though. Leonard (Harvey) Nitz pulled off a brilliant sprint victory at the end of the thirty-one-mile points race on the velodrome to finish with a bronze medal. Tandem sprint riders David Lindsey and Kit Kyle were the B team, yet they advanced all the way to the final before they lost to wind up with a silver medal. On a cold, raw day in the women's thirty-eight-mile road race, Janelle Parks rode through a Rocky Mountain mist to finish surprisingly strong and win a silver medal. Two other women proved to be the country's remaining medal winners—Rebecca Twigg with a silver in the 1.9-mile women's pursuit race, and match-race sprinter Connie Paraskevin, who won a bronze medal.

Some race programs at the 365-yard 7-Eleven Velodrome in Memorial Park, Colorado Springs, which seats 8,200, were sold out, but most programs had vacant seats. Even when the velodrome was sold out, it is worth noting that attendance was only two-thirds of Newark's world championships. The world championship road races held on the Air Force Academy grounds had even fewer attendees distributed over the

9.3-mile course. Unseasonably cold weather and rainstorms discouraged spectators.

Television network coverage in this country was limited as a result
of a breakdown in negotiations with the major television networks.
Corporate advertising painted on the cement velodrome surface became the irreconcilable issue. Network executives, pointing out that
they would be giving away free advertising each time a rider was shown
passing the ads, withdrew from the negotiations.

But while the amount of media attention and number of medals that
U.S. cyclists won did not compare with the Los Angeles Olympics, U.S.
cycling was propelled that summer by Greg LeMond in Europe. The
tremendous publicity he generated overseas after his success in the
1986 Tour de France had a profound effect on the sport in this country.
In 1985, Bernard Hinault and Greg LeMond were teammates on La Vie
Claire (The Good Life) team. LeMond was the dutiful lieutenant who
helped the Frenchman win the Tour for the fifth time, a feat that
elevated Hinault to equal the record of Belgium's Eddy Merckx and
France's Jacques Anquetil.

Hinault performed with great panache in winning his fifth Tour. He
broke away up a climb that connects the upper Rhône valley with the
Abondance valley in a show of strength that gave him a commanding
overall lead.

LeMond's allegiance to Hinault in that race was put to a dramatic test.
Two weeks into the Tour, Hinault was wearing the leader's *maillot
jaune* when he got caught in a pileup during the sprint for the finish
of a stage. He fell face first to the asphalt. His face dripping with blood,
he remounted his bike and pedaled to the finish. He was rushed to a
hospital where X rays showed he had a double fracture of the bridge
of his nose.

Over the next couple of days, Hinault, his eyes blackened, rode in
obvious discomfort as the race approached the Pyrenees, the mountain
chain that presented the greatest obstacle in his quest for victory on
the road to Paris. Hinault's broken nose limited him to breathing
through his mouth, which caused problems when the race went up
mountains a mile and more high. Three days after his accident, the
seventeenth stage went up and down three major climbs that disappeared in the clouds.

Attacks that amounted to a climbing free-for-all in a thick fog resulted in LeMond breaking away on the second climb with three light climbers who rode as though they had wings. Hinault fell behind as the field strung out according to climbing abilities. A Swiss teammate aided Hinault by letting him draft as they got into the second climb, and La Vie Claire team car zoomed up to LeMond, riding gamely with the leaders. LeMond's team coach told him to let the others go rather than risk jeopardizing Hinault's race leadership.

The impetuous American argued. He was second overall and saw this as his chance to make up his deficit on Hinault and become the new race leader. But the coach would not hear any argument from LeMond who finally gave in to sharp orders. He let the three others disappear ahead into the fog. At the finish, he erupted in anger. LeMond got off his bike and broke into tears. When a Dutch television journalist ventured too close, LeMond snapped, "You want a punch in the mouth?"

All of France—and the sporting world—followed the race passionately to see if Hinault could keep the *maillot jaune.* Or if LeMond would take it. What developed was a form of compromise—not tendered but forged in the competition against 144 international professionals. LeMond won a time trial stage, a major victory and his first stage win. Hinault persevered to wear the *maillot jaune* all the way to Paris and win with a margin of less than 2 minutes. On the victory podium in Paris, Hinault announced he would help LeMond win in 1986. That was generous from the man who said the next Tour would be his last so that he could retire on his thirty-second birthday. But bicycle racing is not that predictable; nor is Hinault.

The 1986 Tour de France was hyped in American newspapers, magazines, and weekly CBS television specials. Superlatives described the seventy-third Tour: a record 210 racers were starting the grueling 2,542-mile race over one of the most mountainous courses in Tour history. Americans were proud: for the first time, an all-American team was entered; the 7-Eleven squad was composed of eight from the United States, a Canadian, and a Mexican. And they were prouder still because Greg LeMond, riding for La Vie Claire, was the pre-race favorite. The previous seventy-two Tours had all been won by Europeans.

From the first day, the Tour generated surprises, turning it into the setting for many of the sport's best moments. The staid European cycling community was briefly shocked when 7-Eleven's Alex Stieda of Canada donned the yellow jersey after the first stage. He had broken away on the fifty-three-mile morning run and accumulated enough time bonuses by the finish that even though he was fifth he became race leader. Three hours later in the thirty-five-mile team time trial, Stieda was so spent that he lost the jersey and struggled just to make the time limit to remain in the race.

Then Davis Phinney got in a breakaway in the third stage and won the sprint to claim the stage. The presence of a Hollywood film crew shooting footage for the movie *Yellow Jersey,* starring Dustin Hoffman, got the peloton revved up for the eleventh—and longest—stage, 169 miles.

The race then broke into a monumental battle that will be remembered as one of the best Tours in history. LeMond started the Tour expecting support from the man he had helped the year before, only to find his greatest rival was that very man—Bernard Hinault. Midway through the race, Hinault was in the yellow jersey. LeMond was in distress.

It had become evident to LeMond that Hinault wanted to retire with a record six Tour victories. Hinault is a handsome, muscular man with a square jaw and photogenic features that could make him a movie star. He is also a showman. On the twelfth stage, Hinault attacked on the mountainous road that the Basques call the Cross of Iron. Only the Spaniard Pedro Delgado could go with him. Delgado helped share the drafting as the two increased their advantage over the rest. Hinault rewarded him by easing up near the finish and the Spaniard won the stage. Hinault gladly gave up the stage victory to take over the race—he had the yellow jersey and a lead of more than 5 minutes on LeMond who was—again—in second place overall.

Hinault's strategy and show of strength made him a hero to the thousands who lined the road. They chanted his name and painted it in large letters on the road. Only a few years before the French wouldn't have been so supportive. He won Tours efficiently, but without the overwhelming margins that made the public want to see him cut loose and trounce the competition. Then he had a bad season, underwent knee surgery, and was forced off the Renault-Gitane team. Hinault was seen as a has-been.

He came back in 1984 to form a new team, La Vie Claire, distinguishable in red, white, and black jerseys in a pattern modeled after French artist Piet Mondrian. Hinault the underdog finished second in the Tour that year and won it the next time, becoming more popular than ever. In 1986, the French did not see that he had betrayed LeMond—Hinault was the swaggering Breton showing panache in the best tradition of *La Républic.* His charging up hard climbs was a game of catch-me-if-you-can. And the crowds loved it.

LeMond, for all his talent, was criticized for not showing more of it. In the Giro d'Italia, considered a tune-up for the Tour, he finished fourth—not as good as his second-place finish to Hinault the year before. LeMond was third in the Tour of Switzerland, and came equally close in a few major one-day classics. He was not taking the risks the public thought he should take to win.

It didn't matter that Hinault was finishing twenty-third or forty-eighth in events of comparable stature that season. He had already won more than 200 professional races, including five Tours, three Giros, a world championship, several classics, and that—in the eyes of the French public—gave him license to change his mind about sacrificing for LeMond and to seek instead the record sixth Tour victory.

On the thirteenth stage, with three mammoth climbs under a burning sun up and down the Pyrenees for six hours, Hinault boldly attacked. He fled from the lead group of sixteen, which included LeMond and Hinault's La Vie Claire teammates Andy Hampsten and Canadian Steve Bauer. Hinault soon gained 2 minutes. If he held that lead over the next two remaining climbs before the finish, he would have such a decisive lead over LeMond that the Tour would be virtually over.

LeMond's group, however, included several of the best climbers from other teams, who had reasons of their own for pursuing Hinault. His lead was trimmed to 25 seconds by the time he crested the next-to-last mountain. After a long descent, they faced the final climb, up a mountain called Superbagneres, which led to the finish banner ten miles away. Hinault's chasers caught him at the base of the climb. That left him to make the climb with the others and try again to force his way into the lead.

On Superbagneres, however, it became clear that Hinault had gone too far and had to pay the price. He struggled up the slope and fell farther behind. Hampsten, the wiry teammate LeMond had recruited, proved to be more of a force than anyone expected, and led LeMond at a brisk tempo. He set LeMond up for the final attack that led to LeMond winning the stage alone. When LeMond crossed the line, spectators at the finish held watches to see how much time passed before Hinault got in. More than 4 minutes later, he arrived, his overall lead chopped to a slim 40 seconds.

It was headline sports, and it wasn't over. Three stages later, Hinault got away again in a mountainous stretch with a group that didn't include LeMond. It seemed that La Vie Claire had split—a faction of European riders backed Hinault, and Hampsten and Bauer backed LeMond. Hinault was unable to gain time on LeMond by the finish of that stage. But the tension within La Vie Claire made the race as dramatic off the bikes as it was on them.

By the seventeenth stage, the arduous race had taken such a toll that more than a quarter of the starters had dropped out. More were to quit in this mountainous stage. It was a decisive stage: LeMond got away in a group that did not include Hinault, and the American attacked with others to rip the race apart. By the time LeMond crossed the finish line after nearly 6 hours of racing, he moved into first place in the general classification. He had a lead of more than 2 minutes over Hinault. LeMond at last donned the yellow jersey.

Yet with six stages remaining, LeMond was still anxious. He openly complained that he hoped Hinault would work for him. The next day, the two giants of the race broke away together, much to the delight of the crowds, now densely packed on the roads. Up the climbs, spectators crowded the roads and left the riders only a narrow path to cut through. There were far fewer spectators on the descents, where riders like LeMond and Hinault were clocked at 66 miles an hour.

It turned into a momentous day. LeMond and Hinault built up a 5-minute lead by the time they had the finish banner in sight. Then the two acted like playmates—patted each other on the back, smiled, and waved to the jubilant crowd all the way to the line.

When LeMond got off his bike, he nervously had his sights set on the victory podium in Paris. His compatriots on the 7-Eleven team, however, just wanted to survive until Paris. The repeated mammoth climbs and day-after-day racing had taken its toll on the first all-American team. Eric Heiden was so fatigued that day that his reflexes slowed and he missed a turn at speed down a long descent. His crash was serious enough that he was helicoptered to a hospital where he was treated for a mild concussion. Davis Phinney went out with a broken wrist after falling off his bike. Only half of the ten-member team was still in the race, with the first 7-Eleven rider, Bob Roll, in sixty-third. LeMond's teammate, Andy Hampsten, was in fourth, which also got him the white jersey for top rookie that LeMond had won in his first Tour.

Five stages remained in the Tour, but first came a rest day, the only rest day in the men's Tour. For riders in cycling's major leagues, rest day typically means they go out for a spin of two to three hours. The rest day was followed by another mountainous stage of 112 miles that had no effect on overall standings. But the following day was a crucial point in the Tour. It was the last individual test—a 35-mile time trial over a hilly and twisting course in St. Etienne that would require power, speed, and precise handling skills.

Drama focused on the duel between LeMond and Hinault. LeMond led the Tour by 2 minutes 43 seconds, a lead that could evaporate by the conclusion of a time trial on a course like the one in St. Etienne. LeMond was burning to win the time trial and thus silence critics who said he was not worthy of winning the Tour. Hinault, a time trial specialist, was cheerfully boasting he was feeling super and indicated he could win back the *maillot jaune.*

Just past the 23-mile point, LeMond rounded a sharp right turn too fast and crashed. Suffering only slight abrasions, he quickly got back on his bike and resumed. Then he discovered that his front brake was rubbing against the rim, so he had to stop and replace the bicycle with one from his support car. Hinault had none of these complications and won yet another time trial stage in the Tour. He beat LeMond, in second, but only by 25 seconds, about the same amount of time the American lost in his crash and bike change. LeMond may have lost the stage, but he showed he had the ability and, most important to the French, the character to be a Tour winner.

The rest of the Tour soon descended to flatter ground, and with it went the suspense, as the remainder of the Tour was a ceremonial ride to Paris, with LeMond still clearly leading the Tour in overall time. After they arrived in Paris, Hinault told reporters that he had pushed LeMond to the limit to win so that later he would know how far he could go. Whether that was Hinault's design as mentor or whether he tried but failed to get the record sixth Tour victory, he was still a hero to the French public.

The French, meanwhile, looked upon LeMond differently. He had taken Hinault's best shots and still beat him. Jacques Goddet, co-director of the Tour, wrote in the French sporting newspaper *L'Equipe,* "This was a Tour unquestionably won without complicity by Greg LeMond, a champion representative of his generation, a very nice young fellow who leaves the hope that there are more like him on the other side of the Atlantic."

Goddet called LeMond "a champion representative." The *Washington Post* suggested LeMond was "America's finest athlete." Frank Kramer would have called him the "one good American rider" that would help bring cycling back as a popular spectator sport in the United States.

After a week of rigorous media demands in Paris, and in his racing home base in Kortrijk, Belgium, LeMond flew across the Atlantic to return to Carson City. But first he stopped in Washington, D.C., for a private meeting with President Reagan in the Oval Office.

Accompanied by his wife, Kathy, who carried their son, Geoffrey, LeMond walked up the White House entrance for his five-minute meeting with the president. America's first Tour de France victor presented a yellow jersey to the president. The president gave LeMond a clear glass jar of jelly beans, and two silver cups, boxed and wrapped in gold embossed with the presidential seal.

As soon as LeMond emerged from the Oval Office, he was asked over to a thicket of microphones before a gaggle of reporters from the White House press corps. They all appeared to be seeing a professional bicycle racer for the first time. He took questions at the impromptu press conference and replied with the poise of any member of the Senate or Congress, but with more exuberance.

"I think that meeting with the president is my highest award," LeMond said. "It is probably the biggest honor in my life to be invited to the White House."

LeMond's remarks echoed what Fred Spencer had said sixty-one years earlier, when he and Bobby Walthour II met President Coolidge: "It was a greater thrill than winning the bicycle championship of America. I never thought I would be able to shake hands with President Coolidge. I told the president I considered it a great honor, and I will never forget it."

LeMond smiled and shook his head when asked if there was any ill will between him and Hinault. "Things are all right between us. I have been riding with Bernard for six years. We get along well and he is coming over here to ride in the Coors Classic."

When LeMond was asked if he had a political preference for Republican or Democratic presidents, he smiled again and shook his head. "I am an athlete. I am not a politician. My job is to race bicycles. But I am glad to see the recognition that cycling is getting now. I think my future in cycling is in America."

EPILOGUE

Writing this history of American cycling was like assembling a puzzle. The sport's history is widely scattered, with parts known by those who were involved with different periods, in different sections of the country, while other essentials are reported on the pages of newspapers that went out of business decades ago. Without a successful hall of fame, bicycle racing's heritage has been lost to the general public, as well as to most of the cycling community itself. *The Big Book of Halls of Fame in the United States and Canada,* published in 1977, lists about a hundred halls of fame for sports in this country. Football alone boasts six, from Texas high school players to the National Football League. What about bicycle racing? Attempts to organize a national cycling hall of fame have thus far not met with success.

The memory of days when the sport was robust, when cycling stars were popular heroes, lingers in the minds of an ever-diminishing number of cycling's elders. Career records are glued to brittle pages of scrapbooks packed in steamer trunks in attics and basements, or are stashed away neglected on closet shelves scattered between the Atlantic and Pacific.

America's unofficial hall of fame for those golden days is known only to a few aficionados, in an inconspicuous bicycle shop in Irvington, a Newark suburb. Brennan's Bicycle Shop, one of the oldest in the country, has been at its present location, 93 Madison Avenue, since 1926, and over the years has become the epicenter of the sport's best period in this country. Riders entrusted Pop Brennan and his two sons, Jack and Bill, with photos and newspaper clippings for safekeeping. Then later came more photos, thicker swatches of clippings, more programs, and other ephemera. More volumes of scrapbooks came from widows of the riders, from sportswriters who felt the cycling material was better kept with Pop, and from friends.

Pop Brennan (his real name was John S. Brennan) moved the original shop from a mile away to its present location in 1926 to be closer to the Newark Velodrome. In race programs and newspapers, he advertised with a simple claim: "We fix everything but a broken heart."

Brennan was chief mechanic at the big six-days from Madison Square Garden to Philadelphia, Buffalo, Detroit, Chicago, and St. Louis. He set up his workbench on the inside of the velodrome, at the end of the finishing straight. With three dozen riders in two-man teams racing round and round, accidents and crashes were inevitable. Bent wheels, punctured tires, and general wear and tear were taken care of by the bespectacled man in the black sweater. Hundreds flocked to the inside of the track just to watch him straighten out frames, replace broken spokes, line up wheels, and repair tires.

Jack and Bill grew up in the business and kept the store going when Pop died in 1962 at seventy-four. Jack raced in the 1920s until he fell and broke his arm twice in three months during 1929. The Brennan brothers grew up listening to riders who visited the shop as well as the Brennan household "to bat the fat around" and recapture the drama, action, fatigue, and heroics that they had known up close.

Today Brennan's caters to leisure cyclists. Gleaming bicycles stand in rows inside; some are suspended from the ceiling. Given three days, Bill can make a complete bicycle himself from spare parts in the worn wooden drawers that line a wall. The shop smells of grease and oil like all bike shops. But this is Brennan's Bicycle Shop, and there is something more in the atmosphere. The smell of wintergreen and sweat is in the background, with the faint roar of the six-day audiences on their feet cheering the riders speeding toward the finish of a $100 lap. The ghosts of countless riders stand around or sit on bikes or on the

When cycling's popularity declined after World War II, Pop Brennan and his sons, Bill, on the left, and Jack, adapted to the changing consumer tastes and began carrying balloon-tired bicycles. Meanwhile, the Brennans' shop accumulated more and more news clippings and photos to become the unofficial hall of fame for the sport's best years in this country. (Brennan Brothers)

counter, listening to the Brennan brothers talk. The tools that Pop used, including the large industrial vise he put frames in, are still used every day.

The Brennans are inveterate collectors of cycling memorabilia. A few years ago, they received a call from someone who had inherited a Newark garage and found photos of cyclists on the walls. The Brennans were invited to take all they wanted before the walls were knocked down to make way for a new building.

Jack Brennan opened a photo album to show me what he had taken. The photos were sharp eight-by-tens taken at the Newark Velodrome. The photographer was likely on the staff of one of Newark's three daily newspapers and had used a Speed Graphic camera. Out of one photo peer world champions Robert Spears of Australia and Pete Moeskops of Holland. In another, Oscar Egg, the Swiss ace, smiles.

The photo album is one of several in the Brennans' bike shop, along with numerous scrapbooks. Opening these albums and scrapbooks is like parting the curtain on a colorful era of Americana. Many of the riders traveled so extensively around the country and back and forth to Europe that they had little—and sometimes nothing at all—to show for their efforts. For months at a stretch, they lived with what they carried. Yet each rider was a font of stories that he recounted to the convivial Pop Brennan and his sons.

When Jack Brennan opened a photo album, I felt the ghosts at Brennan's crowding in for a glimpse. The roar of thousands of fans who got inside Madison Square Garden before the fire marshal had the doors barred seemed to rise in a new crescendo. I could smell the freshly laid pine boards of the track. I could hear the Doppler drone of the racers' tires rolling at 35 miles or more an hour over the wooden surface. Somewhere the band was playing a lively rendition of "Me and My Gal" for the first time anywhere.

Jack flipped pages until he found the photo of three riders sprinting around the final turn of the Newark Velodrome in 1920. Their backs were low, their arms bent as they pulled on their handlebars. The stands were packed. Every head was turned to the racers, who were shoulder to shoulder.

The rider on the left was Alf Goullet. On the right was Oscar Egg, the Swiss who held the hour record three times, the third time from 1914 to 1933, the longest of anybody. He also figured out how to make a successful derailleur. Egg reportedly saw an early version in a Paris shop window and studied it closely. Then he went home and made his own. He figured the maker of the derailleur he saw had a French patent, so Egg patented his derailleur in every country in Europe but France. His derailleur, called Oscgear, made him a rich man.

Between the two riders was Eddy Madden, a Newark native who was known as Bees Knees because his knees were so small. Madden, like so many others, was a popular American rider with talent. In 1919, the year he finished third in the national professional championship, he teamed with Goullet to win the Garden's six-day. Madden also won two sixes in Chicago and more in Boston and Kansas City. Yet his name is lost today.

Some of the photos in the Brennans' albums are tinted with water-color for Sunday rotogravure sections where they originally were published. Jack Brennan flipped through the albums, thumping an index finger on the faces of rider after rider, telling their names, where they came from, what their riding styles were like, big races they had won, ones they had blown. His biographical sketches are so vivid that each rider he talked about seemed to wheel off the page and take a solo lap.

As important to the sport as John M. Chapman was, he was a researcher's enigma. He diverted reporters interested in "the bike game" to write about the riders, and thus was never the subject of newspaper or magazine features. I learned about Chapman's youth from a scrapbook that belonged to Iver Lawson, the Speedy Swede, who won the world professional sprint championship in London in 1904. Lawson, a native of Salt Lake City, was as close to Chapman as anyone. He was two years older than Chapman and they apparently met when Chapman went to Salt Lake City. They set the world five-mile tandem record there in 1901, in 9 minutes 44 seconds. It stood as a national record for more than fifty years; riders used to joke that it stood so long because when Chapman took over as promoter he deliberately never held the event.

Chapman and Lawson raced in many of the same events, and traveled twice together to Australia in 1899 and 1900. Lawson kept a detailed scrapbook which includes articles that give insight into Chapman's early years as the Georgia Cyclone. When Chapman retired in 1937, Lawson went back to Utah and left his scrapbook with Pop Brennan.

Another great source was Walter Bardgett, associate editor at *American Bicyclist and Motorcyclist,* who wrote a monthly column, "On the Bell Lap." Bardgett was a walking encyclopedia, and his columns included nuggets about cycling. The *New York Times* in 1925 called him "the dean of cycling critics." As the sport declined during the depression, there was less racing news to comment on and he became the golden era's Homer, chronicling comings and goings, second-career retirements, and deaths of those involved with the sport's best years here.

American cycling's Homer was Walter Bardgett, who entered the sport as an amateur in Buffalo, New York, and went on to compete as an amateur and then professional all around the United States and Europe. Here he is getting ready to start a handicap race, about 1902. (*Jack Simes II*)

Bardgett was a dark-haired man with strong facial features. A native of Buffalo, Bardgett began racing in 1895 at age fifteen for the Buffalo Ramblers Bicycle Club. He turned professional in 1901 and competed around the United States and Europe against the best. He knew Bobby Walthour, Major Taylor, and Frank Kramer from racing against them here and abroad. In one column he recounts racing in 1908 in the French classic from Bordeaux to Paris. That would make him the first American to ride in a European classic. A bad accident that left him with a spinal deformity forced his retirement in 1909.

After 1915, he joined the staff of the magazine where he worked the rest of his life. He was often seen at races. Riders easily picked him out in the crowd—a small stoop-shouldered man wearing a straw hat and carrying a folded-up newspaper in his jacket pocket. "He kept getting shorter and shorter with age," Jack Heid recounted, "but his mind stayed so sharp." Bardgett died at age seventy-three of heart failure in a Miami hospital in 1953.

In researching the sport, I got caught up in the lives of the people who influenced it. One was the indefatigable promoter Billy Brady. He moved from managing heavyweight boxing champion Jim Corbett to managing world champion cyclist Major Taylor to heavyweight boxing champion James Jeffries. Brady had an uncanny flair for picking winners. When Jeffries retired in 1905, Brady shifted to Broadway plays where he continued to pick winners. In 1928, playwright Elmer L. Rice was turned down by more than a dozen producers for his play *Street Scene.* Brady produced it. *Street Scene* lasted for more than 600 performances and won the 1929 Pulitzer Prize. Brady was wiped out after the stock market crash, but later recouped his fortune and went on to produce more than 250 plays.

His association with winners extended to his daughter, Alice Brady, who was a successful stage and screen actress. She won the 1937 Academy Award for Best Supporting Actress for her role in *In Old Chicago.* Brady published *The Fighting Man* in 1916 and his autobiography, *Showman,* in 1937. He died at the age of eighty-six in 1950 in Manhattan.

Another promoter was Harry Mendel, who worked as John M. Chapman's publicist and put on the last Madison Square Garden six-days. Mendel became better known for the press relations work he did in the late 1930s for the Madison Square boxing arena when heavyweight champion Joe Louis was at the height of his career. Mendel then took over as head of publicity for the International Boxing Club and handled press relations for Louis and other champions including Jersey Joe Walcott, Ezzard Charles, and Archie Moore.

In 1955, Mendel was sixty-two when the Boxing Writers Association at their annual dinner presented him with the Jimmy Walker Award "for long and meritorious service to boxing writers." He died the following year of a heart attack in his home in Orange, New Jersey.

One of the most enduring of all riders is Alf Goullet. In 1987, he celebrated his ninety-sixth birthday. Damon Runyon used to refer to him in the *New York American* as "the Babe Ruth of six-day bike racing." Runyon described Goullet as "nine feet high to the strained imaginations of the other riders and growing taller every minute." Runyon proclaimed: "Baseball has Ruth. Pugilism has Dempsey. Six-day racing has Goullet, and in Goullet it has the greatest King of the six-day dynasty. . . . Long live the King!"

Runyon also published a feature on Goullet that his wife Jane liked so much she carried it around in her handbag for years. By the time their two children were in their teens, the clipping was mislaid and lost. Scrapbooks that chronicled Goullet's successes on three continents were lost to a flooded basement. All that survives is a scrapbook from his 1912 season in Salt Lake City.

Goullet was always unduly modest during our numerous interviews. The longest was five hours in his home; my writing hand was frozen to a claw. He never told me that he was one of two cyclists inducted among the original eighty-eight members into Madison Square Garden's Hall of Fame, established in 1968 (his compatriot Reggie McNamara is the other cyclist). Goullet casually mentioned that cartoonist Robert LeRoy Ripley knocked on his hotel room door for an interview the day after he and Alfred Grenda set the world distance record for the six-day in 1914. I went to the Library of Congress, scrolled through microfilm of the *New York Globe* where Ripley worked, and there on the sports page looking back was Ripley's art of Goullet riding his bike. Ripley called him the Human Motorcycle.

After he retired from racing, Goullet worked in the insurance business, and for a while owned and operated a skating rink. In late 1986, he returned to Melbourne for induction into the Australian Sports Federation Hall of Fame. Goullet, who went to Newark to race as a professional in 1910, the year that the Boy Scouts of America was incorporated, stays in shape by walking two or three miles most days, depending on the weather.

When Goullet raced in Salt Lake City during the 1912 season, he roomed with another professional rider, Hardy Downing, whose legacy to American sports was giving Jack Dempsey a start in professional

Alf Goullet, one of the greatest six-day racers ever, was inducted into the Australian Sports Federation Hall of Fame in December 1986. Presenting Goullet with an award at his induction is Rob de Castella, world marathon champion and winner of the Boston Marathon. (*Confederation of Australian Sport, Inc.,*)

boxing. Downing was originally from San Jose and traveled wherever bicycling took him. He used to say that he settled in Salt Lake City because he was snowed in there once after a race. In 1913 Downing retired from cycling and got into boxing promotions with his brother-in-law, Big Jack Price. In 1915 he opened the boxing gym where Jack Dempsey got his start in professional boxing.

On the first page of photos in Dempsey's autobiography, Dempsey is standing in the boxing ring of Downing's gym. Downing's fights were known for their action. "No fight, no pay," was his motto. After 1930, he sold his boxing interests and managed an apartment house.

Downing was well known in Salt Lake City. Newspaper reporters used to write about his fondness for deer hunting, and his belief that

Hardy Downing was a top American professional cyclist whose philosophy was that left hands win fights and right hands sign checks. He retired from cycling in 1914 in Salt Lake City where he opened the boxing gym which gave Jack Dempsey his start in professional boxing. (*Brennan Brothers*)

left hands won fights and right hands signed checks. When illness overtook him in 1960 at eighty-two, Jack Dempsey went to Salt Lake City to visit him in the hospital before he died.

Jackie Clark, the Australian national champion recruited by John Chapman to race in Salt Lake City, was a colorful cyclist who generated a lot of press attention, and had a special attraction with children, according to Goullet. "I've never seen anything like it," Goullet says. "Jackie always dressed nice, in a jacket and starched shirt and collar and tie. When he walked down the street, any kid who saw him walk by would just beat it out of the house to join him so that kid could go back to his friends and say, 'I walked down the street with Jackie Clark.' By the time Jackie got to the trolley barn, there would be a whole bunch of kids walking with him. That happened a lot."

In 1910 Clark married Rena Bray of Salt Lake City. After he retired from cycling around 1915, he had numerous careers. He owned a Newark hotel, sold patent medicine in New York and New Jersey, and sold automobiles in New York City. In 1948, he was busy running a ranch in Las Vegas, but there is no trace of his endeavors subsequent to this.

Alfred Grenda, the durable Tasmanian who won a silver medal in the 1912 world professional sprint championship and a gold in the tandem event, raced until the late 1920s. By then he was nearly forty and was easily spotted by the wool watch cap he wore to cover his balding head. Grenda moved to Los Angeles and ran a gas station there before he settled in Costa Mesa, where he died in 1983 at the age of ninety-three.

Iver Lawson was one of the few riders Chapman looked out for. He worked for Chapman as clerk of the course at the six-day races, and worked odd jobs for him as well. Lawson was a quiet man who did not talk about himself. He was last seen working in 1948 as a card dealer in Provo, Utah.

Eddy (the Cannon) Bald grew up in Buffalo where his father operated a large family butcher business. Young Bald delivered meat on his bicycle and started racing at age sixteen. Five years later, in 1895, he became the country's first professional champion. He repeated as champion the next two years on the rigorous Grand Circuit. Bardgett wrote that Bald was one of the all-time greatest sprinters in this country.

"At the national championships at the Newby Oval, Indianapolis, in 1899, when Tom Cooper won the American sprint title that year, Bald had a match race with Cooper that goes down in the books as one of the best, with Bald the winner," Bargett wrote. "One heat at the mile took 7 minutes and 59 seconds to run, but those who saw the match said that last eighth mile was worth going miles to see with Bald winning in a neck-and-neck battle."

Bald retired from cycling after the turn of the century for a brief career as a car racer. He settled in Pittsburgh where he had a dealership selling Hudson and Essex cars. In 1925 he sold the dealership and retired. He was seventy-two when he died in 1946.

George M. Hendee, the country's first amateur national champion, was popularly known as "Our George" in his hometown of Springfield, Massachusetts. In 1916, he sold his interest in the Indian Motorcycle Company and retired to his country estate in Suffield, Connecticut. Hendee was known for his civic responsibilities. During World War I, he served in the YMCA and was sent to Paris where he headed the YMCA's general post office. After the war, he returned home where he became a patron of Springfield's Shriners' Hospital for Crippled Children and was a prominent Mason. He also raised prize Guernsey cattle on his country estate. Hendee died at seventy-seven in 1943 after a long illness.

Eddie Root, the Bostonian whose taste for the ironic compelled him to insist on riding with Number 13 all his career, was one of the country's famous six-day racers in the early days of the century. He also won many motorpace events. Root was nearly six feet tall, with a lean yet muscular build, and had pleasant facial features.

At various times after he retired, he was chauffeur to Diamond Jim Brady and Al Jolson, but cycling was Root's main activity. He worked as a trainer at six-day races in Louisville and Cleveland. After World War II, he ran a bicycle-rental business in Culvers Lake, New Jersey, until he died in 1956 at age seventy-six.

After Sergio Matteini came back in 1934 from Europe where he had raced professionally for four years, he worked in New York City in his father's upholstery business. In 1960, he and his wife, Vera, moved to Pleasant Valley, New York, where they live. He is a breeder of prize beagles.

Fred Spencer, the national pro champion Calvin Coolidge invited to the White House, is sometimes seen on late-night television with comedian Joe E. Brown in the 1934 Warner Brothers movie *Six-Day Bike Rider.* In a dramatic scene, Spencer gets turned around on the velodrome and rides against the direction of the speeding pack. He rides straight into the others, who fly away like sparks and only narrowly avert disaster.

Dangerous? "I was riding my bike on stationary rollers," Spencer explains. "The camera just showed me riding from the legs up while the other riders went past me."

Spencer retired from bike racing in 1938 and became an engineer. The money he won when the 1920s roared and he was a star went into trust funds that protected him from the stock market crash. In 1977, the New Jersey Sports Writers Association honored him at a banquet with their Hall of Fame Award.

Charley Winter won his last six-day race in Kansas City in 1937, ten years after he won his first one with Fred Spencer in the Garden. Known as the Bronx Strongboy, the burly Winter raced in a total of 104 six-days that logged an estimated 225,000 miles. After his Kansas City triumph, he quit the sport and went into the heating business in New York. In 1977 he retired and moved with his wife, Helen, to Merced, California. He died in late 1985 at eighty-two.

Of all the riders from the glory days of American cycling, the one best remembered years later, despite having spent so much time overseas, was Bobby Walthour, Sr. He returned to the United States in the early 1930s after the German government seized his bank account and career savings. It was a misfortune remarkably similar to the one his aristocratic southern family suffered after the Civil War. Then the family property in Walthourville was confiscated for taxes. When he came back to the States, a special celebration was held in his honor in Atlanta.

Mayor James L. Key ranked Walthour with golf's Bobby Jones and baseball's Ty Cobb as the three men who had done the most to carry the name of Georgia throughout the world.

Walthour settled in New York, where his twin brother, James, had lived for many years. Still lean and wiry, Walthour's only concession to the years was to wear bifocals. He worked for a New York sporting goods company. In 1939, at age sixty-one, Walthour pedaled a bicycle 800 miles from Miami to Atlanta to see old friends and relatives. At a lunch stop in Valdosta, Georgia, a stranger asked if he was Bobby Walthour. When Walthour replied he was, the stranger informed Walthour he had seen him race forty years before and still remembered him.

In 1941 he changed jobs to work in Boston for an automotive magazine. For the next eight years he lived in Jamaica Plains. He contracted cancer in 1949 and died of pneumonia in Boston that year at seventy-one.

Bobby Walthour II fell on hard times during the depression. When the races disappeared, he was left without an income. Two houses he owned in New Jersey were lost to taxes. In 1938, he received a contract for six-day races on the West Coast. With his wife and their three children, he drove west in all he had left—a 1932 Pierce Arrow luxury car, which he had won in a premium during better days in Madison Square Garden.

Walthour stayed in California, but went through lean years. He was a school-crossing guard, and used to wear sunglasses so nobody would recognize him. Then he got a job working as a tram operator at Metro-Goldwyn-Mayer in Culver City. A former peanut vendor in Madison Square Garden who used to watch Walthour race had become a vice-president at MGM. He helped Walthour get a job in the film library. Walthour started as an apprentice, learned the job from the bottom up, and rose to manage MGM's film library and supervise a staff of thirty. Walthour died at Lake Arrowhead in 1980, at age seventy-seven.

Bobby Walthour III says that bicycle racing never attracted him. "I refused to follow my dad's footsteps." Walthour took up swimming at Santa Monica High School where his coaches were Johnny Weismuller and Paul Sadder, who was Weismuller's stand-in for many of the Tarzan movies. After high school he swam for St. Mary's College.

Walthour has been a physical education teacher at Carmel High School for thirty-one years. He coaches swimming and attracted national attention when his team won 103 straight meet victories. After his team won thirty-two straight victories, *Sports Illustrated* ran his picture in "Faces in the Crowd." In 1984, Walthour was named Monterey Peninsula Teacher of the Year. He was cited for having coached thirty-one league champion teams.

Athletics runs in the family. His wife, Joan, is girls' athletic director at Monterey High and has coached the girls' field hockey team to perfect seasons.

Walthour's son, a fourth-generation Bobby Walthour, has taken up bicycle racing to extend the family tradition. In 1986, twenty-year-old Walthour won the USCF northern California district cycling championship for the kilometer. In early 1987, he attended a Federation training camp in Colorado Springs to help him prepare for the 1988 Olympic cycling trials.

Ray Blum lives with his wife, Louise, in Downey, California. His numerous athletic achievements include winning the North American men's outdoor championship in 1950 and, two years later, the North American men's indoor championship. He is a member of the Amateur Skating Union's Hall of Fame.

A versatile athlete, he was what Walter Bardgett described as "a nifty amateur racing cyclist" and won many bike races for decades. In 1981, Jonathan Boyer came back fit from racing the Tour de France and stopped in Los Angeles for a race that Yoplait Yogurt sponsored. Blum finished second to Boyer.

Blum is active in the Orange County Wheelmen's 100- and 200-mile Sunday rides. He continues to race in national age-group championships "to keep my medal collection going."

Don McDermott and his wife, Anneliese, have two sons and two daughters. "I made three Olympic teams," he explains, "and after that, not much else."

A fourth-generation Bobby Walthour has taken up bicycle racing and is upholding the long-standing Walthour tradition of speed and victories. (Bobby Walthour III photo)

In his specialty, the 500-meter (550-yard) speed-skating event, McDermott won a silver medal in the 1952 Olympics in Oslo, and a bronze in the 1955 world championships in Moscow. He is also a member of the Amateur Skating Union's Hall of Fame. McDermott is active in the Edgewater, New Jersey, Lions Club, and is postmaster of Edgewater.

In 1980 the Fitchburg-Longsjo Memorial Race was renamed by the U.S. Cycling Federation to the Fitchburg-Longsjo Classic, one of the few bicycle races in the country to be officially so designated. Through the years, the men's and women's events have drawn such notables as Greg LeMond, Eric and Beth Heiden, Connie Carpenter, and Sue Novara-Reber. At the tenth annual event in 1969, Canadian champion Jocelyn Lovell won a car as first prize. Held every first Sunday in July since 1960, the race has become the oldest in New England and the third oldest in the nation.

Jack Heid and his wife, Julia, raised five children. Heid took up photography, metalworking, skiing in the winter and water skiing in the summer, and continued recreational riding for fitness. He carefully spent the money he earned as a maintenance worker and owned a home in Rockaway, New Jersey, and a chalet in Bushkill, nestled in eastern Pennsylvania's rolling foothills. In 1986 Heid attended the world cycling championships in Colorado Springs where he enjoyed reunions with more than a dozen foreign riders he had competed against. He died at age sixty-two of smoke inhalation in May 1987 when a fire broke out in his Bushkill residence. Heid's bronze medal for third in the 1949 world championships remains the last that U.S. men have won in world championship sprint events.

Gerard Debaets was a man of contradictions and continental charm. The Belgian native became a U.S. citizen in the early 1930s and took to his new nationality by winning the national motorpace championship in 1937. He added the title to his two earlier Belgian national championships. A natural performer, he entertained crowds by building up speed on his bicycle and then removing his feet from the pedals to lie flat with his stomach on the saddle, his arms and legs outstretched as though he were flying down the straight.

Early in the depression, Debaets lost his savings when the Belgian bank his money was in went out of business. He raised two sons while his wife was ill with tuberculosis and confined to a sanatorium. After Debaets retired in the early 1940s, he ran a bicycle shop in Patterson, New Jersey.

He liked to smoke, and kept it up even though his heart continued to bother him. On a Sunday morning training ride with Heid and others in 1956, Debaets's face turned blue and he fell off his bike. The outing ended in a cab ride home. In 1959, Julia Heid was preparing to go to the hospital to have twins when Debaets died of a heart attack at age sixty-one. She gave birth to a girl and a boy, and Heid named the boy Gerard.

Nancy Neiman Baranet, first American cyclist to ride a European stage race, devoted more than a quarter of a century to helping improve the quality of racing in the United States. Elected to the board of the Amateur Bicycle League of America (later the U.S. Cycling Federation) in 1956, she served until 1983. She had two-year terms as treasurer and secretary, and served on developmental program committees. Her contributions to the sport in general and women's cycling specifically came to the attention of *Women's Sports* magazine which in 1978 presented her with the Stay-Free Service to Women's Sports Award.

She and her husband, Nicholas Baranet, moved with their three sons and one daughter to Florida in 1972, where he died in 1984. Baranet still lives in Plantation, Florida, and works as a manufacturer's representative in the food service industry. She is the author of two books: *The Turned Down Bar,* describing her European racing experiences, and *Bicycling,* about recreational cycling. Baranet has also published articles in *Private Pilot, Bicycling,* and *Women's Sports.*

Audrey McElmury, women's world road-racing champion in 1969, retired from racing after a bad crash in 1976. She and her husband, cyclist Michael Levonas, completed their studies for business degrees at the University of Denver that year and moved to Mount Home, Idaho. Michael Levonas is director of the Mount Home School District food service for which Audrey works. Her son, Ian, is a student at San Diego University.

Audrey runs in masters age-group competition for forty and up, in distances from 10 kilometers (6.2 miles) to the 42-kilometer marathon (26.2 miles). She also skis cross country and rides a bicycle with her husband for recreation. The couple co-authored *Bicycle Training for Triathletes,* now in its third printing.

Sheila Young-Ochowicz won a total of six world championship medals between 1972 and 1982, including three golds. Her last medal was a silver at the 1982 worlds in Leicester, England, after which she retired to have a second daughter, Elli.

After she won gold, silver, and bronze medals in speed skating during the 1976 Winter Olympics, Sheila was invited to the White House for a state dinner. "It was like Cinderella at the ball," she says. "We had to find out what to wear, how to properly address people there. I went with my husband, who was my fiancé then, and we sat at a table with President Ford, Mickey Mantle, and Ray Bolger." In 1980 she worked as official spokesperson for the Lake Placid Winter Olympics, did television commentary for ABC Sports' coverage of the Games, and was featured on Wheaties breakfast cereal boxes.

She and her husband, Jim Ochowicz, live with their two daughters in Waukesha, Wisconsin. Her husband is general manager of the powerful 7-Eleven cycling team, which succeeded in capturing three stages of the 1987 Tour de France. Sheila serves on the U.S. Olympic Committee executive board and on the U.S. Cycling Federation board of directors.

Sue Novara was Sheila Young-Ochowicz's greatest rival in women's match sprints and won seven medals in world championships, including two golds, between 1974 and 1980. When the women's road race was announced for the 1984 Olympics, she switched to road racing with promising successes but failed to make the Olympic team. She and her husband, Mark Reber, whom she married in 1977, had a daughter, Kathleen, in 1985.

Sue Novara-Reber, as she is better known today, was hired in March 1986 as national women's coach for the U.S. Cycling Federation. At the 1987 worlds in Vienna, Austria, U.S. women won four medals, including one gold, while the men won none.

Mike Hiltner left Brazil in February 1971 after his marriage broke up and arrived at age thirty back home in southern California. There he saw his first hippies. Their long hair, tie-dyed shirts, bell-bottomed jeans, and casual use of recreational drugs made a big impression on him. Hiltner let his hair grow and stopped shaving. His burr haircut and boyish looks were overgrown with hair. He took time to read and establish his own identity as he worked through layer after layer of his shyness. Hiltner took to wearing a one-piece jumpsuit made of a bright floral, knit fabric that featured wide shoulders, no buttons, and no zippers.

While his new identity took hold, he still had a drive to be a well-known cyclist. In 1975, he went for the round-trip record across the country. Riding the Schwinn Paramount he had used during the 1964 Olympics, Hiltner embarked from the beach of Santa Monica on September 15, pedaled through Palm Springs, into Arizona, and kept going. A van with four support crew followed him. They reached Atlantic City, New Jersey, in eighteen days.

On the way back, confident that he could complete the cross-country double and set a record, he examined his life and decided it was time to lay the old Mike Hiltner to rest and start anew. "It became an obsession while I was out there riding on the way back—to change my name." The name that crystallized was Victor Vincente of America. Victor came from English for winner. Vincente came from the Latin root *vincere,* to win. On October 23, he arrived back in Santa Monica to set a new record for a cross-country trip of thirty-six days.

"I am glad I succeeded in establishing the record," he said. "It just burned in my brain that I was going to change my name. In fact, I thought that if I failed, I would take as my name ten Zs, as in one who is snoring. You know, change my name to ZZZZZZZZZZ. I am not sure I had the courage to do this." Victor Vincente of America laughed as he spoke.

Perry Metzler may be the greatest tragedy in American cycling. Many contend that if he had had any breaks at all, he would have been a superstar. He was a consistent top rider in big regional races in the Northeast in the early 1960s. In 1962, he won the Eastern States Outdoor Track Championship on a portable velodrome in Fair Oaks, New York. Four years later, Metzler was part of a team that Al Toefield led to represent the ABL at a big Pan American meet in Trinidad. "They loved him down there," Toefield recalls. "Perry rode hard and won a lot of races on grass tracks and on an outdoor cement velodrome there. They wanted to keep him, he was so popular."

Cycling offered an alternative to the young man who lived in Brooklyn's crime-infested Bedford-Stuyvesant section. In 1967, he placed well enough in the ABL district championships to qualify for the nationals, and he competed in St. Louis. But unemployed and having to support a wife and two sons, Metzler had to drop out of the sport soon after he returned home. Robbery was the alternative occupation for the area's unemployed men, and Metzler committed a few.

In mid-1968, Metzler went to Chicago and began making plans to move there. He made a down payment on a house for his mother and grandmother, and tried for nine months to find work in Chicago. One month he called on over sixty places. He asked at vocational rehabilitation centers. For a while he got a steel-mill job working early-morning hours two or three days a week until the job was phased out.

His wife joined him in Chicago late in the summer with their sons while Metzler continued to look for work. Finally, Metzler got so discouraged that he decided to rejoin the army. In September 1969, he tried to enlist in Chicago but was rejected because he wrote on the application that he had a wife and two sons. Metzler took a bus to Detroit. He told the army recruiter he was single and had no dependents.

Back in the army, his sense of self-worth returned. He went through basic training again and followed that up with parachute school. He loved making parachute jumps. The army made him a member of its military police unit. Then he got orders for Vietnam.

"I didn't want him to go," says his wife, Patricia Assam Metzler. "I threatened to say that he had a wife and two kids. We had loud arguments over that. Day and night. Perry's mother went crazy with us arguing. But Perry had a lot of pride. He had an enormous amount of pride. In 1967 and 1968 Perry had the only bad part of his life. He got into drugs and theft and he wanted to get out of that. He knew right from wrong. He wanted to get out of the ghetto environment. Bike riding was a way out for him. He was aware of different life-styles. He was so glad to get back into the army. Going to Vietnam was part of being in the army then."

Twenty-nine-year-old Metzler was shipped to Vietnam on February 3, 1970. Eleven days after he arrived, on Valentine's Day, he was on guard duty on a base in Quang Tri when he was killed.

The Pentagon notified the Detroit newspapers of his death, based on his enlistment there, although he was in Detroit only as long as it took to enlist. Pentagon officials promptly notified Metzler's wife, mother, and grandmother, but since they were living in Chicago, away from his New York roots, news of his death took years to reach the cycling community. Metzler's name is engraved on the black marble panels of the Vietnam War Memorial in Washington, D.C.

"Perry had a lot of pride, but the odds were against him," Patricia says. She remained in Chicago where she raised their boys, then ages nine and five, herself. She worked for the city as a support services specialist identifying student aid sources from private and public sources for five years, and then in 1976 went into business for herself.

From time to time she has returned to New York to visit family and friends. "There are streets I walk along in Brooklyn where one person after another calls out to me," she says. "I don't know who these people are, but they knew Perry. People remember me because I was Perry's wife."

BIBLIOGRAPHY

Abt, Samuel. *Breakaway: On the Road with the Tour de France.* New York: Random House, 1985.

Arnold, Peter. *History of Boxing.* Secaucus, NJ: Chartwell Books, 1985.

Baranet, Nancy Neiman. *The Turned Down Bar.* Philadelphia: Dorrance & Co., 1964.

Bardgett, Walter. "The Bicycle Racing Stars of the Nineteenth Century Assn. Reverently Honor the Memory of 'Major' Taylor." *American Bicyclist and Motorcyclist,* July 1948, p. 32.

Borysewicz, Edward. *Bicycle Road Racing: Complete Program for Training and Competition.* Brattleboro, VT: Velo-News, 1985.

Brady, William A. *The Fighting Man.* Indianapolis: Bobbs-Merrill, 1916.

Brady, William A. *Showman.* New York: E.P. Dutton, 1937.

Breyer, Victor. "Arthur Zimmerman—Greatest Pedaller of All Time." *Cycling Weekly,* April 30, 1947, pp. 336–337.

Breyer, Victor. "The Great Parade." *American Bicyclist and Motorcyclist,* December 1955, p. 17.

"Champion on Wheels: Harlem Youth Is Star Cyclist after Only Four Years' Racing." *Ebony Magazine,* September 1967, pp. 108–112.

Coffey, Steve. "Crashes, but Fine Racing!" *Cyclist,* September 25, 1971, pp. 2, 3.

Connor, Dick. "F. Don Miller: The Colonel Leaves a Legacy." *The Olympian Magazine,* February 1985, pp. 4–7.

Dempsey, Jack, with Barbara Piatteli. *Dempsey.* New York: Harper & Row, 1977.

Dickow, Ray. "Round and Round and Round-Steak." *The Butcher Workman,* May 1957, pp. 6–8.

Durso, Joseph. *Madison Square Garden: 100 Years of History.* New York: Simon & Schuster, 1979.

Eisele, Otto. *Cycling Almanac.* New York: 1950.

Eisele, Otto. *Cycling Almanac.* New York: 1951.

Eisele, Otto. "A History of the Amateur Bicycle League of America, Inc." In *Review of Cycling* (Watson N. Nordquist, ed.), 1943 edition, pp. 18–25.

Goullet, Alfred T., and Charles J. McGuirk. "The Infernal Grind." *The Saturday Evening Post,* May 28, 1926, pp. 18–181.

Held, John, Jr. *Outlines of Sport.* New York: E. P. Dutton, 1930.

Hoviss, Joe. "Disney, Nieman and Metzler, National Champions." *The Staten Island Transcript,* September 20, 1957, p. 1.

Keene, Judy. "Marshall Taylor—Bike Champ from Indianapolis." *Indianapolis Magazine,* May 1977, pp. 41–54.

Kieran, John. *The American Sporting Scene.* New York: Macmillan, 1941.

Lacey, Robert. *Ford: The Man and the Machine.* Boston: Little, Brown, 1987.

Levine, Peter. *A.G. Spalding and the Rise of Baseball.* New York: Oxford University Press, 1985.

Litzky, Frank. "Avery Brundage of Olympics Dies." *New York Times,* May 9, 1975, p. 1.

Lucas, Robert. "The World's Fastest Bicycle Rider." *Negro Digest,* May 1948, pp. 10–13.

McCullagh, James C., ed. *American Bicycle Racing.* Emmaus, PA: Rodale Press, 1976.

Morand, Paul. *Open All Night.* New York: T. Seltzer, 1923.

The Most of John Held, Jr. Foreword by Marc Connelly. Introduction by Carl J. Weinhardt. Brattleboro, VT: The Stephen Greene Press, 1972.

Murphy, Charles M. *The Story of the Railroad and a Bicycle: When "A Mile a Minute" Was Born.* New York: Jamaica Law Printing Company, 1936.

Ottum, Bob. "The Lure of the White Noise." *Sports Illustrated,* September 14, 1964, pp. 22–25.

Rickard, Maxine Elliott (Hodges). *Everything Happened to Him: The Story of Tex Rickard.* New York: Frederick A. Stokes, 1936.

Samuels, Charles. *The Magnificent Rube: The Life and Gaudy Times of Tex Rickard.* New York: McGraw-Hill, 1957.

Sinsabagh, Christopher G. *Who, Me? Forty Years of Automobile History.* Detroit: Arnold-Powers, 1940.

Taylor, Marshall Walter. *The Fastest Bicycle Rider in the World: The Story of a Colored Boy's Indomitable Courage and Success Against Great Odds.* Worcester, MA: Wormley Publishing Company, 1928.

Ten Years of Championship Bicycle Racing, 1972–1981. Brattleboro, VT: Velo-News, 1983.

Wedemar, Lou. "The Bike's Here to Stay." *Sports Illustrated,* March 1949, pp. 62–64.

Williams, G. Grant. "Marshall Walter Taylor (Major Taylor)." *The Colored American Magazine,* September 1902, pp. 336–345.

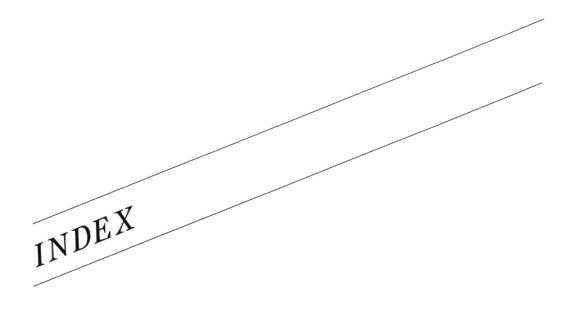

INDEX

Boldfaced page numbers indicate illustrations.